100
OF THE
World's Greatest
MYSTERIES

100
OF THE
World's Greatest
MYSTERIES

E. Randall Floyd

AUGUSTA, GEORGIA

100 OF THE WORLD'S GREATEST MYSTERIES
By E. Randall Floyd
A Harbor House Book/May 2000

For information address:
Harbor House
3010 Stratford Drive
Augusta, Georgia 30909
harborbook@aol.com

Book Design by Lydia Inglett

Library of Congress Catalog Card Number 99-076131

Publisher's Cataloging-in-Publication Data
Floyd, E. Randall, 1947-
100 Of the World's Greatest Mysteries / E. Randall Floyd
First Edition
p. cm.
ISBN 1-891799-05-3
1. Curiosities and Wonders
2.History-Miscellanea
1. Title
001.94
LCCN
Printed in the United States of America
10 9 8 7 6 5 4 3 2

*This book
is dedicated to
Annie Frances Davis*

Contents

Foreword

We mortals are a curious bunch. In the short span of time we've been on this planet, we've struggled to unravel the great secrets of the cosmos. We've built pyramids, gone to the moon, plumbed the depths of the sea and—more recently—conquered cyberspace in our unyielding quest for knowledge.

For all of our grand achievements, however, the universe remains a mysterious and forboding place. We still wonder who we are, where we came from and where we're going. Are we alone in the universe? Is another Ice Age on the way? Did black kings once rule the vine-shrouded jungles of Central America?

Questions like these continue to haunt our dreams, even as we head into the new millennium. It is unlikely we will ever know all the answers—yet, we keep searching for clues. We look to the stars, dig up ancient tombs, resurrect the bones of long-dead beasts.

"Our universe is a sorry little affair unless it has in it something for every age to investigate," the philosopher Seneca once remarked. "Nature does not reveal her mysteries once and for all."

We mortals should be grateful. We need mysteries to keep our lives in balance, to keep alive the fear and wonder. Without mysteries, life would be boring. Who'd want to live in a world without Bigfoot and Atlantis and the Bermuda Triangle?

Around 1899, a group of scientists boasted that every worthwhile invention and discovery had already been made. The new century, they proclaimed, would be a rather dreary time because science had reached a kind of dead-end. "Scientists will no longer be in demand," they predicted.

What a difference a century can make!

During the past 25 years we've learned more about the Earth and the cosmos than all the preceding years of recorded history. Yet, the more we learn, the more we realize how little we actually know about our strange universe and the great mysteries within.

To me, that's a wonderful thing. For, as Albert Einstein said,

> *"The most beautiful thing we can experience is the mysterious. It is the source of all true art and science."*

I want to thank a lot of people for helping make this book possible—most importantly, my wife, Anne, who patiently read and re-read each edited revision; Tharon, a gifted editor and friend; Lydia, without whose help this project would have been too challenging to contemplate; and all the others—friends, relatives, librarians, booksellers, distributors and contributors too numerous to mention in this short space—for reading, editing and encouraging me to go forward with this book.

It's been a wonderful adventure.

—E. Randall Floyd
Augusta, Georgia, 2000

In the
Beginning

The Fires of Heaven

"In the beginning, God created the Heavens and the Earth..."

So begins the most famous creation story ever told, read and memorized by millions of people around the world, from darkest equatorial regions to the shining cities of Heartland America.

Penned more than 5,000 years ago, the Biblical account of the origins of the universe sets forth the compelling notion that all the stars and planets and every creeping thing within the vastness of space sprang into existence on God's command at some remote moment in the past.

One 17th century theologian, Irish archbishop James Ussher, went so far as to calculate the precise date and time of Earth's creation: 9 a.m. on the morning of Oct. 23, 4004 B.C. The French naturalist, Georges Buffon, disagreed, insisting that the world was "at least" 70,000 years old. In 1775, the German philosopher Immanuel Kant boldly speculated that the planet might be "a million, or even millions of, years old."

Amazingly, more than 20 percent of Americans still believe the world was created less than 10,000 years ago.

Today we know those early estimates are billions and billions of years off the mark. Current scientific study suggests that the universe began with a bang between 10 and 15 billion years ago—the result of a titanic explosion that sent showers of celestial dust and gases spewing in all directions.

This was the so-called "Big Bang"—the primeval moment when Nothingness ended and Existence began. George Gamow, a Russian-born American scientist, is generally credited for coining the term in 1946 while studying the distribution of hydrogen, helium and other chemical elements throughout the universe. He theorized that, in the beginning, the universe consisted of a primordial substance called *ylem*— a "boiling sea of neutrons and protons" that eventually exploded and began to expand rapidly.

This process of rapid expansion from a single, primal "cosmic egg" continued for billions of years, gradually slowing and cooling to form stars, moons, planets and eventually life—at least on Earth. In time, say some scientists, the universe will stop expanding altogether and begin to collapse upon itself due to gravitational forces. When that happens, so the theory goes, there will be another big bang—and the process will start all over again.

Even the best-trained scientists are still unsure what caused the Big Bang. Like hooded priests of old trying to understand thunder and lightning, they search the cosmos with powerful telescopes for answers. They count quasars and microwaves, probe black holes and superclusters of galaxies billions of miles away. What inexplicable force sent cosmic shock waves free-wheeling across the void, culminating in the formation of so much matter—galaxies, solar systems, planets, moons and millions of asteroids and other planetary debris?

These scientists are not alone in their curiosity. Since earliest times, people have gazed heavenward and wondered the same thoughts. As they beheld the flickering stars—the ghostly glow of celestial corpses long dead—kings and peasants alike must have asked themselves: "Where did it all come from?" "How was it created?"

Questions like these certainly plagued ancient civilizations, just as they continue to puzzle modern scientists. Without radio telescopes and computer models, however, our ancestors turned to nature and magic and spiritual realms for answers to the great mysteries. Religion was born of necessity, and legends and myths were spawned in an attempt to understand the meaning of it all.

In Africa, the Bantu tribe believe the universe was born one day when the great white god Bambu got sick and vomited up the moon, stars, and animals like the leopard, crocodile, turtle and, finally, some men—including Yoko Lima, who was white like Bambu.

According to the Ainu people of Asia, nothing but demons

and gods existed before the birth of the universe. It was a dark and cold place until Kamui, the chief god, looked down and decided to create worlds and fill them with animals and people. The devil tried to thwart him by swallowing the sun, but failed. When the first people were sent from the darkness to live on Earth, the lesser gods held their noses, crying, "What a terrible smell they make!"

The Apache, too, had wonderful creation myths. In the beginning, nothing existed—no earth, sky, sun or moon, only darkness everywhere, throughout the humming void. From nothingness there suddenly appeared a small, bearded man—Creator, the One Who Lives Alone. When Creator gazed upon the darkness, he felt lonely so decided to create light. Then he made a small child,, who asked that a home be made for her, so Creator made Earth.

The Aztec creation story centers around the Original Mother, a peculiar deity called "Coatlique" (Lady of the Skirt of Snakes"). One day Coatlique became impregnated by an obsidian dagger and gave birth to Coyolxanuhqui, goddess of the moon, and to a group of male offspring who became the stars. The kids could not get along, so there began a bloody battle, after which the cosmos crumbled and fell apart.

Norse mythology also tells of a time before creation, a dark time when restless gods stalked through an icy wasteland called Niflheim. Then one day Ymir, a Frost Giant, was killed, and his body carved up to form the world. His teeth became mountains and rocks and his blood filled the rivers and seas. His skull was placed in the sky to form the dome, and his brains were scattered into the air to form clouds.

From cosmic eggs to skull-faced mother goddesses, creation myths ranged the scope of human consciousness and experience. Emotional, imaginative, brutally decadent and harsh at times, these fables and dreams sought to offer comfort and hope, to help primitive people better understand and appreciate the mysterious universe around them.

In the words of David Adams Leeming, author of *The World*

of Myth, creation myths were important in the development of civilization because they "helped us establish our reason for being, the source of our significance."

Modern science provides us with yet another version of the creation story—the Big Bang, which assumes that the universe began in complete order and harmony but has been moving rapidly toward chaos and apocalypse ever since.

"If this theory appears familiar, it should," states Leeming. "Both the ancient Greek and medieval Christian view of history share much in common with the cosmologists' notion of the history of the universe."

Death of the Dinosaurs

They were big, bad and mean— and always very hungry.

For more than 140 million years, these lumbering monstrosities—the dinosaurs—were the undisputed masters of the planet. Then, approximately 65 million years ago, something terrible happened and they suddenly vanished. To this day, no one knows why.

The fate of the dinosaurs—the largest and most spectacular creatures ever to walk the Earth—remains one of science's greatest unsolved mysteries.

Did a comet or meteorite strike the planet and wipe them out? Did they grow too big to feed themselves and starve to death? Or was it something else—"raiders" from other worlds, perhaps, or a "black hole" that swiped the Earth, that brought doom to these fabulous beasts?

Dinosaurs have both terrified and fascinated people since the mid-19th century when famed anatomist Professor Richard Owen first introduced the term. For centuries, nobody knew about the great prehistoric reptiles that thundered across the landscape millions of years ago. Fossils found on mountainsides and along riverbeds were thought to be the remains of giants drowned in the Biblical flood about 5,000 years ago.

Once the existence of dinosaurs was accepted, scientists and laymen alike wanted to know more about these gargantuan creatures. What were they like? What color were they? What did they eat? How big did they grow? Most importantly, people wanted to know what happened to them.

Some paleontologists think that diseases and parasites—perhaps brought to Earth on an asteroid or meteorite—struck down these mighty animals. Another widely held view points to evidence that cosmic radiation from the sun or some exploding star caused fatal mutations.

There are numerous other explanations, ranging from global warming and starvation to a massive aerial bombardment from space. Some scientists say the dinosaurs became extinct because their brains were too small and their bodies were too large. Others think they just "grew old" and died off.

One plausible theory holds that poisonous gases belched up from volcanoes and shifting continental plates did them in. A few fanciful investigators claim that "raiding parties" from other worlds came down and kidnapped the great reptiles—the first alien abductions.

Finally, there is the possibility that the dinosaurs did not become extinct at all, they merely evolved into creatures that still exist—birds.

Most of these views have been dismissed as idle speculation by paleontologists because they seemed to represent simplistic attempts to explain a big and dramatic event. A growing number of scientists now suspect that a combination of factors might have contributed to the dinosaurs' doom.

Dinosaurs—Greek for "terrible lizard"—came in all shapes and sizes, from tiny, chicken-size creatures who scampered about on two legs, to hulking, tank-like brutes with armor-plated hides and horns. Winged terrors with gaping claws ruled the skies, while scaly, lizard-like behemoths dominated the warm seas. Yet, by the end of the Cretaceous

Period 65 million years ago, not a single one of these creatures was around.

Most paleontologists believe death came from the stars in the form of a large asteroid—perhaps 6 miles wide and weighing a billion tons—that collided with the Earth and obliterated two-thirds of all life on the planet. The impact must have been truly colossal—at least 100 million times greater than the eruption of Mt. St. Helens, more powerful than all the nuclear bombs ever made in the history of the world.

Monstrous tidal waves, spawned by earthquakes that shook mountains and ignited fiery volcanoes, roared across the land, washing away thundering herds of beasts. Ghastly plumes of dust and ash billowed high over the planet, blotting out sunlight and triggering lethal showers of sulfuric acid that lasted for years.

Temperatures around the globe plunged. Massive volcanic eruptions continued to shake the continents, while "Hypercanes"—super-intense hurricanes—blew furiously across the boiling, bone-littered landscape. Darkness settled over the planet.

Those prehistoric creatures not incinerated in the initial blast or swept away in the storms and surging tidal waves must have died slow, agonizing deaths as the air grew thick with poisonous gases and food supplies gave out. As these great herds perished, new masters of the planet began to emerge—small, furry animals that eventually evolved into the creature known as man.

Geologist Walter Alvarez of the University of California, Berkeley, was one of the first scientists to propose that a massive asteroid strike caused the demise of the dinosaurs. His controversial theory found few supporters—until 1980 when he found a massive crater off the Yucatan coast of Central America.

The crater, measuring more than 100 miles wide and 3000 feet deep, contained a layer of iridium—an element extremely rare on Earth but abundant on other celestial bodies. Date testing showed that the iridium was laid down about 65 million years ago, coinciding with the dinosaurs' extinction.

Dinosaurs were not the only victims of this "mass extinction." Many other species were killed off as well, including all marine reptiles such as plesiosaurs, mosasaurs, ichthyosaurs and ammonites, swimming and flying reptiles, sea crocodiles and foraminifera. In addition, many bony fishes, sponges, snails, clams and sea urchins became extinct.

Not all scientists are convinced that an asteroid strike caused the demise of the dinosaurs. Some think the end was a more gradual process that might have begun more than 100 million years ago with dramatic temperature changes and other environmental factors, such as the breakup of continents that diminished food-rich habitats. While this was going on, massive and continual volcanic eruptions darkened the skies with lethal gases and spewed rivers of lava across former grazing grounds.

Even if these other events occurred, scientists believe the *coup de grace* came in the form of a huge asteroid roaring down from space. They say the fate of the dinosaurs was sealed the moment that nameless piece of rock struck home.

Twilight of Neanderthal

Think "Neanderthal," and images of grunting, stoop-shouldered cavemen clad in bearskin loincloths and brandishing clubs come to mind.

That's unfortunate, because new research indicates that this big-brained ancestor who roamed Europe and parts of Africa and Asia more than 150,000 years ago was not the dim-witted brute of yore.

In fact, burial sites in Spain, Croatia, Israel and elsewhere suggest Neanderthals were sensitive, thoughtful creatures who looked after their sick and wounded and tenderly cared for the dead, as evidenced by flowers and other personal items found in some graves. More than a few scholars have gone so far as to say these enigmatic ancestors would probably blend in fairly well in a contemporary crowd—at least as long as he kept his mouth shut.

"Neanderthals were highly resourceful, highly intelligent creatures," says Fred Smith, a Neanderthal specialist at Northern Illinois University. "They were not big, dumb brutes by any stretch of the imagination. They were us—only different."

Scientists have learned a lot about these prehistoric people since the first fossilized remains were discovered in Germany's Neander Valley (hence the German name, "Neandertal" or Anglicized Neanderthal) in 1856. At first they thought this curious creature was the so-called "missing link" between humans and apes. Others thought it was a misshapen freak from the Middle Ages.

The origins of Neanderthal are uncertain, but scientists suspect they emerged as a distinct human form roughly 230,000 years ago in Europe. Skeletal remains show they were stocky, robust and muscular—traits that helped them adapt to long periods of glacial cold in northern Europe.

While their brains were larger than more advanced humans who moved into Europe about 50,000 years ago, they appeared to be deficient in tool technology, art and other customs typically associated with enlightened humans.

Neanderthals roamed far and wide pursuing game and avoiding ice sheets. They journeyed as far north as Britain and as far south as Italy and Spain, probably in small bands of 30 or less. From the Rhine River in Germany they spread toward Central Asia, finally reaching Israel and other the Middle East locations.

Some Neanderthals lived in caves. Others established campsites along animal migration routes, digging holes or trenches for shelter. Never numerous, their total population at any one time probably numbered only in the tens of thousands.

Early in their development, it appears that Neanderthals were scavengers and probably competed with wolves, lions and hyenas for food. Later, as hunting skills improved, they went after bigger game—bison, elk, even mammoths. Evidence found at some sites leads to speculation that these "Dawn Age" people might have practiced cannibalism on occasion.

It has long been suggested that the Neanderthals lacked an incest taboo—universal among all modern human societies—and did not follow an established pattern of mating and marriage between nuclear families. Despite their large brains and impressive foraging skills, it is doubtful that they ever developed symbols for communication or artistic expression.

Contrary to earlier views, Neanderthals did not die out immediately upon the arrival of clever newcomers called Cro-Magnons. Anthropologists have found abundant evidence suggesting Neanderthals were around as recently as 33,000 years ago in Croatia, 30,000 years ago in southern Spain. In other words, these two early human groups—Neanderthals and Cro-Magnon—co-existed for more than 10,000 years.

How did they get along? Was there tension and conflict between the two groups?

Until recently, the common view was that Cro-Magnon, the more advanced group, used refined weaponry and superior tactical intelligence to simply exterminate their slower-moving neighbors in battle.

Nowadays, many scientists lean toward a gradual assimilation theory. This suggests that Neanderthals intermingled with the superior race and, over time, were simply absorbed by the dominant species. Bones found in Croatia seem to confirm that Neanderthals were, in fact, beginning to breed with groups of modern humans arriving from the Middle East.

Other scientists disagree. "They were a different species," argues Fred Spoor of University College in London. "There is no convincing evidence of interbreeding on any significant scale."

Then what happened to this wandering group of people thousands of years before the birth of civilization? If their population was not eradicated by modern immigrants or bred out of existence, why did they suddenly vanish from the world stage? Perhaps they were an evolutionary dead-end from the get-go, destined to become extinct in humanity's long evolutionary march upward. Perhaps the newcomers on the scene—smarter, taller, more artistic and technologically dominant in every way—simply outclassed these enigmatic, stoop-shouldered creatures from the past.

Doomsday Stars

Somewhere far out in space, there is a big chunk of rock with Earth's name on it. Years from now—it could be 50, it could be 50,000—that rock will kick loose from its solar orbit and come crashing down. When that happens, life on Earth could come to a screeching halt—as it has so many times in the geologic past.

Such a catastrophic scenario might seem unthinkable to some, the stuff of science fiction and fantasy. Yet a number of scientists say doomsday voyagers from the distant corners of the solar system are out there—and they may be headed our way.

It is known that millions of asteroids cartwheel through the solar system, ranging from a few feet in diameter up to 50 miles wide. At least 50 potentially death-dealing asteroids regularly intersect Earth's orbit. One monster, Ida, is thought to be the largest, at 278 miles across.

What would happen if Ida or one of her big neighbors crossed paths with Earth? For many scientists, this would be the ultimate nightmare. Computer models show that an earth-crossing asteroid of only 1-mile-wide could wipe out a third of life on the planet. A 6-miles-wide object would have the impact of 2 million Hiroshima bombs, or 320,000 mega-tons of dynamite.

Fortunately, scientists say the chance of Ida slamming into

Earth is zero. But the odds of an encounter with another asteroid of equal magnitude remain high, so high governments around the world have formed "Doomsday Squads" that monitor the heavens in search of potential danger.

Millions of years ago, the Earth was under constant bombardment from asteroids and comets. As time passed the number of collisions became fewer, but the size of the asteroids stayed pretty much the same. Some 500 large meteorites continue to fall to earth each year, while tons of tiny micrometeorites descend daily.

Some scientists think that a colossal rock more than 6 miles wide and weighing probably a billion tons broke from its orbit 65 million years ago and crashed into the coast of Mexico's Yucatan peninsula. The impact wiped out two-thirds of all life, including the dinosaurs.

Comets whirling through the cosmos on their long journeys around the sun also pose catastrophic risks. Scientists speculate that collisions with these "dirty snowballs" have occurred in the past, sometimes resulting in mass extinctions.

In 1994, the world watched breathlessly when a runaway comet called Shoemaker-Levy 9 looped out of orbit and walloped Jupiter. The impact, clearly visible through telescopes, sent shudders through the scientific community, waking up many to the reality that a cataclysmic collision could occur on Earth.

A few astronomers insist strikes by meteorites or death-dealing comets spawned the Biblical story about Noah and other legends of fire and flood.

It is true that practically every race has its own traditions about ancient catastrophes that nearly ended the world. Many of these legends are so similar in detail that it's tempting to assume they all share a common origin.

The Babylonian Epic of Gilgamesh, for example, which is around 4,000 years old and records traditions of an even earlier age, tells of a dark cloud that rushed at the earth, leaving the land shriveled by the heat of the flames.

The legends of the Cashinaua, the aborigines of western Brazil, tell of the time when, "The lightnings flashed and the thunders roared terribly and all were afraid. Then the heaven burst and the fragments fell down and killed everything and everybody."

Besides the story about Noah, the Bible contains numerous other passages that refer to terrible events. Psalms 18:7-15 reports: "Then the earth shook and trembled; the foundations also of the hills moved and were shaken. The Lord also thundered in the heavens, and the highest gave his voice; hail stones and coals of fire…"

Greeks, Romans, Egyptians, Indians, Persians, Norwegians, Chinese and the Mayas and Aztecs of Central America are among the many ancient peoples whose legends deal with cosmic events and cataclysmic disturbances. So do such widely separated cultures as the Celts of Britain and the Maasoris of New Zealand.

What on Earth—or in Heaven—could have caused such seemingly worldwide disasters?

More recently, the late Russian physicist Immanuel Velikovsky promoted a controversial theory that a close-Earth comet encounter lay behind the catastrophe legends of old. He claimed the encounter might have had something to do with the parting of the Red Sea, the eruption of Mt. Sinai and the pillar of cloud and fire that Moses saw moving across the sky. According to Velikovsky, the Book of Joshua describes a destructive shower of meteorites occurring before the sun "stood still" in the sky.

Although most orthodox scientists dismiss the idea of a global catastrophe of the kind described by Velikovsky as "crank theory," they are hard put to explain the legends. For example, Noah's flood supposedly drowned every living thing on Earth—apart from the few survivors on board the Ark. It is now considered likely that this story was based on a real flood that submerged some 40,000 square miles of the Euphrates Valley some time between 5400 and 4200 B.C.

Since ancient times, people have contemplated the heavens with a mixture of fear and wonder. The passing of a comet, crash of a meteorite or other similar celestial event must have been a faith-altering experience for primitive populations. Even today, people still look upon the skies with that same sense of helpless dread.

Scientists who chart the movements of comets and asteroids must occasionally be tempted to shake their heads and say, "If they only knew…"

Adam and Eve in the New World

Anthropologists generally agree that humans evolved in Africa, then migrated to Europe and Asia, eventually crossing the Bering Straits into Alaska before wandering down into the Americas.

This prehistoric journey to the New World has long been the subject of intense speculation among scholars. Until recently, it was thought the migration did not begin until after the end of the last Ice Age, between 12,000 and 10,000 years ago.

The prevalent view was that the journey occurred in several waves, one generation giving way to the next, as these skin-clad hunters armed with crude spears and axes pressed deeper into their strange new world in search of game and who knows what else.

The process must have taken countless ages, whole populations growing up and dying within a few miles of their ancestral birthplace. In time, however—perhaps as recently as 8,000 years ago—their descendants finally reached Tierra del Fuego at the tip of South America.

Now scientists aren't so sure that's the way it happened. New findings in California, Texas, Florida, Central and South

America seem to indicate that human beings have been in the New World a lot longer than previously suspected.

In 1976, workers digging along the marshy banks of a creek in Monte Verde in southern Chile unearthed the remains of a prehistoric campsite that might contain human artifacts older than any before found in the New World.

The discovery sent shock waves rippling around the scientific world. According to some anthropologists who have examined the artifacts, it now appears that the historical record of the Americas will have to be rewritten.

"These were truly dawn people," said Tom Dillehay, an American anthropologist who headed the initial investigation in Valdivia. "We might think of them as Adam and Eve in the New World."

Radiocarbon testing of stone weapons, mastodon bones and hundreds of other artifacts at the Monte Verde site indicate the region might have been home to a band of prehistoric wanderers thousands of years sooner than thought possible.

Human footprints were found, along with remnants of some 45 edible plants. More than one-fifth of the plants came from regions as far as 150 miles away, indicating that the Monte Verdeans either ranged far or traded with other groups.

"The amount of plant foods we found at the site—notably wild potatoes, bamboos, mushrooms and juncus seeds—was astounding," said Jack Rosen, an ethnobiologist from Ithaca College who helped study the site.

These and other prehistoric finds in the region contradict conventional theories about mankind's relative newcomer status in the New World, according to David Meltzer, an archaeologist at Southern Methodist University in Dallas.

"How could people possibly have reached all the way down there from Alaska in a few hundred years?" he asked. "They were pioneering a landscape that was becoming increasingly unfamiliar as they moved south. They had to find water and figure out which plants and animals were edible, useful, harmful or even fatal."

These brave newcomers had to "cross formidable barriers," Dr. Meltzer continued, "and cope with new diseases. And they had to do all this while raising families on a vast continent devoid of other people. All of that takes time."

Primitive tools and charcoal deposits recently excavated at several places in the United States, Central and South America point to the arrival of native Americans in the New World 50,000 years ago or longer.

Linguists and geneticists have long maintained that American Indians are simply too rich in languages and genetic diversity to have had a common ancestry only 12,000 years ago. The variety of cultures that developed in the Americas would have required a much longer period, they say.

Since Monte Verde suggests a much earlier presence, just how and when did they arrive? Could they have skirted the glaciers, coming down along the coast by boat from Alaska? Or could they have migrated through a narrow corridor that might have separated the ice sheets in eastern British Columbia?

Sailing across the Pacific from Asia to South America in numbers large enough to colonize seems too difficult a journey for primitive seafarers, according to some anthropologists. A more likely explanation, they contend, is that these "dawn age" travelers migrated into the lower reaches of North America even before the ice sheets developed—between 20,000 and 75,000 years ago.

The speculation is likely to continue, even as more evidence is brought forth from the ground.

Secrets
of the
Ancient *World*

The Pharoah's Curse

Howard Carter was worried.

For years he had been digging in the dry desert soil with nothing more to show for it than a few boxes of old ancient bones and Bronze Age trinkets.

Now his time was running out. If he didn't find archaeological treasure soon, he would lose his funding. Lord Carnarvon, his primary British backer, had already warned him there would be no more money after this season.

But Howard Carter clung to his dream. He knew that somewhere, buried beneath the shifting sands of the Valley of the Kings, lay the long-lost tomb of an ancient Egyptian monarch named Tutankhamen—and a treasure worth millions.

So the young English archaeologist kept digging, pushing his workers relentlessly beneath the blazing Egyptian sun.

Finally, on the morning of November 4, 1922, Carter uncovered a series of stone steps that led to an apparently undisturbed underground chamber. His spirits soared when he read the name carved above the door: Tutankhamen.

Then he saw another message: "Death shall come on swift wings to him who disturbs the peace of the king."

Carter ignored the strange warning and quickly fired off a telegram to Lord Carnarvon: "At last have made a wonderful discovery in valley…Magnificent tomb with seals intact…"

Accompanied by a team of specialists, Lord Carnarvon hurried to Egypt. It took them several more days to break through the door and clear a rock-filled passage. Then the two partners—Lord Carnarvon and Carter—stood before a second sealed door.

It was Howard Carter's moment of truth. As his wealthy partner and friend peered over his shoulder, the archaeologist chipped at the door until there was a hole big enough for him to flash a light in and take a look.

He wrote: "At first I could see nothing, the hot air from the chamber causing the flame to flicker. But as my eyes grew accustomed to the light, details of the room emerged slowly from the mist: strange animals, statues, and gold—everywhere the glint of gold!"

The chamber consisted of four rooms filled with caskets, vases, a gold-plated throne inlaid with precious stones, gems, furniture, clothing and weapons. In the burial chamber itself, flanked by two black statues, were four gold shrines, one inside the other, and a sarcophagus contained a nest of three coffins.

The inner one, of solid gold, held the mummified body of Tutankhamen, wrapped in a jewel-studded shroud. Over his face was a gold mask inlaid with quartz and lapis lazuli. Across his neck and breast was a garland of cornflowers, lilies and lotuses.

The discovery of the Egyptian boy-king's tomb made headlines around the world. Scholars hailed it as the most significant archaeological discovery of all time. In the following months, however, the excitement was marred by a number of strange events that led many people to believe that King Tut's curse had come true.

Some say it started the very day the tomb was opened. A sandstorm reportedly sprang up suddenly, blinding several workers. As it died away, a hawk—the royal emblem of ancient Egypt—was seen soaring over the tomb to the west, toward the mysterious "Other World" of Egyptian belief.

Superstitious workers said the hawk carried away the soul of the dead pharaoh, who had left behind a curse to punish those who violated his tomb.

The following spring Lord Carnarvon, 57, died from a bug bite. Legend has it that at the exact moment of his death in a Cairo hospital, the city experienced a brief power failure. Back in England on the Carnarvon estate, one of the Lord's favorite dogs began to howl, then suddenly fell over dead.

By 1935, 21 people either directly involved with the expedition or related to someone who took part in the dig had died—all under mysterious circumstances. Among them were Lord Carnarvon's half-brother, Aubrey Herbert, and another relative, Lady Elizabeth Carnarvon. Astonishingly, she too died of an infected insect bite.

Shortly after Lord Carnarvon's death, Arthur Mace, the American archaeologist who had helped unseal the tomb, complained of exhaustion, then lapsed into a coma and died in the same hotel where Lord Carnarvon had died.

George Jay Gould, a wealthy American financier, also visited the tomb and died the same day. Joel Wool, a British industrialist who toured the tomb with Carter, died of a strange fever on his way back to England. Even the radiologist who X-rayed Tutankhamen's mummy—Archibald Douglas Reid—died of "mysterious causes" on his return trip to England in 1924.

The Hon. Richard Bethell, who helped Carter catalog the treasures, was thought to have committed suicide at the age of 49. A few months later, in February 1930, his father, Lord Westbury, hurled himself to death from his London apartment. An alabaster vase from the Pharaoh's tomb was in his bedroom.

An Egyptian prince, Ali Farmy Bey, whose family claimed descent from the pharaohs, was murdered in a London hotel, and his brother committed suicide.

Newspapers headlined the string of strange deaths on a daily basis. Recalling the cryptic warning on the boy-king's tomb, they wrote shocking stories about "King Tut's Curse."

While professional archaeologists scoff at the idea of King Tut's curse, the fact remains that dozens of lives were strangely affected by the discovery. In the seven years after the tomb was opened in 1922, a dozen people who had been involved with the project were dead—victims, some believed, of the dead Pharaoh's curse.

Most investigators say the deaths were coincidental and had nothing to do with a superstitious curse. Bug bites, for example, are common in Egypt and without proper medication, victims frequently die from infection. Some of the deaths were linked to dangerous molds inside the ancient tomb.

Ironically, the man who might have had most to fear from the curse—Howard Carter—lived for another decade. His death in 1939 was attributed to natural causes.

Yet, stories about the strange curse did not go away. In 1966, another death made headlines, this one following a decision by the Egyptian government to allow the pharaoh's treasure to be sent to Paris for exhibition.

For years, Mohammed Ibraham, the Egyptian director of antiquities, had dreamed that a "terrible fate" awaited him should Tutankhamen's treasure be allowed to leave the country. Shortly after the decision was made to send the exhibition to Paris, Ibraham was struck by a car while crossing a street outside his Cairo office.

He died two days later—another victim, some say, of the pharaoh's curse.

The Talking Colossus

In ancient times, people traveled to Egypt from vast distances to gaze upon the pyramids and Sphinx and other architectural marvels. But the most famous tourist attraction was a pair of gargantuan statues that stood guard over the capital city of Thebes for more than 3,000 years.

What made the statues so popular was the fact that one of them—the so-called "Vocal Memnon"—could talk.

The phenomenon was reported by thousands of visitors, including the great Greek geographer Strabo. Many came to worship and pray at the base of the statue. Some described the sound as "like the blow of mighty winds." One worshipper said it was more like the "voice of a sweet goddess crying out for a lost child."

According to another Greek geographer, Pausanias, the statue spoke every day at sunrise, usually after a large crowd had gathered at its feet to pay homage.

"Every day at sunrise, it cries out," he wrote in *Guidebook of Greece*, the only guidebook to have survived from the ancient world. "One would compare the sound most nearly to the breaking of a harp or string."

Many witnesses believed that they had heard the voice of Memnon, the legendary king of Ethiopia, who was said to have been slain by the Greek hero Achilles in the Trojan War.

On the legs and base of the "talking" statue were many inscriptions of the names of distinguished visitors, often with lengthy messages. The inscriptions, written mostly in Greek and Latin, reveal the firm belief of the visitors in the miraculous sound.

Archaeologists believe the pair of statues—known as the Colossi of Memnon—are really twin statues of the Pharaoh Amenophis III, who reigned from about 1417 to 1379 B.C. Carved from red sandstone, they tower 64 feet above the ground, with shoulders 20 feet broad and fingers more than 4 feet long.

In 27 B.C., an earthquake struck Thebes with great force, damaging one of the statues. The giant split across its body, and the upper part of the magnificent structure was hurled to the ground.

Soon after the earthquake, reports began to circulate that the damaged statue had begun to "talk"—usually around sunrise every day.

For 200 years, visitors marveled at the talking statue. Then, early in the third century, a Roman emperor—Septimius Severus—who ruled from A.D. 193 to 211, went to Thebes and ordered the damaged statue repaired.

After the statue was repaired, however, a strange thing happened—it never spoke again.

How, then, did the statue "speak?"

One theory holds that the sudden, fierce heat of the sun

expanded the cold, damp stone unevenly along the cracked surface. This might in turn have set up vibrations that were interpreted as a melodious voice.

Another theory is that the sound might have been caused by a current of expanding air making its way through a damaged section of the stone.

Skeptics attribute the phenomenon to human intervention—an ingenious subterfuge to guarantee that gifts and offerings would continue to pour into the shrine.

Perhaps the Theban priests were expert ventriloquists. Or perhaps they concealed someone at the base of the statue before dawn. If so, they must have been incredibly skilled or lucky to have kept up the deception for so long.

Beneath the Lair of the Sphinx

French explorers digging near Giza, Egypt, 150 years ago were astonished when they uncovered an enormous stone statue that seemed to be part lion, part god and part pharaoh. Scholars identified the statue as the famed Sphinx, known to the ancient Greeks, Romans and Arabs, but forgotten for centuries.

The discovery was hailed as the "find of the century" and sparked an international debate about the enigmatic origins of the Sphinx, its purpose and the myriad of ancient secrets supposedly buried beneath its massive, out-stretched paws.

Most scholars think it was built 4,600 years ago as a memorial to Chephren, son of Cheops, architect of the Great Pyramid. But that can't be true, say some Egyptologists who argue that the sculptured beast is much older than the nearby pyramids and was built at least 12,000 years ago.

One such thinker was French mathematician R.A. Schwaller. In the 1930s he published a paper outlining his theory that ancient Egyptian science and culture was far older than previously believed by modern scholars. Dr. Schwaller's hunch is linked to water markings around the base of the Sphinx that he thinks were laid down at least 10,000 years ago—long after the great stone edifice was built.

Dr. Schwaller was convinced that "a great civilization must have preceded the vast movements of water that passed over Egypt, which leads us to assume that the Sphinx already existed, sculptured in the rock of the west cliff of Giza—that Sphinx whose leonine body, except for the head, shows indisputable signs of water erosion."

American author John Anthony West, a respected Egyptologist who conducts research and frequent tours of the Sphinx and nearby pyramids, agrees with Dr. Schaller's findings. For one thing, he says there hasn't been enough moisture on the Giza plateau in 5,000 years to account for the extensive erosion evident on the body of the Sphinx.

"You really have to go back to before 10,000 B.C. to find a wet enough climate in Egypt to account for weathering of this type and on this scale," West said. "It therefore follows that the Sphinx must have been built before 10,000 B.C., and since it's a massive, sophisticated work of art, it also follows that it must have been built by a high civilization."

West quickly dismisses any notion that wear and tear of the Sphinx might have been caused by wind or sand erosion.

"If the Sphinx was really built in the Old Kingdom, and if wind erosion was capable of inflicting such damage on it in so short a time-span, then other Old Kingdom structures in the area, built out of the same limestone, ought to show similar weathering," he said. "But none do—you know, absolutely unmistakable Old Kingdom tombs, full of hieroglyphs and inscriptions—none of them show the same type of weathering as the Sphinx."

Professor Robert Schoch, a Boston University geologist and specialist in rock erosion, agrees with West. He convinced some professional peers at the 1992 Convention of the

Geological Society of America that the weathering of the Sphinx was not caused by wind-scouring, but by thousands of years of heavy rainfall long ages before the Old Kingdom came into being.

"I'm not saying that the Sphinx was built by Atlanteans, or people from Mars, or extraterrestrials," Dr. Schoch explained. "I'm just following the science where it leads me, and it leads me to conclude that the Sphinx was built much earlier than previously thought."

If his theory as a geologist conflicts with that of archaeologists, historians and Egyptologists about the rise of ancient civilizations, "then maybe it's time for them to re-evaluate that theory," he noted.

So who built the Sphinx if it wasn't the pre-dynastic Egyptians?

According to Graham Hancock, British author of *Fingerprints of the Gods*, "the riddle is linked in some way to those legendary civilizations spoken of in all the mythologies of the world. You know—that there were great catastrophes, that a few people survived and went wandering around the earth and that a bit of knowledge was preserved here, a bit there…

"My hunch is that the Sphinx is linked to all that. If I were asked to place a bet I'd say that it predates the breakup of the last Ice Age and is probably older than 10,000 B.C., perhaps even older than 15,000 B.C. My conviction—actually it's more than a conviction—is that it's vastly old."

John Anthony West expects that "some day" archaeologists will find a hidden passageway beneath the Sphinx—a hidden lair that will prove the vast age of the monument once and for all.

"It's down there," he said. "We've got the evidence to prove it."

That "evidence" centers on seismological research conducted in the early 1990s, which West said revealed the existence of a "substantial" underground chamber.

Dr. Zahi Hawass, the archaeological director of the pyramids, and many other scholars who have spent decades scrutinizing the pottery, tombs, hieroglyphics and other ruins from the Giza plateau, take strong issue with "outlandish" theories about prehistoric civilizations in Egypt. In Dr. Hawass's opinion, not a single object found there can be interpreted as coming from an advanced civilization that predates about 3200 B.C.

"Anyone is free to believe anything he wants," Dr. Hawass said, "but I call people like him (West) Pyramididiots."

Such comments only inflame West's intense desire to keep searching for clues to prove that his theories are correct and those of mainstream Egyptologists like Dr. Hawass are way off base.

"All I know for sure on the basis of our work on the Sphinx is that a very, very high, sophisticated civilization capable of undertaking construction projects on a grand scale was present in Egypt in the very distant past," he said. "Then there was a lot of rain. Then, thousands of years later, in the same place, pharaonic civilization popped up already fully formed, apparently out of nowhere, with all its knowledge complete."

While the debate continues to rage, the enigmatic, red stone monument stands gazing across the Nile, timeless and tranquil, as inscrutable and mysterious today as it was when its unknown builders laid the first stone.

A Dark and Cruel Past

The ancient Cathaginians, rulers of the western Mediterranean for more than 500 years, were a proud and prosperous people. From their North African kingdom near Tunis, they roamed the seas, establishing colonies and conquering any nation bold enough or reckless enough to stand in their way.

In 186 B.C. the empire's greatest leader, Hannibal, crossed

the Alps and laid waste to much of Italy. When the long campaign bogged down, Rome counterattacked, eventually conquering Carthage itself and bringing to an end one of the ancient world's oldest and most glorious empires.

The conquest also opened one of history's darkest mysteries.

For years, it had been rumored that, beneath their courageous and industrious image, the Carthaginians were a "cruel and hard" people who practiced hideous religious rituals, including child sacrifices. It was alleged that they purchased or captured children from other nations for the sole purpose of offering them to Baal Hammon, their principal deity.

The Greeks were the first to postulate about this dark side of Carthage, following an attempt by Agathocles to capture the powerful city-state in 310 B.C.

"Lately," wrote Diodorus, the noted Greek historian, "instead of sacrificing children from the best families to the god, they had been buying children from other nations, rearing them in secret and then sacrificing them."

To be sure, much of what is known about the Carthaginians was handed down by their conquerors, most notably the Greeks and Romans, who might have had their own reasons for depicting their ancient foe in a less than flattering light. Plutarch called them a "dark and gloomy people, subservient to their rulers, harsh to their subjects."

Others called them cowardly and cruel, obstinate and superstitious.

Many 19th century European historians found the horrible rumors hard to believe. No ancient people could have been that cruel or superstitious, especially the courageous Carthaginians, proud descendants of the long-vanished Phoenicians of Tyre and Sidon.

In 1862, historians were outraged by a book written by Flaubert that described the horrific details of child sacrifice practiced by the Carthaginians.

"There were in Carthage several brass statues of Baal

Hammon," Flaubert writes in *Salammbo*. "The outstretched hands were inclined toward the earth so that a child placed on them could not lie there but rolled off and fell into the fiery pit below."

The dark legend has been confirmed by archaeology.

Child sacrifice at Carthage apparently did not cease with the Roman destruction of the city. Tertullian, a second-century Christian, reported that it continued for hundreds of years, that children in that part of Africa were sacrificed in public to Saturn until the priests themselves were crucified in 37 A.D.

But, said Tertullian, this execrable sacrificial ritual of children continued in secret until his own day. Most tragic of all, he wrote, was that the parents themselves brought their offspring to the bloodthirsty god.

To be sure, the Carthaginians were not the only ones who partook of this hideous practice. Kingdoms and nations throughout the ancient world, including the Israelites and other Biblical peoples, ritualistically killed children for a variety of reasons.

According to scholars, children were often sacrificed as a means of population control in times of famine and stress. Phoenicians, for example, threw their children onto bonfires in times of crisis. King Mesha of Moab sacrificed his oldest son during a war against Israel, in the hopes that the god Chemosh would save his kingdom from destruction.

Diodorus of Sicily wrote that when the Carthaginians "saw their enemy encamped before their walls…they selected 200 of the noblest children and sacrificed them publicly."

Some historians have suggested that Carthaginians and other ancient peoples resorted to child sacrifice as a means of consolidating family wealth among the upper class. They also theorize that infanticide was a widespread method of preventing poverty, similar to the Greek and Roman custom of leaving unwanted children exposed on hillsides.

Newborns were frequently chosen for the ritual, but in Carthage evidence suggests that older children—1 to 3 years of age—were preferred. Sometimes the children were related, as many of the urns found at the Tophet—the largest and oldest cemetery in Carthage—suggests.

No one knows how, when or exactly why the grim practice of child sacrifice originated. In all likelihood, the ritual began at the dawn of time as a means of coping with an uncertain world full of mystery and wonder.

By ancient times, however, the custom of slaughtering children to appease gods had become an everyday part of life. Many passages from the Bible, in fact, indicate that Yahweh, god of the Israelites, called for the ritualistic blood offerings of children.

"Consecrate to me every first-born," God instructs Moses in Exodus 13:1-2, "the first issue of every womb among Israelites is mine." Then, in Exodus 22:29, Yahweh orders, "The firstborn of your sons you shall give to me."

Based on the archaeological record, however, the Carthaginians appear to have been the only society that made child sacrifice a routine part of their culture—a "dark and cruel" people indeed.

The Shining Kingdom in the Jungle

For six long months French naturalist Henri Mouhot had been hacking his way through dense, crocodile-infested swamps of northern Cambodia in search of rare birds and exotic plants.

Nearing exhaustion and running low on supplies, the weary explorer was on the verge of declaring his mission a failure when, early one January morning in 1860, he came upon an astonishing sight—great sandstone towers rising high above the trees.

Intrigued, Mouhot pressed on to discover fabulous temples and terraces half-hidden in the weeds, huge stone causeways and walls and wondrously carved pinnacles covered in elaborate sculpture. Extending as far as the eye could see was a magnificent city with hundreds of daringly constructed towers and the remnants of vast artificial waterways and broad monumental highways.

And everywhere was colossal sculpture—elephants, lions, serpents, kings and queens and hundreds of figures from Hindu religious epics. Most impressive of all, perhaps, were the temples—hundreds of crumbling stone edifices covering at least 25 square miles.

One large temple, believed by some researchers to be the largest religious monument in the world, appeared to represent the Hindu cosmology with beautifully crafted bas-relief statues of dancing queens and devatas.

Mouhot had just laid eyes on Angkor Thom, the fabled lost city.

"It is greater than anything left to us by Greece or Rome," Mouhot declared in his diary. "To obtain any idea of its splendor one must imagine the most beautiful creations of architecture transported into the depths of the forests in one of the more remote countries of the world."

Angkor's most notable monument lay more than a mile outside the walls of the city Angkor Wat, one of the most beautiful and famous shrines in the world. Built in the 11th century by King Udayadityavarman II and renovated by King Jayavarman VII at the end of the 12th century, the vast temple ruins are surrounded by a 4-mile long moat—once stocked with crocodiles and poisonous snakes—in an almost perfect square.

The main temple is a bewildering complex of lakes and libraries, cloisters and galleries, shrines and stairways. Spiraling stone steps lead to crumbling terraces and platforms where proud nobles presided, where robed priests once raised their arms heavenward and called out to the angels to protect the population from demonic spirits. Lonely, rickety ramparts still guard the silent city from long-dead invaders.

When local people were asked who had built these remarkable structures, they shrugged and said variously it was the "work of the giants" or it was the "work of Pra-Eun, the king of the angels."

Others claimed Angkor was created by the Leper King, or that it simply "made itself." Some said the city had stood in the jungle since the beginning of time and would remain their forever.

Mouhot concluded sadly that the inhabitants of the mysterious stone city "seemed destined to remain hidden among the chaos and ashes of the past."

Two years after his discovery, the naturalist died of tropical fever. But in 1866 the French government began a systematic study of Angkor Thom, the ancient capital of the great Khmer Empire that flourished for five centuries before fading 400 years ago.

By 1885 certain rulers and time-lines had been identified, but major questions remained: Who had built the city and why? Why did the empire collapse? Where did the original occupants go?

Archaeologists are still seeking answers to those questions. Some think that natural disasters—prolonged droughts or even heavy flooding—might have brought down the once mighty empire. Others suspect that brutal invaders from the north overran the kingdom, killing off most of the population and enslaving the rest.

Today, the descendants of the once-proud Khmer continue to inhabit Cambodia's Northwestern province of Siem Reap, content to eke out a living among the steamy jungles and swamps of their ancient homeland. When outsiders ask them about the glorious past of their ancestors, they smile and say the day will come when the old ones return to reclaim their shining kingdom in the jungle.

Mighty Zimbabwe

High atop a windy plateau in southern Zimbabwe stand the crumbling remains of a stone city that has intrigued explorers and scholars since its discovery in the late 1800s.

Local tribesmen call the massive granite stoneworks "Zimbabwe," which means "venerated houses" or "stone houses" in the Bantu language, but nobody knows who built them, when or why.

European scholars theorized that the ruins had been constructed by some advanced civilization far to the north, possibly the Phoenicians or Egyptians. Another suggestion was that "Great Zimbabwe," as the ruins came to be known, may have been the site of King Solomon's legendary mines.

Scattered over sixty acres, the complex is dominated by a huge, walled enclosure dubbed the "Acropolis" because of its hilltop site. Three structures are included in the complex—a majestic, fortress-like series of walls, labyrinthine passages, steps and corridors; a magnificent temple in another walled enclosure more than 100 yards long and 70 yards wide; and a series of lesser buildings, known simply as the Valley Ruins.

German archaeologist Karl Mauch is thought to have been the first white man to gaze upon the ancient ruins. He came upon the imposing formations while tracking through the brush in 1871.

In his diary, Mauch wrote: "On the third of September 1871 we ascended this hill. It is about two miles long, fairly high with a bare top from which there is a magnificent view in all directions. At first my guide ventured gingerly on to the summit and then, one after another, walking like cats on hot bricks, we followed.

"Suddenly, in an easterly direction about five miles away, could be clearly seen a hill on which were great walls built apparently in European style."

When the German entered the lost city, he found evidence of a rich and powerful civilization. One thing was certain, however—the builders could not have been Africans, because the local population—the Karangas—lived in modest mud huts and possessed few of the skills and wealth necessary for the construction of such an architectural marvel.

No, it had to be someone else—some powerful people or civilization now long vanished. The legendary Christian monarch Prester John came to mind, as did the ancient Egyptian cities far to the north.

The German explorer's discovery stimulated interest in long-lost cities and civilizations on the "dark continent." Soon waves of archaeologists and tourists were flocking to what was then called Rhodesia to investigate and marvel at Great Zimbabwe's brooding walls and temples. Treasure hunters came in droves, searching for gold and other valuable artifacts.

Experts believed the ruins were a byproduct of the gold trade that flourished in the region thousands of years ago. Most scholars supported Mauch's theory that Great Zimbabwe had been planned and built as a trading post by skillful architects and workmen imported from either Egypt or Phoenicia.

But could the African Acropolis really have been built thousands of years ago? To many archaeologists, this seemed doubtful, especially after a Scottish expert, David Randall-MacIver, concluded that the stone structures were only hundreds instead of thousands of years old, and that they were the work not of foreign workers but of Africans.

These findings, announced early this century, were upheld by an English archaeologist, Gertrude Caton-Thompson, who, in 1929, wrote that "examination of all the existing evidence gathered from every quarter, still can produce not one single item that is not in accordance with the claim of Bantu origin and medieval date."

Zimbabwe's age continued to be debated, but evidence found in deposits dated by carbon-14 analysis suggests that work on the Acropolis, the earliest settlement on the hill, did not begin until the second or third century A.D. By about 1200 the area was controlled by the ancestors of the present Shona people, the Mbire, who were skilled miners, craftsmen and traders.

When and why was the flourishing trading and religious center of Great Zimbabwe abandoned?

Historians are now fairly certain that by the start of the 16th century, the inhabitants of the ancient city simply ran out of food and timber supplies. Climatic changes, such as a series of droughts and crop failures, could have sent the population fleeing to safer, more producer regions.

One local legend says a god came down to earth and took the people away. Like many another god, the visiting deity promised he would return someday to get the rest of his people.

Stonehenge Decoded

Of all the world's great mysteries, none has haunted the popular imagination more than Stonehenge, that brooding circle of giant stones towering over a windy, desolate plain in southern England.

Nobody knows who built Stonehenge or why. In many ways, the origin and purpose of the megalith remains as mysterious as it did when Roman legions overran the British Isles more than 2,000 years ago.

Was it a temple of the sun? A royal palace? A magic shrine? An observatory for studying the heavens?

Some have even suggested it was a gigantic computer built centuries before the Greeks mastered mathematics. By aligning the stones with astronomical formations, it is possible to mark the passage of time and predict future events—or so it is said.

Until recently, many people thought Stonehenge was built by a mysterious class of Celtic priests known as Druids. According to legend, the Druids, clad in white robes and adorned with sacred mistletoe leaves, used the temple as a place of worship and as a site for bloody human sacrificial rituals.

But modern archaeology has determined the mysterious structure situated on Salisbury Plain in the county of Wiltshire predates the Druids by more than 1,000 years and was built in several stages over a period of several centuries.

Stonehenge owes much of its mystical reputation to a 12th century historian, Geoffrey of Monmouth, who linked it with legends about King Arthur and Camelot. He also claimed that the magician Merlin used magic to transport stones from Ireland that were used in the site's construction. Ever since, the place has been the scene of much mystery and magic.

Even though many people continue to believe Stonehenge was built by the Druids, most experts now agree the assemblage was built and rebuilt by a series of Neolithic peoples who inhabited the area over a period of some 2,000 years.

According to some authorities, construction probably started around 3000 B.C. when a group of a new Stone Age people arrived in Britain. At that time, Stonehenge was little more than a circular ditch and bank about six feet high with a broad entrance. Around this formation were 30 smaller, but still immense, upright stones forming an outer circle, with 30 slightly smaller lintels making up a continuous level ring, its surface about 16 feet off the ground.

Several centuries later, a highly developed Bronze Age group known as the Beaker Folk are credited with hauling and erecting the estimated 82 original bluestones, monoliths each weighing up to 5 tons, which they probably brought by sledge roller and barge from the Prescelly Mountains in southern Wales.

Refinements to Stonehenge were made 50 years later by another Bronze Age group known as the Wessex.

It is possible that Stonehenge remained a center of some sort even into Roman times, though most experts say it is doubtful that it was used by the Druids, who favored groves and streams for their mystical worship services.

One British investigator, author Daniel Cohen, explains: "If it had been a center of Druidic resistance to the Romans, the Romans probably would have had it torn down. As it was, they simply ignored it."

Gradually, Stonehenge fell into disuse, and its original purpose was forgotten.

Part of the mystery centers around its construction. For example, many experts wonder how a pre-Roman, barbaric people like the Britons were able to build such an elaborate assembly without the required technology.

Even more puzzling are the so-called bluestones. As previously noted, these enormous slabs, each weighing about five tons, could have come from only one place—the Prescelly Mountains in Wales, some 130 miles from Stonehenge. The question is how did they get there?

"The easiest way to move these stones would have been by water," said Cohen, "and the most direct route would have involved floating the stones on rafts over 215 miles of waterways, then dragging or rolling them overland for another 125 miles or so."

The point is, added Cohen, the construction of Stonehenge was a local project involving native labor, ideas and technology. He admitted, however, "there is a possibility that builders from more advanced Mediterranean cultures may have helped."

Similar groups of megalithic stone circles have been found throughout Western Europe, from the misty fens of Sweden and the Shetland Islands in the north, to Spain, Portugal and Malta in the south. One source estimated that at least 50,000 Stonehenge-like assemblies have been located, while countless thousands of others were destroyed by Christian zealots who saw them as pagan ceremonial centers. Many others were simply pushed aside to make way for highways, houses and parking lots.

During the Middle Ages, Christians viewed these colossal monuments as evil, the handiwork of devils and demons, of wizards or of the giants who walked the earth before The

Flood. In later times, people thought they were simply crude copies of the more polished monuments of the Middle East and Homeric Greece. The designs, they said, had been brought by missionaries preaching a new religion, or by merchants following the trade routes which brought amber from the Baltic and tin from Cornwall to the Mediterranean world.

In 1963, American astronomer Gerald Hawkins claimed to have found a simple, yet complex, answer to the Stonehenge enigma. In his book, *Stonehenge Decoded*, Professor. Hawkins theorized that the ancient collection of rocks once served as a kind of prehistoric computer, its primary function being to make "intricate calculations" of sunrises and sunsets, the movements of the moon and the eclipses of both sun and moon.

While modern archaeology has answered many questions about Stonehenge, many secrets remain.

Alpine Iceman

In the fall of 1991, two German hikers trekking across a glacial region of the Tyrolean Alps near the Austrian-Italian border came upon a grisly sight.

Frozen in the ice and drifting snow was the badly decomposed body of an oddly attired man, armed with a copper ax, knife, long bow and leather quiver bulging with flint-tipped arrows.

Suspecting foul play, the hikers hurried down the mountain and informed the police. Only later did they learn that the desiccated corpse they discovered was that of a man dead for more than 5,300 years.

The discovery of the "Alpine Iceman" made headlines around the world. Some anthropologists compared the significance of the find to the discovery of ancient Troy and King Tutankhamen's tomb.

For the first time, scientists had an opportunity to study the well-preserved remains of a Stone Age European.

The iceman's attire—deerskin vest, leather loincloth, bearskin leggings and a conical cap made of fur—provided valuable clues to a long-vanished culture.

The dark-skinned iceman, a male probably in his late 20s or early 30s and stood 5-feet, 2-inches tall, carried an impressive arsenal of Stone Age technology, including a 6-foot bow, flint scrapers, awl, flint knife with string sheath and a copper ax bound with leather.

Elated scientists hailed the find as a "time capsule" of everyday Stone Age life. Other items found on the body included a braided grass mat; a coarsely-woven grass bag; a birch bark container with a raw blackthorn berry in it, indicating that the Iceman died in the late summer or early autumn; a leather pouch; and a flat marble disc threaded onto a necklace decorated with 20 leather straps.

There is evidence to suggest he was clean-shaven, sported curly brown hair and wore an earring. Worn teeth indicates he probably ate coarse ground-grain, or that he regularly used his teeth as a tool.

Almost immediately, questions arose pertaining to the iceman's authenticity. Skeptics declared it an elaborate hoax, comparable to the Piltdown Man. One expert asserted that the body was that of a transplanted Egyptian mummy, while another insisted it was the mummified remains of a pre-Columbian American.

But an international research team, writing in the journal Science, dismissed the possibility of fraud as "highly unlikely." The authors based their conclusion on analysis of DNA samples taken from the iceman's muscle, bone and connective tissue, which seem to confirm he is a genuine European from the late Stone Age.

"There are relatives of the iceman all over northern Europe," commented Dr. Bryan Sykes, an Oxford geneticist who took part in research led by the University of Innsbruck.

Still, many unanswered questions remain. Who was he? Where did he come from? What was he doing wandering around glaciers more than 10,300 feet above sea level?

"It just doesn't make sense," said one American member of the research team. "Considering the way he was dressed, he was prepared for the harsh altitude in an L.L. Bean kind of way. But the thing that eludes us is what he was doing up there in the first place."

Perhaps he was a farmer or a shepherd, say some archaeologists, or a trader or prospector. Others suggest he was a village outcast, perhaps a criminal on the run or exiled.

Since X-rays revealed some broken ribs, at least one researcher—Dr. Konrad Spindler, author of *The Man in the Ice*, believes he got into a fight in a village below and this led to his injury and flight into the mountains.

But Lawrence Barfield, an archaeologist at the University of Birmingham in England who specializes in prehistory, thinks otherwise. In an interview published in *The New York Times*, Dr. Barfield said, "A more economical explanation would be that he was already up in the mountains with his sheep when an accident prevented his descent to the valley before the snow came."

Even before genetic studies confirmed his authenticity, Dr. Barfield pointed to one artifact that he says clearly refutes the idea of fraud—a small antler point inserted into a lime wood handle used in retouching flint tools.

"No one thinking to perpetrate a fraud would have thought to include this particular tool in the iceman's kit," Dr. Barfield said.

At least 15 radiocarbon tests have verified the age of the iceman's body, and that it had lain encased in ice since the time of the pyramids. While the unfortunate iceman has taught us much about that far-off age, it is doubtful that scientists will ever understand the tragic fate that befell the young traveler so long ago.

"In This Sign Shalt Thou Conquer"

Rome was worried.

For centuries the great empire had maintained peace and fostered prosperity throughout its sprawling realm, from the shores of the Mediterranean to the forests of Germany.

Now, in the third century of the Christian era, barbaric warlords and political instability threatened to topple the empire. Galloping inflation added to its woes, as did marauding bands of soldiers that ravaged the countryside, slaughtering civilians and Republican Guards who got in their way.

Unhappy people turned to magic and pagan gods in an attempt to cope with the horrific changes sweeping across the land. Some embraced strange new religions that promised salvation in the next world. Many believed that a single, all-powerful supreme god was the answer to their prayers, rather than the old Olympian deities.

To stem the growth of Christianity, Rome's rulers had resorted to harsh punishment and executions. In the name of Jupiter, Apollo, Minerva and other "immortals" who had held sway in the empire's capital for centuries, Christians were routinely beaten, tortured, mutilated, decapitated, imprisoned and thrown to the lions.

Then, all at once, it stopped. Almost overnight Jupiter and his consortium of old gods were gone, replaced by Christianity as the official state religion. What happened to bring this mystifying event about?

Some scholars credit Emperor Constantine with the sudden change. According to an account written shortly after Constantine's death in 337 by Bishop Eusebius, it happened in October 312, when the emperor was marching on Rome to reclaim it from his rival, Maxentius.

As Constantine approached the city, he looked up and saw

"with his own eyes the trophy of a cross of light in the heavens, above the sun, and bearing the inscription, "In This Sign, Shalt Thou conquer." According to Bishop Eusebius, the emperor was "struck with amazement, and his whole army also, which followed him on this expedition and witnessed the miracle."

That very night Christ is said to have appeared to the emperor in a dream, carrying the same sign he had seen in the heavens and commanding him to lead his army forward to victory. At dawn the next day Constantine ordered workmen to fashion a standard made of gold, studded with precious jewels, and bearing a monogram symbolizing his fealty to Christ.

Behind the ensign—and, according to some accounts, with a special sign of the cross painted on every shield— Constantine's soldiers defeated the enemy at Milvian Bridge on the River Tiber. Constantine entered Rome victorious, and from that day on, a committed Christian.

Or was he? Some scholars suspect that Constantine never truly abandoned his pagan ways, even though he ascribed his spectacular military success to the vision of the Christian cross and much later in life was baptized into the Christian faith.

One view holds that the emperor continued to worship the sun god Mithras, the religion of his father and several emperors before him. Other scholars point to the fact that Constantine scratched pagan symbols from his coins and even removed his statues from pagan temples as proof of his conversion to Christianity.

During his long reign, Constantine saw to it that Christians were treated fairly, even though he continued to tolerate paganism as well. He enacted many laws favorable to Christians, prayed everyday and enjoyed the company of Christian bishops.

The evidence, then, seems overwhelming that Emperor Constantine did believe in the Christian god. The Edict of Milan—which granted Christianity the same rights as all other legitimate religions—and his baptism seem to support this view.

Did Constantine have the experience that Eusebius describes?

Scholars have wrestled with that question for more than 1,600 years. Many skeptics want to know why—and how—such a startling revelation could have been kept secret until after the emperor's death. How, too, they wonder, was it possible to create an elaborate bejeweled standard in a single morning, almost on the very day of battle?

And why, after being converted to Christianity in such a miraculous way, was the emperor not baptized as a Christian until the last year of his life?

Historians believe that in an age of superstition, stories about divine visions were bound to gain currency. Everybody at the time, pagan or Christian, believed in miracles; and the wonder of Constantine's conversion as narrated by Eusebius had a tremendous impact not only on the bishop's contemporaries but also on many generations to come.

There can be little doubt, however, that something happened to the emperor on the eve of his entrance into Rome. Some scholars have suggested that his "vision" may have been caused by what meteorologists call the "halo phenomenon," in which ice crystals in the upper atmosphere form light rings around the sun.

Very occasionally, such rings interlock in a pattern that can suggest a cross to some viewers.

In any event, Constantine was certainly not a Christian before the battle at Milvian Bridge. But scholars say the victory convinced him of the power of the Christian faith—and he never forgot it. After unifying the Western Empire under his own rule, he moved quickly to help the poor and repressed Christians, who now suddenly saw their religion elevated to great heights of power and prestige.

And, for the rest of his life, Constantine's imperial armies marched behind the sacred labarum, the name given the banner on which Constantine's monogram of Christ was inscribed. And they never failed to emerge victorious *in hoc signo* (in this sign.)

The Man in the Mud

In the summer of 1950, peat-cutters working among the acid-rich bogs near Tollund Fen in northern Denmark uncovered the naked body of a well-preserved body man with a noose around his neck.

Police were called in to investigate, but the corpse was no recent murder victim. Radio-carbon testing showed the dark, leathery-brown body crowned with a shock of reddish hair to be at least 2,000 years old.

The find was similar to hundreds of other bodies pulled from the deep bogs of northern Europe in recent years. What made the Tollund discovery so unusual was the high degree of preservation and serenity of the corpse.

"His face wore a gentle expression," wrote Professor Peter V. Glob, the Danish archaeologist called in to examine Tollund Man, as the victim came to be called. The eyes "were slightly closed, lips softly pursed, as if in silent prayer."

Some say he was the victim of an ancient execution. Others contend his death was part of a ritualistic sacrifice to pagan gods.

Dr. Glob, a leading authority on the so-called "Bog People," suggested Tollund Man might have been a priest who volunteered to be strangled with a ceremonial rope and buried in the peat to honor a northern fertility goddess during a winter festival to hasten the arrival of spring.

"It was on just such occasions that bloody human sacrifices reached a peak in the Iron Age," Dr. Glob wrote.

But Dr. Glob and other investigators are quick to make distinctions between Tollund Man and the hundreds of other Iron Age bog burials scattered throughout northern Europe. While most victims found in the bogs died extremely violent deaths—strangulation from either hanging or garroting, visible blows to the head or from multiple stab wounds to the heart—Tollund Man apparently suffered no brutal treatment at the hands of his executioners.

"This one (Tollund Man) bore no signs of violence other than the marks of the noose," he said. "The Nordic peoples, until they turned Christian many centuries later, associated hanging less with punishment than with offerings to their gods."

Adding to the mystery was the fact that Tollund Man had no calluses and was well-groomed and stripped before being deposited in the bog. This, say investigators, is a clear indication that the victim was of high social standing, perhaps even a leader.

During the Middle Ages, superstitious peat-cutters usually associated bog people with evil and quickly reburied them in consecrated soil. Many peasants avoided the lonely bogs because they feared encounters with the devil.

It wasn't until after World War II when modern dating technology became available that scientists learned the antiquity of the bog people.

Altogether, some 890 bodies have been recovered from bogs in Denmark, Germany, England, Wales, Scotland, Ireland and elsewhere in northern Europe. The best documented and most numerous are the Danish finds, particularly in north and central Jutland.

The Danish finds include Tollund Man, whose celebrated head now rests in the Silkeborg Museum in central Jutland, and an equally famous neighbor, Grauballe Man, whose throat was slashed from ear-to-ear sometimes around 100 B.C.

A few finds are truly ancient. One is from the Mesolithic period, about 3000 B.C. Other specimens are surprisingly recent. At least one is a strapping man staked into the bog with birch staves as late as 1360 A.D.

The remarkable state of preservation of the bog people has been attributed to the unique chemistry of a peat bog.

"Everything is anaerobic in bogs," explained Dr. Hayden Pritchard, a botanist at Lehigh University and the Wetlands Institute of New Jersey. "Particularly at the lower levels there's almost no life because there's no oxygen. You need oxygen to degrade flesh."

The question archaeologists hope to answer some day is why so many Iron Age people were thrown into the bogs and murky waterways of northern Europe. Were these human deposits made to appease pagan gods, as many suspect, or were they barbaric forms of punishment?

Some researchers theorize that these dark places of earth and water had religious significance, perhaps some special meaning to the people of that far-off age. Perhaps they were seen as gateways to the next world, or—at worst—tunnels to the hellish regions below.

Star-Crossed Voyagers

In Africa, members of a poor, cave-dwelling tribe of farmers claim that fish-like "gods" from the sky visited them thousands of years ago, leaving behind a unique mythology rich in astronomical knowledge.

According to Dogon tradition, these cosmic creatures originated in a star system called Sirius—the "dog star"— some 8.7 million light years away. They came in a "flaming ark" that made a whirring dust storm as it landed, while a huge glowing object—presumably the mother ship—waited above.

The Dogon claim the extraterrestrials' purpose in coming was to civilize the people of Earth.

Mythologies of other ancient lands—Babylonians, Egyptians and Greek—mention amphibious gods bent on similar star-trekking missions. Many tribal myths in the New World tell of similar encounters with watery deities, some of which rose from the depths to tame and educate heathens.

It wasn't until the early 1950s that the outside world discovered the secrets of the Dogon, who inhabit a bleak and formidable region of Mali some 300 miles south of

Tombouctou, (formerly Timbuktu). That was when two French anthropologists who had lived among the tribe from 1946 until 1950 were initiated into their religious order.

In a paper titled *A Sudanese Sirius System*, the Frenchmen—Marcel Griaule and Germaine Dieterlen—recounted the Dogon belief that ancient spacemen gave them knowledge of a "dark star" in the constellation Canis. The existence of such a star—a dense, heavy companion to Sirius known as Sirius B—had been suspected by scientists since the mid-19th century, but was not described in detail until the 1920s.

Long before, the Dogon knew the star—invisible to the naked eye—was made of matter heavier than any on Earth and moves in an elliptical orbit, taking it 50 years do so.

It was not until 1928 that Sir Arthur Eddington postulated the theory of "white dwarfs"—stars whose atoms have collapsed inward, so that a piece the size of a pea could weigh half a ton. Sirius B is the size of Earth, yet weighs as much as the sun.

Is it possible that the Dogon learned this complex theory from some knowledgeable space traveler? Or did they learn it from some more plausible source—a traveler from Egypt, perhaps, or a modern European visitor?

The late Dr. Carl Sagan openly criticized the notion that ancient star-men "dropped out of the sky" and landed in such a desolate location. He considered it far more likely that the Dogon gained their knowledge from traveling Europeans around 1930—a time when details of Sirius, its tiny companion star and other astronomical data later related to Griaule and Dieterlen had become common knowledge in the Western world.

Oriental scholar Robert Temple thinks otherwise. Author of several books on the subject, Temple believes that the knowledge shown by the Dogon cannot be explained away as coincidence or diffusion—knowledge passed on through contact with outsiders. In *The Sirius Mystery*, he points out that the Dogon have an extraordinarily detailed knowledge of the solar system.

For example, they said the moon was "dry and dead," and—without benefit of a telescope—they drew pictures of Saturn with rings around it. They knew about the moons of Jupiter as well, and they recorded the movements of Venus in their crude temples.

Temple concludes that the Dogon might have learned about Sirius and the fish gods from the Egyptians, who probably passed down the information to the Babylonians, Greeks and other ancient cultures.

But where did the Egyptians get such detailed information about the cosmos?

While most cosmologists shrug off theories of extraterrestrial connections, Temple suspects intelligent beings from outer worlds, perhaps the region of Sirius, visited Earth in antiquity and imparted such knowledge.

It is worth noting that the Dogon tribe is believed to be of Egyptian descent. After migrating from Libya centuries ago, they settled in West African, bringing with them astronomical lore traceable to pre-dynastic Egypt before 3200 B.C.

The Dogon insist their knowledge was delivered by cosmic voyagers long ago. Their mythology suggests they learned it from Nommos—amphibious, repulsive-looking beings who arrived in a fiery ark. The Nommos, who lived mostly in the sea, are depicted as partly fishlike and, at least in a general way, reminiscent of merfolk.

Ancient Babylonian mythology makes reference to similar star-born creatures called Oannes, while earlier societies gave them different names. The Sumerians, for example, called them Enki.

The Dogon also speak of a second star orbiting Sirius, at right angles to Sirius B. They call it *emme ya* ("sun of women"), but this celestial object is presently unknown to science. Dogon tradition holds that this second star is the home of the Nommos.

The Hairy Ainu

The first Western visitors to reach Japan's northern islands were surprised to discover a primitive race of people who bore a physical resemblance to Europeans.

The discovery came in 1854, shortly after American Commodore Matthew Perry persuaded Japan's rulers to abandon their centuries-old policy of near-total isolation and open borders to the outside world.

Soon, newspapers in America and England were full of strange stories about tall, white-skinned men and women with blond hair and greenish eyes whose eyelids lacked the small fold of skin from the upper eyelid that covers the inner corner of the eye in many Asian people.

The white-skinned people were found on Japan's northernmost main island, Hokkaido, and on Sakhalin and the Kuril Islands farther north.

They called themselves Ainu (pronounced "Eye-noo") meaning "man" in their language. The Ainus—or "Hairy Ainus," as they came to be called because of their thick and often wavy beards and abundant body hair—represent an anthropological enigma. While their physical appearance clearly sets them apart from Asian neighbors, their language is unrelated to any known tongue.

The first known reference to the Ainu is found in a Japanese account written in 642. They became regular trading partners with Japan in the eighth century, specializing in hide, fur, fish oil, feathers and dried fish in exchange for metal tools and luxury goods.

Despite their Caucasoid appearance, they are separated by thousands of miles from their nearest possible relatives, and surrounded by Asian peoples.

Who are the "Hairy Ainu?" Where did they originate? How did they come to be where they are?

Nobody knows—not even Japanese anthropologists who

have spent almost a century studying the Ainu culture. Ainu legends claim that their ancestors "fell from the sky." Their way of life, however, closely resembles that of the people of the west coast of the Pacific Ocean.

Some authorities believe the Ainu is one of many small, mysterious groups of people, remnants of early races that are fast fading into extinction.

Many Ainu customs are found nowhere else in the world—such as the men's use of ceremonial moustache-lifters in drinking, the tattooing of women around their mouths, and the absence of rites marking important stages in a person's life, including puberty.

While bears played an important role in their religious ceremonies, the Ainu believe the natural world is dominated by spirits, both good and bad. At the start of each new fishing season, they honor their complex pantheon of gods with elaborate rituals—feeding the sea with tobacco and sweets.

But if the Ainus have continued to fascinate their supposed relatives in the West, they have mostly inspired contempt and impatience in their neighbors, the Japanese. Since the 16th century, the Ainu—now numbering about 25,000 in population—have lost most of their ancestral lands to settlers from other parts of Japan.

All research indicates that the Ainu have lived on the Japanese islands since earliest times. Hokaido ("quiet earth where the peoples live") and Honshu contain many places bearing Ainu names, including the sacred volcano, Fujiyama, named for their fire goddess, Fuji.

But the Japanese trace their own ancestry to a vanished race they call the Jomon people. According to tradition, the Jomon, originating on the Asian mainland, arrived long ago from the south—perhaps on a long-submerged land bridge to Korea—whereas the Ainus arrived from the north.

Emerging into nationhood, the Japanese pushed the Ainus farther and farther north, and finally off Honshu. Near the end of the 19th century they began to displace them on Hokkaido.

The Japanese have long held that their ancestors occupied the islands thousands of years ago. But that belief has lately been challenged by the findings of American anthropologist Christy G. Turner III.

An examination of fossilized teeth in Japan shows that modern Japanese probably immigrated to Japan from China—several centuries after the arrival of the Ainu.

Piri Re'is Map

Deep below Antarctica's quivering icecaps lie the frozen remains of an ancient civilization that ruled the world thousands of years before the coming of the Mesopotamians or Greeks.

So say a number of scholars who contend that this long-vanished kingdom at the bottom of the globe might have been the "father of all cultures," perhaps even the Biblical Garden of Eden.

Much of their evidence is based on an obscure 16th century map said to be drawn from an even older map used by Christopher Columbus when he set out to discover the New World in 1492. The so-called Piri Re'is map—named after the famous Turkish admiral who created it in 1513—shows not only the Atlantic Ocean and North and South America, but also what some believe to be the continent of Antarctica.

"The map confirms that an advanced Ice Age civilization flourished in the region we now call Antarctica and is now buried thousands of feet below the snow and ice," says Charles H. Hapgood of Keene College, an expert on ancient maps. "This culture, at least in some respects, may well have been more advanced than the civilizations of Egypt, Babylonia, Greece and Rome."

At the time of its drawing, the Piri Re'is map—drawn on gazelle hide and featuring a web of lines crisscrossing the

Atlantic—was said to be the most accurate map in the world. But the fading parchment was forgotten until 1929, when it turned up in the archives of the Imperial Palace in Constantinople (Istanbul), Turkey.

The rediscovery of the map created a sensation. After studying the document, Capt. Arlington H. Mallery, a retired Navy officer and expert on ancient maps, concluded that the map revealed a part of the Antarctic coast called Queen Maud Land—a region covered with a thick mantle of ice for thousands of years.

Capt. Mallery theorized that Piri had in his possession maps of Antarctica based on information gathered at a time before ice covered the continent—a little more than 10,000 years ago. Moreover, Mallery said, it was clear that the mapmakers had access to information gathered from the air!

In his book, *Maps of the Ancient Sea Kings*, Prof. Hapgood suggests that thousands of years before the pyramids, there flourished a civilization that possessed a technology far superior to anything known until modern times.

"Some of the geographical knowledge, for example, had been passed on, often in garbled form, to the geographers of Greece and Rome, and had finally wound up in the Imperial Palace at Constantinople," he wrote. "It was from such information that Piri Re'is had obtained his picture of Antarctica before the last Ice Age."

To bolster his theory, Prof. Hapgood cites a number of archaeological sites in Europe, Africa, Asia and South America that he thinks were inspired by common Ice Age ancestors. These ancestors, whether native to this planet or stranded survivors from another world, possessed navigational and technological skills far superior to the peoples of ancient, medieval or recent modern times, the professor added.

"Now this was extraordinary," he told *Fate* magazine in 1966. "In the first place, nobody is supposed to have discovered Antarctica until 1818, 300 years after Piri Re'is, and it is regarded as unthinkable that the Greeks, Romans,

Babylonians or Phoenicians could have sailed that far. In the second place, the ice cap in Antarctica is supposed to be millions of years old, and therefore to have been in existence long before man evolved on earth."

The professor maintains that source maps used by Piri to compile his controversial document were themselves based on earlier maps, compilations of which were made at the Great Library of Alexandria, Egypt. The puzzle, he suggests, is not so much how Piri Re´is managed to draw such an accurate map of the Antarctic region more than three centuries before it was discovered, but where the original source for the document came from.

Noted map experts at the U.S. Navy Hydrographic Office who verified the authenticity of the ancient map: "It's so accurate only one thing could explain it—a worldwide aerial survey."

Since flying machines weren't invented until the 20th century, thousands of years after elements of the Piri Re´is map were published, the question that begs to be answered is: Who did the aerial survey?

Some investigators think they might have been voyagers from another world, sent to earth perhaps on an exploratory or colonizing mission.

"That's simple logic," explained Capt. John Brent, a Naval Academy graduate and authority on the Piri Re´is map. "A race far more technically advanced than we are today existed on earth thousands of years ago."

But something must have happened—a disastrous accident, perhaps, or a war on their home planet—that stopped the mission. Survivors of that mission, Capt. Brent said, remained on earth and fell into a primitive state. Memories of their advanced world beyond the stars remained alive in legends and myth.

Proof that earth was visited in prehistory by beings from outer space can be found in the Piri Re´is map, according to Swiss researcher and author Erich von Daeniken.

"Unquestionably," said Von Daeniken, "our forefathers did not draw these maps. Yet there is no doubt that the maps must have been made with the most modern technical aid—from the air."

The White Horse of Uffington

A colossal piece of artwork etched deeply into the side of a wind-swept hill has been a source of wonder for the people of western England for more than 2,000 years. Known as the White Horse, the drawing is steeped in mystery and legend.

No one knows who created the 370-foot-long horse or why. One theory holds that the figure—thought to be the oldest such "hill art" in England—dates from the Roman invasion in 55 B.C. Another, advanced by celebrated British archaeologist Stuart Piggott, suggests that the horse represents an ancient Celtic demigod.

Until recently, a popular notion was that the slender, gracefully curving figure is not a horse at all, but a dragon—the mythical dragon supposedly slain by St. George on nearby Dragon Hill. A bare patch of chalk upon which no grass will grow is purported to be where the dragon's blood spilled.

One legend suggests that the White Horse commemorates Alfred the Great's victory over the Danes in 861. Modern scholarship, however, now attributes the work to a Bronze Age tribe known as the Belgae—perhaps built as a shrine to some forgotten dead leader.

For centuries, the White Horse has been one of the West Country's most popular—and enigmatic—tourist attractions. Located on a lonely hilltop near Wantage, the colossal carving is actually one of dozens of similar chalk renderings in the region. Another nearby drawing is the Giant Warrior of Cerne, which also dates back to the time of the Romans.

Though their motives continue to be debated, the creators

of the White Horse accomplished a mammoth piece of art-work. Placed well up the steep slopes of a 500-foot hill—known locally as Uffington Castle—the horse was con-structed by carving deeply through sod to the solid chalk surface of the downs of the Wessex Hills.

The swaths in many areas are actually terraces—banked up in some places—and the horse's eye is a leveled platform raised above deeper trenches in the chalk.

The club-toting Cerne Giant is of simpler construction—ditches scratched into the sward. But the giant's proportions are impressive, pacing out at 180 feet from head to toe, and 167 feet across from the tip of the club to opposite hand.

One of the earliest recorded accounts of the White Horse and Cerne Giant is an entry in the Cartulary of Abbingdon Abbey. In 13th and 14th century documents, the horse is mentioned several times in connection with accounts of near-by land tenures.

Left to nature, the horse and giant would have disap-peared under weeds long ago. Every seven years, however, the local country folk turn out to trim the vegetation and clean out the gouges that comprise the equine figure.

Although the tradition has been going on for some 2,000 years, not one of these faithful attendants has ever been able to explain the local compulsion to preserve the White Horse.

The cleansing, or "scouring" of the chalk outlines appears to have been a lively event in the often dreary lives of the West Country folk. The occasion usually coincided with Whitsuntide, which is celebrated the seventh Sunday after Easter.

The scouring was accompanied by festivals and merry-making, and the caretakers of the Cerne Giant danced around a maypole—raising a hearty hue and cry from local clergy-men who decried the celebration as pagan rites.

Churchmen were especially scandalized by local lore that advised barren wives to sleep overnight upon the virile Giant to magically induce pregnancy.

Rites such as these suggest to some archaeologists that the chalk horse and giant probably trace back to animistic religious practices of the ancient Celts.

One popular legend holds that if you stand upon the horse's head and make a wish, it will come true.

The Dreaded Vikings

Of all the terrors that plagued medieval Europe, none was more dreaded than the sight of a Viking warship bearing down on a Christian stronghold. Such encounters were enough to make even the most stout-hearted defender of the faith turn and run.

Amid a hail of flaming arrows and slashing broadswords, the howling bands of bearded, blood-thirsty invaders would descend, killing, raping, plundering and burning everything in their path.

"From the wrath of the Northmen, O Lord, deliver us!" became a common lament as Vikings pressed south, east and west, conquering and pillaging from Ireland to Byzantium.

One ninth century French chronicler likened a Viking invasion to "the end of the world...Fire and blood and death everywhere."

Christian Europe first became painfully aware of their heathen Scandinavian neighbors to the north in the eighth century when ship-borne raiders sacked the monastery at Lindisfarne in northeastern Ireland. Isolated Viking raids continued into the next century, chasing monks and villagers away from far-flung outposts of western Europe and as far east as the Black Sea and Constantinople.

Medieval monks depicted the Norsemen as pagan devils, brutal and careless. They saw them as in league with Satan, more beasts than men, horrific heathens without conscious or spirituality. Whenever the warning went out that a Viking ship was approaching, everybody fled rather than confront the "mindless savage brutes."

But is it all true? Were these rugged blond warriors who swept down out of the North the brutal barbarians of legend? Or was their fire-and-thunder reputation merely the invention of enemies who sought to malign them?

Some scholars say the Vikings have been given a bad rap. Modern historians now see these Scandinavian raiders as traders and explorers, settlers and poets and extraordinarily gifted artists and craftsmen.

"Consider the fact that all of the reports handed down about attacks were from churchmen, the only Europeans who could read or write in those days," commented Magnus Magnusson, an Icelandic archaeologist and expert on Viking history.

Even when describing victories over Vikings, Magnusson said such reports "tend to exaggerate their opponents' numbers and ferocity. When dealing with the sack of churches, no words could be too black."

Unfortunately, since Vikings were illiterate, there are no documents telling their point of view.

"Modern scholarship is gradually revealing a different picture of the Vikings," Magnusson pointed out, one that challenges the traditional notion that Vikings were "cruel and savage assassins, intent only on raiding the wealth of a serenely Christian Europe."

To be sure, the Vikings did pillage and destroy, especially churches and monasteries.

"From their pagan point of view," said Dr. Gwyn Jones, an American researcher of Viking history, "the Christians must have appeared unbelievably stupid, cramming their churches with gold and silver ornaments, and leaving them undefended except by monks and priests."

But, he added, "the Vikings did not just leave smoking ruins wherever they went before passing on the fresh pastures for plunder. They were builders as well as destroyers."

For example, he said the Vikings were among the finest

artists and craftsmen of their age, excelling in animal carvings, metalworking, shipbuilding and naval technology.

"They brought with them new ideas and products that in many ways helped transform the drab economies of 'Dark Age' Europe."

Furs, cattle, dairy products and amber were among the many Viking products traded with neighbors to the south. Perhaps their most important contribution, according to some scholars, was the notion of colonization.

In time, Viking explorers spread out among the lonely, uninhabited islands of the North Atlantic. Settlements sprang up on Iceland and Greenland. By the 10th century small groups were staking claims along the fog-shrouded shores of the North American continent—the first known European voyagers to the New World.

Giant Heads of Easter Island

Dutch Admiral Jakob Roggeveen could not believe his eyes.

Looming over the ragged shoreline in the near distance were hundreds of colossal giants, their massive, helmeted heads erect and unmoving as the admiral's ship drew dangerously close to the small, uncharted island in the middle of the South Pacific.

Was this some lost race, the admiral wondered—the "giants in the earth" mentioned in the Bible, perhaps?

Sailing closer, the admiral was relieved to find that the giants were only stone statues and that the naked, heavily tattooed men who walked among them were mere mortals.

The date was April 5, 1722. Since this was Easter Sunday, Admiral Roggeveen named his discovery Easter Island and sailed away.

Almost half a century would pass before Europeans sailed this way again. And it took another century before European explorers committed to an extensive survey of the remote island, some 2,700 miles east of Tahiti and 2,550 miles west of Chile.

The Europeans were amazed at what they found—hundreds of gigantic statues, some more than 66 feet tall and weighing as much as 50 tons—lying scattered all over the island.

Most of the stone statues no longer stood erect, as had been observed by Admiral Roggeveen. Instead they littered the rocky ground like gigantic boulders. Only a few rose mysterious and god-like, their granite expressions frozen in the salt-laden breezes that swept in from the gray sea.

What the startled Europeans wanted to know was: Who built the colossal stone statues—called moa—and why?

Scientists believe Easter Island was first settled at least 1,600 years ago, perhaps earlier, by Polynesian explorers. Thor Heyerdahl, however, suspects that pre-Inca people from Peru might have migrated to this far-flung outpost. As evidence, he cites freshwater plants and vegetables found on Easter Island that are native to the Andes, as well as similarities in religious customs and the existence in both places of fair-skinned, red-haired people.

Wherever their origins, it appears that, at least for the first few centuries, these hearty newcomers built smaller statues similar to pre-Columbian works found in South America.

At some point the islanders resorted to carving the massive moi, an undertaking that required enormous demands on labor and resources. Nobody knows why, but some islanders today think the heads were monuments to dead rulers and were once infused with benevolent supernatural power they called mana.

Some mystics claim that Easter Island was part of a lost continent and contend the stone monoliths possess magnetic healing power, similar to the standing stones found in Britain and elsewhere in the world. Others suggest that it was mysteriously joined to ancient Egypt or that its original inhabitants came from outer space.

The works were apparently created by craftsmen of a culture known as Long-ears, people who extended their ear lobes by inserting heavy disks in them. A second, distinctive group of people who shared the island are known as Short-ears, because they did nothing to their lobes.

Ancestor-worshipping Long-ear islanders believed that when a tribal chief died, his soul, an internal force called mana, could be captured for the future benefit of the community by carving giant statues as a dwelling place for the mana.

The massive, stylized figures that resulted are majestic, yet disturbing. The heads are immense, their expressions brooding and disdainful, their ears grotesquely elongated, their chins jutting and powerful.

Arms hang rigidly at the sides of legless trunks. Hands extend stiffly across protuberant bellies. The heads, once crowned with enormous stone hats, appear flat and roughly chiseled.

Although carving began early, the craze reached its highest expression in the 14th and 15th centuries. More than 1,000 statues have been found, most between 12 and 15 feet tall and weighing an average of 20 tons.

The giant statues were apparently carved from volcanic rock found in the dormant crater of Rano Raraku, one of Easter Island's three volcanoes. More than 300 "heads" were chiseled from the crater, then lowered down its slope and somehow maneuvered into upright positions.

Inside the crater archaeologists found some 400 uncompleted statues. Obsidian hatchets and chisels, abandoned by the ancient sculptors, were also found in the crater.

Mystery continues to surround the creations because the culture of their creators was destroyed.

For much of its early history, the Long-ears and Short-ears flourished side by side on their island paradise, lush with coconut palms and forests. After centuries of peaceful coexistence, however, the clans clashed.

Civil war followed civil war, reducing the population from

some 20,000 to 4,000 by the early 18th century. The winners of the ravaged island were the Short-ears clan.

The great unanswered question is how the island's inhabitants transported the monuments or erected them on bases. Theories that logs were used as rollers were discounted, after tests showed that Easter Island soil could not support trees of the size required for such an exercise.

Another possibility considered was that vines woven into ropes were used to haul them into place. But this, too, was ruled out after it was proved that vine ropes could not stand the strain of pulling 30-plus tons of rock.

Aside from how the work was done, there is another mystery: Who did the work? Some authorities say there was never sufficient labor available on the island at any one time to assemble the colossal statues. Others say the primitive islanders lacked the engineering know-how.

Even though archaeology has shown that the statues are fairly easy to carve out of volcanic rock, some experts doubt the island's population would have been sufficient to carve the colossal creations and roll them into place.

"Even 2,000 men, working day and night, would not be nearly enough to carve these colossal figures out of the steel-hard volcanic stone with rudimentary tools—and at least a part of the population must have tilled the barren fields, gone fishing, woven cloth, and made ropes," said Erich von Daeniken, author of *Chariots of the Gods*.

The solemn stone faces give no answers. The truth about Easter Island's secret past may never be known.

New World
World
Realms

Voyagers From Beyond the Sea

Early on the morning of Oct. 12, 1492, a young Spanish sailor on lookout duty aboard the *Santa Maria* spotted something white and shimmering on the far horizon.

"Land! Land!" he shouted to weary shipmates.

At daybreak the ship's commander, Christopher Columbus, rowed ashore and promptly named the new land San Salvadore (Holy Savior)—presumably out of gratitude for a successful voyage across the Atlantic Ocean.

Besides his crew, the only witnesses to the momentous landing was a band of Taino Indians peeking from the jungle as Columbus claimed for his queen the tropical island 400 miles southeast of Florida called Guanahani by its inhabitants.

Thus was born one of the world's greatest myths—that Columbus "discovered" America. Historians—and most children—now know that numerous other groups of Europeans, Asians and perhaps even Africans preceded Columbus to the New World by many centuries. In fact, it now appears that the great Admiral of the Seas might have been a regular Johnny-come-lately to trans-Atlantic travel.

Asians were first, emigrating in successive waves across a now submerged land-bridge in pursuit of Ice Age quarry like giant bison, elk and woolly mammoths. In time—perhaps over a 50,000-year period—these hearty nomads explored and settled vast regions of the Americas, from Alaska to South America and the islands of the Caribbean in between.

Some established magnificent civilizations, like the Aztecs and Maya of Central America and the Inca of Peru. Others retained more primitive lifestyles and became the ancestors of the Sioux, Choctaw, Creek and hundreds of other tribes. By the time of Columbus's arrival, the Indian civilizations of America were indeed ancient.

Scholarly debate continues about which group of people came next. Some experts believe a variety of pre-Christian era sailors—Greeks, Egyptians, Phoenicians, Libyans, and Romans—made frequent trips across the Atlantic, either on purpose or because they were blown off course. Iberian warriors and fur-clad Celts are also thought to have sailed across the mysterious, monster-haunted sea in search of Paradise or to flee the long blades of *berzerkers* howling down from the North.

Coins, religious objects, rune tablets, stone forts and other puzzling artifacts seem to indicate that America was a popular place among Old World travelers thousands of years before Columbus's heralded landfall. In fact, historians and archaeologists now think that the Atlantic Ocean might have been a veritable freeway linking the old and new worlds in ancient and medieval times.

Dr. Joseph Mahan, a Georgia archaeologist, thinks he has found evidence that ancient Hebrews reached the hills of Tennessee in the first century AD. Mahan bases his claim on a rock tablet found in Loudon County in 1889. Inscriptions on the tablet, unearthed along with nine human skeletons in a single mound, were translated to read: "A Comet for the Jews"—an obvious reference to one of the skeletons who had been the group's "comet," or leader, according to Cyrus Gordon, a Semitic languages expert who worked with Mahan on deciphering the tablet.

Barry Fell, now retired from Harvard University, has long argued that North America was explored and settled thousands of years ago by various groups of Europeans and Africans. In his book, *America B.C.*, Dr. Fell points to hundreds of stone tablets, graves and other bits of evidence in North America linking them with trans-Atlantic voyagers, from ancient Egyptians to Celtic tribes from Ireland.

Even though ancient mariners might have lacked the technology for such long maritime journeys, experts such as Dr. Fell and Dr. Mahan believe luck and skilled seamanship probably accounted for many of the trips. Plagues, droughts and invasions by enemies might have been their motivations.

Until fairly recently, not much attention was paid to the old Viking sagas about "Vinland" and Leif Ericksen's legendary travels into the wild land of the Skraelings. But in the 1960s, Norwegian archaeologists working in Newfoundland found the timbered remains of a 1,000-year-old Viking settlement—proof that several groups of Norsemen explored and attempted to settle the frigid wilds of North America at least four centuries before Columbus.

Even before the Vikings, stories circulated about a sixth century Celtic monk named Saint Brendan who sailed across the Atlantic Ocean in search of "the promised land of the saints," a fabled region thought by some scholars to be the Southeastern United States coast or the Caribbean islands. Sailing in a 36-foot boat constructed of wood and ox hide, the voyagers discovered many fascinating worlds, including an island where the sheep were white as snow, another where birds chanted prayers with them, and another covered with fire and ice.

A few days later they sailed through "coagulated waters" (the Sargasso Sea?) before entering another sea so clear they could see fish curled up on the bottom like cats. They called the strange world "The Fortunate Isles."

As incredible as it seems, some modern scholars think there might have been a grain of truth behind Saint Brendan's voyage. It is known that Viking raiders were swarming over Ireland during the time of the saint's supposed exodus and that many monks fled for their lives—often by sea.

It is also known that these monks—who were the finest Christian scholars west of Byzantium—had knowledge of island refuges far to the west. They also possessed advanced maritime skills, having often sailed to the Shetlands and Faroes and finally to Iceland—perhaps even to Greenland. From there a voyage to North America was but a relatively easy trip.

Two centuries later, a Welsh prince named Madoc is said to have landed near what is now Mobile Bay, Ala., after fleeing his homeland during a civil war. According to tradition, the small band of Welsh went on to build stone forts and to colonize parts of the Southeastern United States. They intermarried with Indians and, over the course of time, were forgotten about—except in legend and myth.

One particular legend among the Cherokee people told of a race of white Indians who lived along the Ohio River near Clarksville, Ind. Could these have been the descendants of the lost Welshmen under Madoc's command? Local treasure hunters claim to have found ancient coins and European armor, some bearing the Welsh coat of arms, while Indian legends describe a great battle between red Indians and white Indians on the Ohio River's Sand Island where all the white Indians were slain.

Although fantasy and fact often blend when examining records concerning pre-Columbian voyages, some scholars believe it is only a matter of time before the history of America will have to be re-written to take into account cultural contacts between the Old and New Worlds.

"There is more to America's past than appears upon the surface," Dr. Fell wrote. "A strange unrest is apparent among many of the younger historians and archaeologists…a sense that somehow a very large slice of America's past has mysteriously vanished from our public records."

When Black-Faced Emperors Ruled America

Long before Christopher Columbus made his historic landing in America, dark-skinned monarchs from the coast of Africa reigned over jungle kingdoms in eastern Mexico and other parts of the New World.

So say a growing number of archaeologists who contend that various groups of African mariners "discovered" America more than 2,000 years before the arrival of Europeans.

The most visible signs of a pre-Columbian African presence in the New World are the great stone heads of Mexico unearthed in 1939 by archaeologist Matthew Stirling. Some researchers suggest that these colossal sculptures, some weighing more than 40 tons, are stone portraits of African kings who settled Mexico at least 3,000 years ago.

Carved by Olmecs—the first New World Indians to develop an advanced civilization—the giant heads appear to be Negroid in character, with bulging noses and thick lips.

The Olmecs are generally considered to have given rise to other great civilizations that developed in Central America, including the Mayan and, much later, the Aztecs. Certain Aztec rituals—including human sacrificial ceremonies—are similar to some African bloodletting rites.

Dr. Ivan Van Sertima, a linguist and anthropologist at Rutgers University, believes that Africans, regardless of how and when they arrived, played a key role in the development of that first New World civilization. He also asserts the first wave of immigrant Africans probably came from the region to the south of Egypt called Nubia—now the Sudan.

Few mainstream anthropologists agree with Dr. Van Sertima's theories about pre-Columbian African voyagers. Michael Coe, a Yale archaeologist and leading expert on the Olmecs is one of them.

"The heads don't sell me," Dr. Coe said. "I don't think they look African at all."

Dr. Coe and other critics of Dr. Van Sertima's theories do concede there might have been occasional contacts when African sailors or fishermen were swept off course into the currents that flow westward to the Caribbean. But, they insist, the shipwrecked Africans—assuming there were any—had no lasting impact on any native Americans they met.

Dr. Coe also maintains that the broad noses and full lips of the statues grew out of an artistic technique limited by a lack of metal tools that could carve deeply and by a desire to avoid protruding or thin facial features that might break off.

"I hope nobody a thousand years from now thinks that people had two noses and three eyes in our time just because Picasso painted people that way," he quipped.

But many of those who have seen the heads say they do look like black Africans.

"Why, then," Dr. Van Sertima asked, "did the Olmecs make terracotta figurines that are also plainly (negroid), even down to the hair texture, and why did they paint these faces black?"

In his book, *They Came Before Columbus*, Dr. Van Sertima raises the possibility that the Nubians possessed seafaring technology and experience that would have enabled them to make trans-Atlantic journeys. To emphasis that point, he recounted Thor Heyerdahl's classic drift voyage from Morocco to Barbados aboard the *Ra*, a papyrus reed boat resembling ancient Egyptian craft, that successfully rode the currents from Africa to the New World.

Although the original African contingent may have been assimilated into Olmec culture, Dr. Van Sertime believes there were later African arrivals. Perhaps the most significant of these came much later, 1310 and 1311, when the vast and wealthy African civilization of Mali on the west coast of Africa was at its height.

"Nearly 200 years before Columbus, the scholars at Timbuktu (in Mali) were saying the world was shaped like a gourd, and that if you traveled far enough in one direction, you would eventually come all the way around to your starting point," he noted.

Extant Arab documents and oral tradition reveal how one Mali king—Abubakari—sent several maritime expeditions on exploratory voyages into the western sea. At least one expedition never returned.

Did the African voyagers perish at sea? Or did they reach the New World?

Dr. Van Sertima is convinced that survivors of these early

expeditions intermarried with New World Indian populations and influenced the development of native American cultures.

"I'm not suggesting that the Olmec culture was created by outsiders," he said. "I'm sure native Americans were always in the majority and were the major forces behind their culture. All I'm saying is that Africans were, too, and that they contributed certain things to the Olmec culture."

Crystal Skull of Doom

Few objects in the world have stirred as much speculation and fear as the so-called "Crystal Skull of Doom," a beautifully fashioned artifact supposedly found in the ruins of an ancient Mayan city.

Some believe the 11-pound, highly polished skull possesses supernatural powers. More than a few observers have gone mad while in the presence of the skull, while others reported mysterious tinkling noises and strange, exotic scents.

A number of people who scoffed at the skull's powers have reputedly been struck dead—including one worker who supposedly mocked it.

Frank Dorland, a noted art restorer who studied the skull over a six-year period, noted that the skull produces an "elusive perfume" and that images of faraway mountains and temples sometime appear within its shine.

No one knows how old the skull is or where it came from. Scientists aren't even sure what it's made of, but the crystal is similar to quartz crystal formations found in California.

Erich von Daeniken, author of *Chariots of the Gods*, thinks the skull is very old and cited it as an example of advanced ancient technology.

"Nowhere on the skull is there a single clue showing that a tool known to us was used," he wrote.

The skull supposedly was found in the 1920s under an altar in the ruins of the Mayan city of Lubaantun in British Honduras. Although other crystal skulls from Central America exist, none is said to match this one for quality of workmanship or sophistication.

Moreover, the crystal from which it was made seems to have come not from Central America but from Calaveras County, Calif., but this is by no means certain.

The skull was first brought to public attention in the mid-1950s by Frederick Mitchell-Hedges, a well-known explorer-archaeologist. Mitchell-Hedges said his adopted daughter, Anna, found the skull while poking through Mayan ruins at Lubaantun.

He claimed the skull was "used by the high priest of the Maya to concentrate on and will death," and that it was "the embodiment of all evil."

Nonsense, say skeptics, who contend that Mitchell-Hedges purchased the skull from an anonymous English owner in the 1940s, then fabricated the story about his daughter finding it.

"Perhaps as a way of gaining publicity for it and enhancing its allure," theorized Daniel Cohen, a writer who has researched the skull.

Then there was the following cryptic message, left behind before Mitchell-Hedges' death: "How it came into my possession I have reason for not revealing."

Anna, who inherited the skull, insists her father's story is true, that she found the skull while on an expedition in the jungle. However, there is no evidence that she ever visited British Honduras.

Even those who doubt Mitchell-Hedges' story are hard-pressed to account for the skull's mysterious origins and haunting, other-worldly beauty and craftsmanship.

While some think the skull is of Aztec origin, others say the object is far more anatomically accurate than the usual skulls of Mexican origin.

Viracocha:
The Magnificent Stranger

Of all the legends of pre-Columbian Americans, none was more mysterious than that of Viracocha, a tall, bearded, pale-skinned god who supposedly wandered the Andes centuries before the Spanish arrived.

According to stories handed down to Spanish chroniclers, Viracocha arrived shortly after the Earth had been destroyed by a great flood. Clad in sandals and a long, flowing cloak, this mystical traveler moved among the people, casting miracles and occasionally bringing down the wrath of heaven.

"There suddenly appeared, coming from the south, a white man of large stature and authoritative demeanor," one Spaniard wrote. "This man had such great power that he changed the hills into valleys and from the valleys made great hills, causing streams to flow from the living stone."

He added, "They say that this man traveled along the highland route to the north, working marvels as he went and that they never saw him again. They say that in many places he gave men instructions on how they should live, speaking to them with great love and kindness and admonishing them to be good and to do no damage or injury to one another, but to love one another and show charity to all."

Viracocha went by a number of names—Huaracocha, Con, Con Ticci (or Kon Tiki), Thunupa, Taapac, Ttuypaca and Illa. In Mexico he went by the name Quetzalcoatl—the plumed serpent god. Among the Mayans he was known as Kukulkan, also a reference to "plumed" or "feathered serpent." In Palenque they called him Votan, Zamna in Izamal.

He was invariably described as a scientist, an architect of unsurpassed skills, a sculptor, an engineer, a teacher and—most of all—a great physician who healed the sick, restored sight to the blind and brought the dead back to life.

All great pre-Columbian civilizations—the Olmecs,

Toltecs, Aztecs, Mayans and Incas—claim their version of Viracocho introduced them to the concepts of mathematics, science and the arts.

Assuming that he was real, just who was this mysterious, pale-skinned stranger who supposed worked wonders in ancient America?

Theories abound. Some suspect he was a European, perhaps a Christian missionary who had been shipwrecked along the coast of South America centuries before the arrival of Columbus. Other say it was Christ himself who had become incarnate in the Americas and wandered about—tall, white, lean and bearded, offering the Gospel to the natives.

He also had another side to his nature, however, a wrathful side. On occasion, he produced "strange weapons of heavenly fire" to destroy his enemies. Arriving in a hostile village once, he reportedly raised his hands and threatened to bring down a rain of fire and thunder unless the inhabitants put down their weapons and accepted him as their lord and savior.

One legend described Viracocha as being accompanied by "messengers" of two kinds—faithful soldiers (huaminca) and shining ones (hayhuay-panti). Their role was to "carry the lord's message to every corner of the world."

Many of the old stories say that Viracocha/Quetzalcoatl/ Kukulkan had arrived from somewhere very far across the "Eastern Sea," while others note he descended from heaven in glowing clouds. Ancient Indians revered him as the god of life and divine wisdom.

Some scholars have compared him to the English King Arthur, both real and mythological, half man and half god in one and the same being. Early Spanish friars thought he might have been the apostle Saint Thomas.

It was with "great sadness" that he climbed aboard a raft of writhing serpents one day and sailed away from whence he came, promising to return.

Why did this magnificent stranger leave? Some legends say he had been driven off by a malevolent god named

Tezcatilpoca, whose name meant "Smoking Gun," or "Smoking Mirror" and whose cult demanded human sacrifice.

It seemed that a near-cosmic struggle between the forces of light and darkness had taken place in Mexico, and that the forces of darkness triumphed.

The Amazons

Hostile encounters with natives were nothing unusual for Spanish conquistadors searching for gold along the Amazon River in the 1500s.

But nothing had prepared them for the attack that occurred in 1541 as a 60-man force led by Francisco de Orellana pressed up the Rio Negro, a crocodile-infested tributary of the Amazon.

"Out of nowhere," wrote Orellana, "there suddenly charged into our midst a band of screaming, well-armed women who fought so courageously they put our own soldiers to shame."

Orellana described the women as "the fiercest warriors I have ever seen. They were very white and very tall, with long, braided hair wound about their heads."

He added, "They are very robust and carry bows and arrows and do as much fighting as 10 Indian men."

Such a foe, the Spaniards were quick to conclude, could only be Amazons, the mythical tribe of women that Christopher Columbus, Hernando Cortez and other conquistadors believed ruled the jungles of the New World and by whose name its greatest river is known.

Legends of these women warriors armed with golden shields and silver axes had been around since ancient times. Writing in the fifth century B.C., the Greek historian Herodotus claimed the Amazons lived on the south coast of the Black Sea—a misty, monster-choked region visited by Hercules and Theseus. He said the Amazons regularly invaded Europe and the Middle East. The name means "without breast," derived from the women warrior's practice of lopping off their right breasts to make them better archers.

Other historians, including Plutarch and Diodorus of Sicily, described these fierce female as expert with horses. They worshipped mares and routinely performed "wondrous" maneuvers while charging into battle at a full gallop—leaping from one horse to another, dancing in the saddle and firing arrows from a standing position.

Such acrobatics have led some scholars to theorize that the Centaurs, the legendary half human-half horse warriors of Greek mythology, were actually descriptions of Amazons on horseback.

These "menacing maidens" who supposedly waged constant war against male-dominated societies, replenished their numbers by mating with men from other tribes, keeping the daughters and killing male infants.

Scholars have long suspected there was some truth to the legends. In early Germanic tribes, women often followed their men into battle. During the Crusades, Eleanor of Aquitaine, Marguerite of Provence, Florine of Denmark and other queens and female nobles led armies into battle.

Myths about Amazons also appear in Africa, China, the Middle East and elsewhere. In the mid-1990s, American and Russian archaeologists excavating graves near Pokrovkia in Kazakhstan in the Eurasian steppes uncovered evidence suggesting there may be something to the old tales.

Buried in the graves alongside the remains of robust, bow-legged women were swords, bronze daggers, stone-tipped spears, well-crafted shields and other weapons of war.

"These women were warriors of some sort," Jeannine Davis-Kimball, a leader of the excavation said. "These finds suggest that Greek tales of Amazon warriors may have had some basis in fact."

The body of one young woman still contained an arrow in her chest cavity—a strong indication she died in battle.

These graves and others recently uncovered in Germany, the Middle East and elsewhere strongly support the notion that Amazons existed, according to Dr. Davis-Kimball and other researchers.

Elizabeth J.W. Barber, an archaeologist at Occidental College, said "most people assumed that if a grave had weapons, the skeleton was a man—now they can't be so sure."

Claudia Chang, an anthropologist at Sweet Briar College in Virginia, agreed. "Probably, we've been carried away with the macho image of the nomad," she said, adding that research now shows that women in these ancient cultures sometime "had an active role in warfare and in the political structure."

In the New World, reports of powerful, female warriors had been around since the arrival of Christopher Columbus. Gonzalo Pizarro wrote of "ten or twelve Amazons fighting in the front rank of the Indians" who killed many of his soldiers.

Father Cristobal de Acuna gave an extensive account of female warrior tribes in his book, *New Discovery of the Great River of the Amazons.* Stories by other South American explorers, conquistadors and priests in Brazil, Venezuela, Peru, Chile and Argentina mention first-hand encounters with women in battle or second-hand reports of women warrior tribes.

As in the Old World, most of these reports were not taken seriously until the 1960s when a team of archaeologists documented strong evidence that powerful matriarchal societies existed throughout the continent.

Nazca Lines

In1926, American archaeologist Alfred Kroeber made a startling discovery in the desert of southern Peru. Barely visible in the pale-yellow soil were long faint lines—which formed huge rectangles and other geometric shapes that seemed to end on the far horizon.

Some of the lines curved and arced into magnificent stylistic renderings of animals, including monkeys, spiders, hummingbirds and even a whale, as well as flowers, hands and spirals, ranging in size from a few feet to 600 feet across.

Even stranger, one particular drawing showed a spider completely unknown in that part of the world at the time.

Kroeber knew he had found something special—an ancient roadway, perhaps, or even some kind of primitive astronomical calendar. He theorized that the complex of lines stretching for more than 37 miles had been made by the Nazca Indians about 2,000 years ago.

But why? What was the meaning of this sprawling, abandoned plain, with its strange lines and haunting figures?

The mystery deepened when the archaeologist and others who studied the markings realized that the patchwork of lines was invisible at ground level. Only at a great height—from an airplane, for example—are the intricate lines and circles recognizable.

Swiss investigator Erich von Daeniken theorized that the Nazca plain was built as a landing strip for ancient spacecraft.

It was here that "prehistoric man communicated with beings from outer space," the controversial author-researcher concluded in his best-selling book, *Chariots of the Gods*. "Why else would anyone build something so elaborate that can only be seen by modern aircraft passing high in the sky?"

What intrigues more conventional scholars was not the making, but the purpose of the lines. In 1941 another American archaeologist, Paul Kosok, spearheaded an investigation that discovered many new drawings. From these he was able to plot the lines and patterns.

His conclusion: the lines were intended for astronomical observations. His theory inspired a German mathematician, Maria Reiche, who has devoted her life trying to unravel the mystery of the Nazca lines.

Like Dr. Kosok, she believed that the lines pointed to prominent stars or to the sun, enabling the Nazca to calculate dates. She contends the animals and other figures may represent star constellations, and so the whole extraordinary web of markings was probably a huge calendar.

A British movie-maker, Tony Morrison, went to Peru in 1977 to film a documentary on the work of Maria Reiche. He was convinced that the answer lay in the customs and religion of the ancient Nazca, a people whose culture had been absorbed into the Inca empire in the 15th century, only to be virtually wiped out in the Spanish conquest.

Morrison found a Peruvian archaeologist who believed that the lines were ceques—an Indian word for pathways made for religious purposes. The filmmaker went on to discover that a Spanish chronicle dating from 1653 told how Indians at the Inca capital at Cuzco venerated shrines placed along lines radiating from the Temple of the Sun.

In his book, *Pathways to the Gods*, Morrison suggests that the Nazca drawings were probably sacred representations of gods and animal spirits, while large cleared areas were probably sites for religious gatherings.

The enigma of the Nazca lines is not totally resolved.

Mystery of the Mounds

Explorers pushing westward in the late 18th century were astonished by the presence of large man-made mounds, tens of thousands of them, scattered along the Ohio and Mississipi River systems and throughout the Southeast.

Many of these artificial hills resembled the pyramids of ancient Egypt and Mesopotamia, but some were constructed in the shapes of animals.

The most spectacular discovery was a long, sinuous grass-covered serpent mound, writhing more than a quarter-mile atop a ridge near the modern-day town of Peebles, Ohio.

Speculation about the mounds abounded in the 19th century as waves of pioneers made startling new finds. Near East St. Louis, Ill., for example, settlers came upon an amazing sight—a huge, truncated pile of earth resembling the Great Pyramid of Egypt.

Awed by the size of these earthen formations—and mindful of the sophisticated technology required to construct them—the settlers thought it was unlikely that ancestors of the primitive Woodland Indians who inhabited the region could have built such imposing structures.

Instead, curious observers contended that the mounds were products of a more "noble race"—Romans, perhaps, or maybe Greeks, Phoenicians or even medieval Welshmen.

Others believed the mounds must have been constructed by descendants of the survivors of the Biblical flood, or by migrants from the lost continent of Atlantis. A few attributed them to the lost tribes of Israel mentioned in the Old Testament.

One man who supported the "noble race" theory was William Pidgeon, a thin, bespectacled trader and collector of Indian artifacts. He had devoted most of his adult life to discovering the lost secrets of the people he believed had once inhabited the Americas. His passion in the budding new field of archaeology took him through North and South America in search of evidence.

In the 1830s Pidgeon found what he thought was concrete proof that pre-Columbian explorers from Europe had reached the New World and were responsible for the megalithic earthen monuments.

On a bluff overlooking the Little Miami River in Ohio, he found a huge man-made hill, known locally as Fort Ancient—the "stupendous and wonderful remnants of a lost civilization." A decade later, he traveled by boat across the network of streams and lakes west of the Great Lakes. His quest: to interview Indians along the way, with an eye toward unlocking secrets of the mysterious builders of the mounds.

At the trading settlement of Prairie La Crosse on the upper Mississippi, he met De-coo-dah, a medicine man who immediately warmed to this eccentric man with an insatiable curiosity about the "old ways and times" when gods came to earth and built their palaces and temples.

At trek's end, Pidgeon was convinced that the mounds could only have been built by some "superior" race—a mysterious, lost people he called The Moundbuilders. In all likelihood, these enigmatic builders had been European in origin, but he saw striking architectural, religious and linguistic parallels with ancient Egypt.

Cyrus Thomas, a government ethnologist, was one of the first scientists to cast serious doubt on the Moundbuilder theory. After studying more than 2,000 Indian sites in the eastern and northwestern United States, he concluded that there had never been a lost race of Moundbuilders, that the architects of the mounds and the Indians had been one and the same people.

Thomas' thorough fieldwork, backed by exhaustive archival research, produced the first comprehensive study of North American Indians. Modern archaeologists—who generally share Thomas' view—divide the mound builders into three broad cultures: Adena, Hopewell and Mississippian.

Named after a mound site in Ohio, the Adena culture was centered in the upper Midwest and existed between 1000 B.C. and 200 A.D. Its people built burial mounds and animal effigies, including the awesome Great Serpent Mound of Ohio.

The Hopewell culture, which overlapped and eventually replaced Adena, flourished between 200 and 550. Skilled artisans and traders, the Hopewell and their immediate successors built most of the great earthen effigies and fortlike structures that so amazed Pidgeon and other early archaeologists.

The last and greatest of the mound-building cultures was the Mississippian, which began about 600 and dominated aboriginal society for the next thousand years. Its achievements were best represented by Cahokia, a major pre-Columbian metropolis at the present site of East St. Louis.

The Mississippians were unfortunate enough to witness the arrival of whites in the person of Hernando de Soto and his conquistadors, who crossed what is now the Southeastern United States in 1539. The Spaniards left a trail of death and destruction in their wake. Within a generation of their passage, the region's Indian population was decimated by smallpox and other diseases.

While the mystery of who built the mounds has apparently been solved, scientists are still unsure as to why these elaborate edifices were constructed.

But that's another story.

Drake's California

Almost three decades before the settlement at Jamestown, a fiery little English mariner named Francis Drake sailed into a "faire and good baye" somewhere along the California coast and dropped anchor.

Drake, the legendary "plunderer of the Spanish Main," called the place "Nova Albion" (New England) and proceeded to stake the claim of his sovereign, Queen Elizabeth I, by nailing an engraved metal plate to a post.

The date was June 17, 1579. Unknown to the flamboyant adventurer, his action was setting the stage for a historical dispute that still rages.

"The question everybody wants to know is: where exactly in California did he land?" asked Alan Villiers, a mariner himself and historian who has written extensively about the Drake voyages.

The quest for Drake's original landfall has led historians and archaeologists in entirely different directions. Some scholars who have researched the matter insist the famed "humbler of the Spanish Armada" took in at San Francisco Bay to repair his leaking flagship, the 75-foot *Golden Hind*.

Others say it was farther north, perhaps near Bolinas, while a few claim it was somewhere in-between. Drakes Bay at Point Reyes National Seashore is frequently mentioned as another possible site.

"Many seafarers favor the estuary at Drakes Bay, for they know and I know that the Golden Gate could be a difficult spot to find and enter in the days of sail," noted Villiers.

About the only thing experts agree upon is that, before landing at California, Drake had sailed north along the Oregon coast—perhaps as far as Vancouver Island, British Columbia—in his search for a Northwest Passage to the Atlantic.

"Then he turned south," explained Villiers. "Under the weight of the tons of plunder, the *Golden Hind* was literally coming apart at the seams."

Somewhere along the California coast he stopped and built a stockade to protect his treasure while repairs to the ship were made. Local Indians worshipped the commander "as if he were a god," according to Villiers.

The controversy surrounding Drake's landfall heated up in 1974 when archaeologist Charles Slaymaker excavated an English coin from an old Indian mound near the northern end of San Francisco Bay. A glass bead, unearthed at the same site, convinced Slaymaker and others that San Francisco Bay was the disputed spot.

Not so, said Raymond Aker, president of the Drake Navigators Guild, a group devoted to the study of Drake's voyages. Aker notes that in the three months before pulling in at what is now California, Drake had been gathering booty along the Pacific coast of the Americas—which had been, until his sudden appearance, a peaceful Spanish enclave.

"But he wasn't coming from the south when he saw this place," commented Aker. "He was coming from the north, where he had hoped to find a way back to the Atlantic. His ship was leaking. He had to repair her. He needed a safe place to careen her. The estuary of Drakes Bay fit the bill."

Scrutiny of Drake's own logs might have resolved the dispute. Upon returning to England, though, after completion of his 118-day voyage of 9,700 miles—the longest unbroken passage made to that time—Drake gave them to Queen Elizabeth. They have not been seen since.

One map produced by Judocus Hondius in 1589 plots Drake's trip and spots where he anchored. The map, produced 10 years after Drake's discovery of California, has been used by various scholars eager to prove their own case about landfall.

In 1936, a man on a stroll near San Francisco Bay picked up a plate of brass whose message, signed "Francis Drake," claimed Nova Albion for Elizabeth. The 8-by-5-inch plaque has an opening in one corner that tallies with one journal's description, "a piece of sixpence (bearing Elizabeth's visage)...shewing itself by a hole made of purpose through the plate."

A few days later another man claimed he had been the first to find the plate, near Drakes Bay, but later chucked it from an open car where it was discovered—or rediscovered.

The question of the plate's authenticity has yet to be resolved, despite extensive metallurgical, microscopic and textual analyses. Some researchers feel the case is already proved; others are just as adamant that the plate is a hoax.

Meanwhile, the controversial artifact rests in the Bancroft Library of the University of California at Berkeley.

Drake spent 37 days in Nova Albion, then put to sea and headed home. The 35-year-old admiral and privateer would go on to fame and fortune as the first Englishman to circumnavigate the globe.

For his efforts, the beloved "sea dog" was knighted by Queen Elizabeth—an act that goaded the Spanish into war. In 1588 Drake played a leading role in destroying the Spanish Armada.

Eight years later the red-bearded raider came down with a fever while prowling the Caribbean in search of treasure and died. His body was placed in a lead coffin and dropped into the sea off the Panamanian coast.

Titans of Tiahuanaco

Long before the arrival of gold-seeking conquistadors, a mysterious race of blue-eyed warriors with white skin is thought to have ruled vast regions of South America.

Known as the Tiahuanacans, these enigmatic people built fabulous monuments and stone castles among the lofty crags of the Bolivian highlands before vanishing on the eve of the European conquest.

Their capital city of Tiahuanaco—known as the "city in the clouds" because of its location almost three miles above sea level—flourished from about 100 B.C. to A.D. 1000. Since the inhabitants left no written records, most of what is known about the Tiahuanacans comes from Indian legends recorded by the Spanish 400 years ago.

Some scholars contend that the Tiahuanacans might have originated in Europe or northern Africa, having arrived in South America after being blown off course in storms.

A number of historians and archaeologists say they might have been descendants of the Phoenicians, an ancient sea-faring people who traveled widely. Others trace their origins to Irish monks who sailed across the Atlantic Ocean in hide-covered boats in the sixth century.

In recent years, a number of scholars have suspected that the Tiahuanacans might be linked to Chinese or Japanese mariners who explored the western coast of South America 2,000 years ago.

Norwegian scientist Thor Heyerdahl, theorized that the Tiahuanacans might owe their ancestry to ancient Egyptians who crossed the Atlantic more than 2,500 years ago, settling first in Guatemala and Mexico before moving into South America. In 1970, Dr. Heyerdahl re-created such a voyage by building a vessel of papyrus reeds (which he named the *Ra*) and sailing from north Africa to Barbados in the West Indies.

One thing is certain—the founders of Tiahuanaco were master craftsmen.

Over a gateway of the main entrance is a carving that provides a clue to the origins of Tiahuanaco's civilization. It depicts a creator-god (whom the Incas later called Viracocha) with tears on his cheeks.

According to Indian legend, the creator-god and his followers were white-skinned, blue-eyed people who arrived at Tiahuanaco about 500 A.D. They taught the Indians architecture and agriculture and erected stone statues.

About 500 years later, the legends say, Indians from the coast invaded Tiahuanaco. Most of the white people were slaughtered, but their leaders and a few others escaped to the shore and sailed away across the Pacific Ocean.

Another clue is a statue of a man, twice life-size, near the Kalasasaya. Now called The Bishop, it holds an object that looks like a book, yet books were unknown in South America before the Spanish conquests in the early 1500s.

From these clues and legends, and from archaeological evidence, scientists have sketched an outline of Tiahuanaco's history. Apparently, two sets of outsiders took part. There was already a primitive culture in the area when the first group arrived, about 500 A.D. The newcomers were probably peaceful members of an advanced civilization who taught the natives new skills. Within a couple of centuries Tiahuanacan influence spread over an immense area, from Ecuador to northern Argentina, as well as the coast of Peru.

The second wave of invaders, in about 1000, wiped out the great city. Its empire lay in fragments for 200 years until the Incas reassembled it in their continent-spanning conquests.

Even after all these centuries, many of their great stone

buildings still stand, along with artificial mounds and elabo-rately-carved monuments that weigh hundreds of tons. The largest masonry structure looms 50 feet above the ground and measures 700-by-700 feet. Another building, known as the Kalasasaya, contains a stone block that weighs more than 150 tons.

Tiahuanaco, located in Bolivia on the Peruvian border a few miles south of Lake Titicaca, is all the more incredible when one considers that it was built without benefit of wheels, rollers or beasts of burden. Using only stone tools, primitive builders were able to transport enormous boulders from the nearest quarry, 25 miles away across rugged terrain. The boulders were chiseled into massive blocks, then used to build the vast structures.

But questions remain: Who were the mysterious white-skinned strangers that tradition says raised Tiahuanaco to great heights? What really happened to them? Were they descendants of roving mariners from ancient Egypt or Phoenicia—or were they perhaps the progeny of Irish monks who fled their war-torn homeland centuries before the birth of Christopher Columbus to seek refuge in the New World?

Scientists continue to probe the silent stone ruins in search of answers to these and other questions about the enigmatic Tiahuanacans and their ancient stone city in the clouds.

Giant Balls of Costa Rica

In the mid-1930s, workers clearing ground for the United Fruit Company in a remote region of Costa Rica came across an astonishing sight—hundreds of perfectly spherical stones, some measuring 8 feet in diameter or more and weighing up to 16 tons.

As the workers hacked and burned away the forest, they

found hundreds more of the strange balls, some half-buried, others lying on the surface.

Experts brought in to examine the strange spheres were at a loss to explain the origin of the stones or their means of construction.

"It was," in the words of one archaeologist, "as if they had mysteriously fallen from the sky."

For years, that's exactly what many Costa Ricans believed. Even today, scientists still don't know what to make of Las Bolas Grandes—the so-called Giant Balls of Costa Rica, which many consider to be one of archaeology's greatest unsolved mysteries.

Since their discovery, tens of thousands of the stones have been found, many of which now grace the gardens, parks and public buildings of the capital city of San Jose.

Samuel Lothrop of the Peabody Museum was one of the first Americans to examine the mysterious stones.

"They're a fantastic sight," Dr. Lothrop noted in the 1940s, adding that they are "clearly man-made...because the granite from which most of them were fashioned did not occur naturally in the area where they were found."

According to British scientist and author Arthur C. Clarke, the strangest thing of all is that many of the stones are "so damned perfectly round."

He added, "The largest ones, in particular, are so smooth and round that it is almost impossible to believe that they had been fashioned without some kind of mechanical aid."

Experts who have investigated the spheres confirm that none of the stones deviate in the slightest from a given diameter. This precision implies that the men who made them had a superior knowledge of geometry and possessed the appropriated technical implements.

Dr. Luis Diego Gomez, director of the Museo Nacional in Costa Rica, favors the idea that the stones represent the sun, moon or the whole solar system. Others theorize they may simply be grave markers.

Local legends say the balls fell from the sky long ago. Some describe them as "tear drops of the gods," while others claim they are the unborn souls of children yet born. One version holds that the balls have astronomical significance.

Archaeologists generally reject all these notions.

"In these latitudes the sun has been represented in all ages as a golden orb, wheel or disk, and never as a ball—neither among the Incas, the Mayas, nor Aztecs," commented one researcher.

Most scientists who have studied the stones contend they must have been brought from mountains many miles away.

"To carve a sphere 8 feet in diameter, the ancient masons would have had to start with at least a 9-foot cube of rock, and whole teams of people would have had to turn it as it was rubbed smooth with other stones," Clark said. "Then they, or others, would have had to roll the completed balls to the mountain ledges or the far banks of rivers where they were found."

Researchers say it's only a matter of time before fresh clues will emerge from the ground that will shed new light on the enigmatic stone balls of Puerto Rico. Until then, they will remain a mystery.

Enchanted Lands, *Lost* Worlds

Beyond the Horizon

Legends tell of a wondrous land far beyond the sea, an enchanted realm of peace and beauty where there is no war or poverty, where the streets are paved with gold and scented breezes blow sweet and fresh.

Plato called this place Atlantis, while others referred to it as Lemuria or Mu. To the Spaniards it was known as Cibola, the Seven Cities of Gold. Irish Celts dreamed of an Isle of Youth—Tir nan Og, while their Scottish kinsmen dreamed of an Isle of the Dead where weary souls found eternal rest among the gods and spirits of their ancestors.

These earthly paradises went by other names—Ogygia, Meropis, the Garden of Hesperides, Eden, El Dorado, Prester John's Kingdom, Engel-land and Avalon.

During the Middle Ages, it was widely believed that Paradise was on an island somewhere far beyond the horizon. Here, animals talked and cavorted among the gods. Sailors returning from long voyages often told stories that seemed to reinforce a universal belief in that far-off mystical realm.

In the eighth century, a band of Irish monks led by Saint Brendan said they sailed west and saw islands of fire and ice. They camped on the back of a large whale and, sailing on, encountered talking beasts and strange human-like creatures with long, curling tails that slept at the bottom of the sea.

Stories like these, kept alive by dreamy poets and minstrels, fired the popular imagination while offering fresh hope to oppressed underclasses everywhere. Some scholars think such fables actually led to the great age of exploration in the 15th and 16th centuries.

One of the most famous of the fabled realms was Avalon, the legendary burial ground of England's semi-legendary King Arthur, who is believed to have reigned over the Britons before the Saxon conquest. So wondrous was this place the Celts called it the Isle of the Blessed.

Glastonbury, in England, is often associated with the Isle of Avalon and with stories of Arthur's passing. Many believe the remains of Arthur and Queen Guinevere—if indeed they existed at all—lie in the ancient cemetery of Glastonbury Abbey.

Glastonbury Tor, a curious, conical hill set in rich meadows, was surrounded by swamps and marshes around 500, the assumed time of King Arthur, and may have been the fabled Isle of Avalon.

In *Morte d' Arthur*, Sir Thomas Malory suggests that Camelot, King Arthur's legendary court, was in Winchester. Other suggestions, based on folklore, have placed Camelot at Colchester, for which the Roman name was Camulodunum, or near Tintagel, in Cornwall, where the River Camel and the market town of Camelford are situated.

The most noted site, backed by archaeological evidence, is Cadbury Castle in Somerset that looks over the Vale of Avalon toward Glastonbury. The castle—the remains of an Iron Age fortified hill—is near the village of Queen Camel. John Leland, an antiquarian of Henry VIII's reign, wrote that local people often referred to the hill on which the fort was found as "Camalat."

It has also been claimed that the nearby River Cam was the scene of King Arthur's last battle, Camlann, which is referred to in Historia Britonnum, written by the ninth century British historian Nennius.

Over the years, farmers in the region have reportedly unearthed skeletons and other artifacts west of Cadbury Castle that indicated that a great battle had indeed been fought there.

The legend of King Arthur being only wounded in battle, eventually recovering and returning to rule in a golden age, has a parallel in another medieval myth about the land of Ogygia.

Plutarch (A.D. 46-120), the Greek writer-philosopher, wrote that Ogygia was in the west, a place of enchanting beauty beneath the setting sun. There, it is said, sleeps Cronus, the Greek Titan, who castrated his father, Uranus, and devoured most of his children for fear of being usurped.

Like England's legendary King Arthur, the Aztec's Quetzalcoatl and Germany's Barbarossa, Cronus would one day awaken to rule in a golden age.

Ancient Greek poetry says that Ogygia is a "sweet-scented" land where youth reigns, a land of plenty where the golden age lasts forever.

Spell of Atlantis

Since ancient times, men have dreamed of lost cities and vanished civilizations, of glittering kingdoms beyond the horizon with forgotten secrets and fabulous treasures there for the taking.

But for all the mystical allure of these fabled lands, none rivals the spell cast by Atlantis, the legendary island kingdom in the Atlantic which, according to ancient and medieval accounts, sank in a cataclysmic upheaval about 12,000 years ago.

The location of Atlantis has been lost to the ages. The Greek philosopher Plato put it somewhere in the "Great Ocean, the Western Sea whose swelling waves rose beyond the Pillars of Hercules"—a watery realm known today as the Straits of Gibraltar.

Fanciful seekers of the lost paradise have tried to find it in a bewildering variety of places—Tibet, the Andes, Australia, the Caucasus, South Africa, the Amazon Basin, Libya, Cuba, Florida, the Basque country, India, Morocco, Egypt, Mexico, Ceylon, China, the North Sea, Indonesia—even the Gobi Desert.

It would seem that a continent like Atlantis—larger than Europe, with beautiful cities, advanced technologies and an enlightened, utopian government—would have left behind more clues!

Most of what is known about the ancient kingdom comes from two of Plato's dialogues, *Timaeus* and *Critias*. Written around 370 B.C., the dialogues were supposedly based on information handed down from 200-year-old records of the Greek ruler Solon, who had heard of Atlantis from an earlier Egyptian priest.

Plato described Atlantis as a "wonderful empire" which had apparently conquered vast regions of the world, including Egypt. When an attack against Greece failed, however, Atlantis ran into trouble. "There occurred violent earthquakes and floods," Plato wrote, "and in a single day and night of misfortune all your warlike men in a body sank into the earth, and the island of Atlantis in like manner disappeared in the depths of the sea."

Thus ended the days of Atlantis, a noble, sophisticated society that had defied the will of Zeus and was destroyed.

The philosopher's story of the sunken continent captivated following generations. While some Greek thinkers—Aristotle and Pliny, primarily—disputed the existence of Atlantis, Plutarch and Herodotus wrote of it as historical fact. Atlantis, the antediluvian world, became entrenched in folklore all around the world, charted on ocean maps and sought relentlessly by explorers down through the ages.

During the Middle Ages, as wars, plagues and famine ravaged Europe, the story of Atlantis was all but forgotten. It wasn't until the 15th century that the legend was rediscovered, thanks to explorers and imaginative cartographers who included Atlantis on their maps.

When America was discovered, it was frequently identified with Atlantis, even though dry land obviously conflicted with the legend of a sunken continent. Many continued to believe, however, that the mountain peaks of the Azores, the Cape Verde Islands, the Canaries and Madeira were the true visible remains of the lost kingdom.

Of all the champions of the Atlantis story, none defended it more vigorously or more passionately than a failed business-man-turned-politician from Philadelphia, Ignatius Loyola Donnelly. In 1882, more than 2,300 years after Plato first wrote about Atlantis, Donnelly published *Atlantis: the Antediluvian World*, an instant international success that followers viewed as the Bible of Atlantology.

According to Donnelly, Atlantis was the world that preceded the Great Flood of the Bible. The people of Atlantis, he wrote, were handsome, prosperous, technically advanced sun-worshippers. Their oldest colony was probably Egypt, whose civilization reproduced that of the mother kingdom.

Borrowing heavily from contemporary science in constructing his theory, Donnelly spoke of the Atlantean kingdom as the original Garden of Eden, the Elysian Fields, the home of powerful kings and queens who were later to become the gods and goddesses of the Egyptians, the Greeks, the Phoenicians, the Hindus, the Scandinavians and the Indians of North, Central and South America.

Atlantis was also said to be the original home of the Basques, who are racially and linguistically different from other Europeans, and of the scattered tribes of white Indians who were occasionally seen in places like Venezuela. Pale-skinned pre-Columbian gods of the New World might also have been Atlanteans, as were the Guanches, cave-dwelling aborigines of the Canary Islands who were wiped out by the Spanish.

At the height of its glory, Atlantis was a "fair and wondrous" land, with magnificent mountain ranges, lush plains and a variety of exotic animal life—including elephants that, according to some accounts, were trained to fly through the air. The capital, built at the very center of the island, was remarkable for the scale and splendor of its handsome buildings, statues made of gold and canals.

Then came that terrible day 12,000 years ago when the entire island, along with most of its inhabitants, was destroyed by a series of earthquakes and tidal waves.

When Atlantis perished "in that terrible convulsion of nature," a few citizens escaped in ships and on rafts, bearing the dreadful news to the nations of both east and west. Hence, the stories of the Great Flood, which are told all over the world.

As Donnelly saw it, these Atlantean refugees planted the seeds for the creation of many new civilizations—India and Central America, as well as Egypt and elsewhere.

Donnelly had been drawn to the Atlantis story while serving as a U.S. Congressman. He spent countless hours in the Library of Congress, poring over the latest books and scientific journals dealing with geology, history, folklore, world literature, religion and linguistics. As his interest grew, so did his obsession: Atlantis had to exist, he felt. How else to explain the many similarities between the Old and New Worlds—botanical, biological, architectural and cultural?

Why, he wondered, did so many American and European animals and plants look alike? Why the coincidence of pyramids, pillars, burial mounds and ships appearing on both sides of the Atlantic?

Donnelly's answer was that everything had originated on Atlantis—the Terrestrial Paradise, the Isle of the Blessed, the Pure Land, the original Garden of Eden—then spread to the rest of the world.

"I cannot believe," he wrote, "that the great inventions were duplicated spontaneously…in different countries. If this were so, all savages would have invented the boomerang; all savages would possess pottery, bows and arrows, slings, tents and canoes."

In short, he concluded, "all races would have risen to civilization, for certainly the comforts of life are as agreeable to one people as another."

But to prove his theory once and for all, Donnelly knew what he needed.

"A single engraved tablet dredged up from Plato's island would be worth more to science, would more strike the imagination of mankind, than all the gold of Peru, all the monuments of Egypt, and all the terra-cotta fragments gathered from the great libraries of Chaldea."

So far the ocean has yielded no such tablet. Twelve-thousand years after it supposedly sank into the sea, the doomed continent of Atlantis remains nothing more than a glorious myth.

Giants in the Earth

The notion that a long-vanished race of giants once lived on Earth is an old one, predating the Bible, which states "there were giants in the Earth" in the days before the great flood survived by Noah and his kin aboard the ark.

Ancient drawings on rock walls from Spain to India have given weight to this theory, as have legends and stories handed down by Scandinavian tribes and Bushmen of Australia. The Sumerians of Mesopotamia also believed in a primordial race of giants, as did the Inca, Aztec and other pre-Columbian peoples of the New World.

As recently as the Middle Ages, it was commonly believed that giants had once ruled empires from the steppes of Central Asia to the frozen wastelands of Norway. Who else could have built Stonehenge and other colossal stone ruins scattered across Europe, northern Africa and the Mediterranean?

Some legends suggest these beings were descended from star-gods who walked the Earth countless ages ago.

Nobody knows what happed to these supermen of old. Some say they returned to the stars. Others say they simply died off, leaving nothing behind but their bones and legends.

Long ago, the Patagonian coast of South America may have been home to a mysterious race of giants. According to legend, these giants ruled their remote kingdom with an iron hand, forever waging war on diminutive populations to the north.

The first Europeans to encounter the warlike titans were

members of Portuguese explorer Ferdinand Magellan's crew who anchored at Port San Julian on the Argentine coast in June 1520.

Pigafetta, a member of Magellan's staff, wrote: "One day a giant appeared on the beach. This man was so tall that our heads scarcely came up to his waist, and his voice was like that of a bull."

Magellan's men captured two of the giants, intending to take them back to Europe, but they died in chains en route.

In 1578, after docking at Port San Julian, British explorer Sir Francis Drake skirmished with "men of large stature" before retreating with heavy losses. Fourteen years later, another European explorer, Anthony Knyvet, passed through the Magellan Strait and reported seeing "huge Patagonians" standing over 10 feet tall. He also claimed to have found several dead bodies measuring 12 feet tall.

Other explorers reported encounters, but by the turn of the 17th century the giants began to disappear. According to researcher John A. Keel, "The giants may have been thinning out or moving further inland to escape the encroachment of the militant Europeans."

However, Commodore Byron, skipper of the Dolphin, is supposed to have had a peaceful meeting with the giant tribe in 1764. After anchoring in the Magellan Strait, the crew of the Dolphin saw hundreds of natives, some of "monstrous" proportions.

"One of them, who appeared to be a chief, came toward me," wrote the commodore. "He was of gigantic stature, and seemed to confirm the tale of monsters in a human shape."

By the time Argentina and Peru had been settled in the 19th century, the old stories about giants had all but disappeared. Speculation continues, however, even to this day.

For example, on May 16, 1966, the *London Daily Mirror* reported that a "ferocious band of savages" measuring more than seven feet tall "are terrorizing neighboring tribes in the Amazon jungle."

Could these savages be descendants of the Patagonian giants who had moved inland to escape European civilization?

Back in Europe, 17th century workers digging in a sand quarry in southern France found what scientists believed were the remains of the last giant. Eighteen feet down, the workers found a coffin 30 feet long, 12 feet wide and 8 feet deep. Inside were the bones of a giant no less than 25 feet tall, with shoulders 10 feet across. Its skull, according to one report, was 5 feet long and 10 feet around, with eye sockets as big as dinner plates.

Unfortunately, most of the bones crumbled to powder soon after they were exposed to air. All that remained were two fragments of the lower jaw, three teeth, three vertebrae, a shoulder blade, part of a thighbone, the humerus bone of one arm and a few assorted pieces.

An engraving of the sarcophagus identified the body as Theutobocheus Rex-King. Theutobocheus was a semi-mythological ruler who had led barbarian tribes against Roman legions at the battle of the Galaure River, close to the site of the find.

According to a tablet enclosed within the tomb, King Theutobocheus was slain in combat and ordered buried in the coffin by Gaius Marius, the victorious Roman general.

News of the giant Theutobocheus spread quickly, and in due time what was left of him arrived in Paris, chaperoned by Pierre Mazuyer, the first scientist to analyze the remains. Not one to miss an opportunity, he put the bones on public display and quickly made a fortune.

When Nicholas Habicot, a respected and popular professor of medicine at the University of Paris, heard about the giant, he decided to investigate. His examination indicated that the bones were the real thing.

In a pamphlet summarizing his findings, the master surgeon wrote that the shape and composition of the bones left no doubt that they had come from a human male.

It wasn't until the 19th century that the issue was settled by

Baron Georges Cuvier, a fossil expert at the Museum of Natural History in Paris. The bones of "King Theutobocheus" were not really those of an ancient warrior after all. Rather, said Cuvier, they were the remains of an extinct elephant.

He did not blame Mazuyer and Habicot for their mistake: They were completely unaware that such animals once roamed the land.

Quest for El Dorado

Soon after the discovery of the New World, stories began circulating throughout Europe about the existence of a legendary city of gold in the Andes. Incredible riches awaited whoever was lucky enough to find the fabled city called El Dorado.

According to some accounts, El Dorado was presided over by a king so rich he dusted himself with gold every morning then washed it off in a sacred mountain lake in the afternoon. Worshippers tossed in offerings of gold, silver, emeralds and other precious objects.

So persistent and so compelling were these tales of el hombre dorado—the Gilded Man—that legions of gold-hungry explorers set off in search of the fabled realm of gold.

What followed was a genuine horror story as the bearded fortune hunters raped, robbed and plundered the jungles and mountains in their obsessive quest for gold and silver. The foolhardy quest ended the reputations—and lives—of many of those who sought vainly for the glittering prize.

"That was because they were searching for something that did not exist," said Casper Montibelli, an expert on the El Dorado myth. "It was a land that seems to have been based not even on legend but on the misinterpretation of a legend."

Initial failure didn't stop them from coming, however. And as they plundered their way into South America, Spaniards, Germans and other European treasure hunters were thrilled by the promise of great riches just over the next hill or across the next river.

Exaggerated accounts of El Dorado handed down by the sun-worshipping Chibeha Indians who lived in the 8,600-foot-high plateaus near present-day Bogota fired their imagination. The Chibehas, it was said, venerated gold as the sun god's metal. They wore golden ornaments and for centuries had covered their buildings with sheets of the precious metal.

As the tales spread, El Dorado came to be thought of as a city of gold. It was even shown on ancient maps of Brazil and the Guyanas, though its location was always vague.

In the 1530s several more expeditions went in search of El Dorado. But the mountains were nearly impassible, and they were forced to turn back when they ran out of food.

One ill-fated expedition led by Ambrosius Ehinger—a German sent by the Spanish government to establish a commercial colony in 1529—suffered a particularly brutal fate. After two terrible years, the Europeans were destroyed by the jungle—and by hostile Indians. Ehinger was killed by an arrow and only a handful of survivors made it out of the snake-infested wilderness.

But the legend of the fabulous city still tantalized fortune hunters, and the very words constantly on their lips, "El Dorado," became synonymous with "The Golden Place," and its true meaning—"The Gilded One"—was ignored.

In 1535, Sebastian de Belacazar, veteran of the Inca conquest and founder of Quito, Ecuador, spent a small fortune in an unsuccessful attempt to find the "Golden Man." Soon dozens of different stories merged into one hypnotic legend that drove the gold-seekers on.

One year after Belacazar's miserable expedition, Gonzalo Jimenze Quesada led 900 men inland from Santa Marta on

Colombia's northern coast. The invaders found some gold along Colombia's Cundinamarca plateau, but local Indians told them the sacred realm of the Golden Man was further north, where a greater abundance of gold and emeralds could be found.

Quesada eventually discovered Lake Guatavita, the reported site of the sacred ceremony. According to legend, tribesmen would smear their chief with a sticky resin and blow gold dust over him until he glistened from head to foot—literally an El Dorado. Then he was conducted in a magnificent procession to a raft at the edge of the lake. From there the chief would ride to the center of the lake, plunge into the icy water and rinse the priceless dust off his body.

Arriving at Lake Guatavita, Quesada and his men found no Golden Man—or gold. The treasure—if there was any— lay on the bottom of the lake, situated almost 9,000 feet above sea level in the crater of an extinct volcano.

While references to El Dorado continued to appear on maps well into the 18th century, the active hunt was really over. At the beginning of the 19th century, Prussian natural scientist and traveler Alexander von Humboldt conducted an extensive reconnaissance of South America. He retraced the routes of most of the El Dorado seekers and found what they found—nothing.

Exciting news was made in 1966 when two farm workers dug up an exquisite model raft made of solid gold in a small cave near Bogota. On board the raft were eight tiny oarsmen rowing with their backs to the regal golden figure of their chief.

But Lake Guatavita still refuses to yield its golden treasure.

Although some gold and emeralds were found in the muddy banks, the icy depths of the lake were never plumbed. So far as is known, the offerings to El Dorado—the Gilded One—are still at the bottom of the sacred lake.

Kingdom of Prester John

In 1221, fantastic rumors swept through Western Europe that a mighty Christian monarch was waging a holy war against the Moslem infidels of Central Asia.

This mysterious monarch—known only as Prester John— was said to be marching westward to relieve the beleaguered Crusaders, who were clinging precariously to parts of the Holy Land.

Some even believed the gallant conqueror would visit Europe once the eastern war was over.

European hopes were shattered, however, when another rumor reached them that the eastern warlord was not a Christian monarch at all, but the legendary "Beast of Asia," Genghis Khan.

This was not the first story of the coming of Prester John, nor would it be the last.

For centuries, stories persisted about a fabulously wealthy priest-king and his mysterious land in the East, where peace and justice reigned and poverty and vice were unknown. During the Middle Ages, this fabled land was known as the Kingdom of Prester John.

Prester John's palace was supposedly built of crystal and roofed with precious gems. The priest-king, who claimed to rule over 70 nations, slept unguarded on a bed of sapphires because a magic mirror kept him informed of secret plots. Rivers surrounding his capital city were filled with gold and other precious stones.

A fountain of youth supposedly kept the king young and strong, but one source put his age at 562 years. Within his kingdom lived elephants and lions and golden monkeys. There also existed a vast array of exotic species, including horned men and centaurs, one-eyed giants, satyrs and fauns, women who performed acrobatic tricks on horseback, and a bizarre race of three-eyed humans who slept with their heads in the ground.

The origins of the Prester John myth are obscure, but there is some evidence that it started as a legend of the Nestorians, a Christian sect who traveled and traded from Syria to China. Some investigators think the stories might have been started by Bishop Hugh of Gebal, Lebanon, in the 12th century.

In 1165, Byzantine Emperor Manuel I received a long, detailed letter from someone who signed himself, "Presbyter Johannes," who claimed to a descendant of the Magi of old—the wise men who saw the star of Bethlehem. Copies of the letter were sent to Pope Alexander III and to the Holy Roman Emperor, Frederick Barbarossa.

The mysterious author boasted that he was "King of Kings," and "ruler of rulers." He further stated that he presided over a crime-free and vice-free kingdom, where "honey flows in our land and milk everywhere abounds."

Page after page, Prester John repeated how wonderful and powerful he was. "If thou canst count the stars of the sky and the sands of the sea, thou canst judge the vastness of Our realm and Our power," the letter said.

Who was this enigmatic leader? Where was this sprawling and powerful kingdom?

Our knowledge of Prester (a corruption of "Presbyter," or "priest") John comes from information contained in almost 100 manuscripts, written in several languages, including Hebrew, which are scattered throughout the libraries of Europe. Scholars believe the nucleus of the story is rooted in historical fact—yet it now seems impossible to distinguish fact from fiction.

Some authorities have placed John's kingdom in China, others in India. A number of accounts gave Africa as his realm because of his frequent reference to elephants and black kings.

Some modern scholars have suggested that "John" is merely an incorrect rendering of "Zan," the royal title of Ethiopia. Marco Polo identified Prester John with the Khan of the Kereit, a tribe in Mongolia, which was then Nestorian Christian.

Prince Henry of Portugal was one of the first European leaders to seek out the enigmatic John, hoping their two armies could form a gigantic pincer around the Moors and crush their ancient enemy. Henry's passion to explore the unknown was driven, in part, by this desire to discover an inland route to Prester John's kingdom.

In 1177 Pope Alexander III even dispatched his personal physician to the East with a letter to Prester John. The man was never heard from again. Over the following centuries, numerous other European envoys tried to locate Prester John's domain—all to no avail.

That's because Prester John and his fabled kingdom never existed in the first place, argues Daniel Cohen, author of Mysterious Places.

"Prester John is almost certainly a deliberate fabrication, a bit of medieval romance of the mysterious East literature," he said, adding that some of the elements "seem to have been drawn from the Sinbad stories."

Like many legends of that period involving enchanted lands, Prester John's kingdom gradually fell out of interest. Then, in1221, interest was revived when information reached Rome from a prominent churchman, the Bishop of Acre. He shed new light on the mystery by reporting that King David of India was alleged to be a grandson of John.

In the early 1900s, speculation about the fabled kingdom was rekindled when Portuguese missionaries in Ethiopia found ancient Christian banners and swords. Tradition holds that the artifacts belonged to a godlike Christian king who lived long ago—proof, insist believers, that Prester John once ruled that far-off desert kingdom.

Speculation about Prester John and his fabled realm will likely continue, even if only in myth and fantasy. It can be argued, however, that the mysterious "King of Kings" from the east profoundly affected the geographical knowledge of Europe by stimulating interest in foreign lands and sparking the great voyages of exploration and discovery.

Lost Colony of Roanoke

For more than four centuries, the world has pondered the enigmatic fate of a small band of English men, women and children who sailed to the New World to launch a colony but disappeared in the Virginia wilderness.

Roanoke Colony, the brainchild of Sir Walter Raleigh, was to be a shining example of Renaissance ingenuity and courage and a bold challenge to Spanish primacy in the Americas. The 117 colonists sailed from Plymouth in 1587 to start their new settlement. The new land was billed as a paradise, a "most pleasant and fertile ground, replenished with goodly Cedars, and divers other sweete woods, full of (grapes), flaxe, and many other notable commodities."

The natives were said to be "gentle, loving and faithful." There was also talk of gold—lots of gold—and the possibility of finding a northwest passage to the Orient that would make them all rich.

Earlier attempts to establish colonies in Virginia had ended tragically. Sir Walter's half-brother had perished at sea after an ill-fated effort to plant settlers in what is now Newfoundland. A similar attempt two years earlier near Roanoke had come to nothing when the colonists abandoned the colony and a handful of soldiers left to guard the post had been massacred.

Colonial officials had every reason to think this second expedition to Virginia would be successful. To head the colony, Sir Walter had appointed his friend, the famous artist John White. Governor White had visited Virginia on a previous voyage and was expected to be a "bolde and resourceful" leader of the settlement.

In Raleigh's time, Virginia referred to much of the land lying north of Spanish-controlled Florida. Named after Elizabeth I— the "Virgin Queen"—the colony was set up to serve as a base while explorers sought the fabled passageway to the Far East.

Many who had come before had hoped to find gold, just as the Spaniards had to the south in Mexico and South America. Gold meant they could return to England as wealthy men and women.

Instead of gold and a linkup with the Pacific, however, the Roanoke Islanders found hardship and death. Trouble began almost immediately with the Indians. While the Croatan tribe remained basically friendly, others resented the white intruders and occasionally lashed out.

In 1587, White sailed to England for fresh supplies. Among those he left behind were his daughter, her husband, and their newborn daughter, Virginia Dare—believed to be the first child of European parents born in the New World.

Before departing, the governor left instructions that should the remaining colonists be forced to leave the settlement in his absence, they were to inscribe their destination in a "conspicuous place."

As fate would have it, war broke out with Spain and he was unable to return for three years. A grim sight awaited the governor's arrival at Roanoke. The tiny outpost had been ransacked and destroyed, and its population had vanished.

The only clue to the colonists' whereabouts was the single word "Croatoan" carved into a tree—an indication, perhaps, that the settlers had fled to Indians by that name on a nearby island after supplies ran out.

But the Croatoans expressed no knowledge of the colonists. The same went for other tribes in the area. The settlers had simply disappeared. Devastated by the grim loss—and with a storm coming on—the dispirited governor sailed back to England, never to return.

What happened at Roanoke? How could an entire colony disappear without a trace?

Some researchers theorize they were either captured or killed by Spanish soldiers who either marched or sailed up from St. Augustine to eliminate the unwanted English presence. Since none of the settlers' boats were found, a few historians say they might have tried to sail away, only to be lost at sea or captured by pirates or Spaniards.

Most scholars, however, contend the colonists fled inland and either joined up with friendly Indians or were wiped out in the process.

Anthropologist Charles Hudson of the University of Georgia supports the view that the Roanoke settlers moved onto the mainland where food and water was more plentiful. They intermarried with local Indians and, in time, were assimilated into the Indian culture.

Evidence of this migration has been found among certain tribes along the Lumber River in North Carolina. The Lumbees, for example, claim to be descended from the long-lost white settlers—and many have the blonde hair, blue eyes and pale skin to prove it.

Pioneers pushing inland along the Lumbee River in the 18th century were startled to confront these English-speaking Indians who dressed like white frontiersmen and lived in remarkably comfortable houses. Some could even read and write and claimed white gods had taught their ancestors how to "talk in books," which probably meant to read.

Could these Lumbees be descendants of the lost colonists at Roanoke?

In the 1930s, the president of Brenau College in Georgia raised a new possibility—some of the colonists probably migrated to Georgia. Dr. Haywood Pearce Jr. said a freshly excavated stone in his possession contained Elizabethan markings, including the initials of Eleanor White Dare— Governor White's daughter, who had been among the missing colonists.

As news of the stone spread, others with Eleanor's initials began turning up in Georgia and elsewhere—49 in all. The rocks were verified by stonecutters, geologists and experts in Elizabethan English for authenticity.

"I subjected them to every scientific test I could command," Dr. Pearce explained.

A panel of historians led by Dr. Samuel Eliot Morison spent months examining the relics, finally concluding: "The preponderance of evidence points to the authenticity of the stones."

But in 1940, a journalist commissioned by the *Saturday Evening Post* uncovered evidence suggesting the stones were a hoax—that Dr. Pearce, Dr. Morison and other investigators had been duped into believing they were authentic.

For one thing, the geologist who tested the stones later admitted to reporters that markings on at least one of them had been carved quite recently. The authority on Elizabethan English then revealed that some of the words found on the stone "probably" had not been introduced into the English language until later.

The final blow came when it was learned that one of the first men to find a stone had been accused of faking copies and trying to sell them to museums.

The mystery of the Dare stones, as the press called them, had been solved.

No so, however, the true fate of White's daughter, her family and the hundred or so other tragic colonists of Roanoke Island. Their strange disappearance ranks as one of the world's greatest mysteries.

"The Once and Future King"

For more than a thousand years, legends have been told of a noble High-King who gallantly defended Celtic Britain against an impossible array of enemies, including giants, witches, dragons and a hoard of heathen invaders from across the eastern sea.

This semi-mythological ruler was known by a number of names, most notably Arthur, son of Uter Pendragon of Cornwall. Wise and strong, Arthur and his beautiful wife, Queen Guinevere, supposedly lived in a shining castle perched at the far end of the realm called Caerleon—or, Camelot.

It was a time of magic and myth, a time when chivalrous young knights like Galahad, Tristram, Gawain and Lancelot rode off in search of glory and to accomplish great deeds in the name of their king and lord. One of their most famous missions was to find the Holy Grail—the divine cup used at the Last Supper, also said to contain a few drops of blood spilled by Christ as he lay dying on the cross.

According to legend, the holy goblet was taken to Britain by Jesus' tin-trading uncle, Saint Joseph of Arimathea, who founded a small church at Glastonbury in Somerset. Somewhere along the way—perhaps in the Forest of Broceliande—Saint Joseph and the Holy Grail disappeared; their fate remains one of the world's greatest mysteries.

Arthur's best friend and advisor was an enchanter and prophet named Merlin. It was Merlin, according to some accounts, who helped Arthur become king—first by giving him the power to withdraw the magical sword Excalibur from a stone, thereby proving he was the "true" king, then by enabling him to defeat a host of supernatural demons and monsters that sought to prevent his ascendancy to the throne.

Little is known of the real Arthur. Most historians speculate that the Arthur of legend is probably based on a British war-chief of the sixth century named Roman Artorious. He was likely a leader of the Romanized Britons who battled Saxon invaders from around 450 onwards.

One of the earliest chronicles that mentions Arthur by name is the *Historia Britonum (History of the Britons)*, supposedly written by a Welsh monk named Nennius about two centuries after the hero's death. In the 12th century another Welshman—Geoffrey of Monmouth—first gave literary form to the Arthurian stories in his *Historia Regum Britanniae (History of the Kings of Britain)*. In this chronicle Geoffrey fused history and legend to create a highly imaginative world of pagan gods and virtuous warriors who waged constant battle against heathens and the forces of evil.

The *Cambrian Annals* written in the 10th century say that

Arthur defeated the Saxons at Mount Badon in 516, and also mentions the Battle of Camlann, in southwestern England, where Arthur was mortally wounded. The fallen leader's body was mysteriously spirited away to the mythical Island of Avalon, thought by some to be modern Glastonbury, where he could be healed, then returned to the throne at some point in the future.

Some say that Camelot—named after the pagan king Camaalis—was located near Tintagel, Arthur's reputed Cornish birthplace. Modern researchers have sought to place the legendary castle at the ruins of Cadbury Castle, an Iron Age earthwork fort near Glastonbury in Somerset. Sir Thomas Malory put the castle in Winchester, while Geoffrey of Monmouth placed it at Caerleon, on the Usk River near the Welsh border.

The romantic world of King Arthur reached new levels of popularity in the 15th century with publication of Malory's *Morte d'Arthur (Death of Arthur)*, a highly imaginative chronicle heavy on fantasy and light on historical substance. Still, it provided new generations with highly romanticized accounts of King Arthur and Camelot, Queen Guinevere, Merlin, the Knights of the Round Table and their adventurous search for the Holy Grail.

Was Arthur a real king—or merely a myth? Some say he was neither, theorizing that the legendary figure was actually an amalgam of several historical characters, including Anwn (alias Arthun), a Welsh ruler who conquered Greece, and Athrwys (alias Arthwys) the king of Glywyssing and Gwent.

During the Renaissance, Tudor monarchs vigorously defended the story because of their royal claim to Arthur's heritage. Some scholars have argued that Arthur was actually a Scottish king named Artur, the son of King Aidan of Dalriada, born in the 550s, while others say he was really King Cerdic, founder of the Saxon dynasty of Wessex.

Another theory is that the historical Arthur was descended from Lucius Artorius Castus, a second century Roman general stationed in Britain. Since many of Arthur's battles took place in northern Britain, Arthur's name has sometimes been linked with King Arthwys, who ruled over a large kingdom in the Pennines.

In the end, King Arthur—the man—died on the field of battle at Camlan while defending his throne against Mordred, a rebellious nephew. But the legendary Arthur lived on, as his Christian Celt followers quickly fled—some say to the mountains of Wales, others to Brittany in France. There stories were whispered and sung about their fallen king's valor and goodness—stories that became more glorified with each telling until truth and legend blended in a mythical haze.

In 1191 the remains of a king and queen were found in the ruins of an abbey at Glastonbury—the same ruins said to have been built by Saint Joseph. An inscription on the tomb read: "Here lies Arthur, the once and future king."

Fin,
Fang and
Fantasy

Bigfoot and His Hairy Kin

In every mountain range in the world, stories are told of shambling, manlike creatures that stalk the snowy gloom, occasionally wandering down from higher elevations to terrorize remote communities.

In the Gobi desert they are called meti. Elsewhere in Asia their names are Shookpa, Migo and Kang-Mi. To the people in the northwestern United States the creature is Bigfoot, while in the foothills of the Canadian Rockies the phantom monster has been known as Sasquatch since ancient Indian times.

For centuries, Himalayan Sherpas have referred to these enigmatic beasts as yeti, or "abominable snowmen." In Australia, the aborigines called them yowee.

Whatever the name or habitat, descriptions are roughly the same—heavy, hairy, foul-smelling and tall, sometimes 10 feet or more. They usually walk upright on two legs and sometime utter fearful cries, especially when confronted by humans.

No yeti, Bigfoot, Sasquatch, yowee or other creature matching their description has ever been captured. Nor has sufficient evidence come forth to convince the scientific world that such a creature really exists.

Yet sightings continue by credible witnesses—explorers, missionaries, even scientists. People who believe in the existence of these legendary beasts point to the gorilla, nothing more than a myth in much of the world until its discovery in the early 1800s. Many believe it's only a matter of time before one of the elusive creatures is killed or captured.

No one claims to know what these strange creatures are. Some believers suspect the legendary beast might be a living representative of *Gigantopithecus*, a giant primate that existed from a half million to 5 million years ago. Is it possible that some of these prehistoric ape-men survived in remote regions of the world?

For centuries, the mountain people of Nepal and Tibet

have feared the yeti, a creature said to have supernatural powers and the strength of 10 men. Other than its size, the yeti's most striking feature is its face—usually described as round and white, with thin lips, intelligent eyes and other humanoid features.

In one form or another, yetis have been in and out of the news since 1832, when Nepal's first British resident, B.H. Hodson, described a hitherto unknown creature that "moved erectly, was covered in long, dark hair, and had no tail."

The first Westerner who claimed to have seen the yeti was Lt. Col. C.K. Howard-Bury, leader of a British reconnaissance expedition to Mount Everest in 1921. On Sept. 22, the expedition found a group of large, humanlike footprints in the snow near Lhakpa La in Tibet. Since the prints were three times the size of a normal human foot, Lt. Col. Howard-Bury concluded that they were made by a large bear or wolf. His Sherpa guides disagreed, informing him that a metoh or mehteh kangmi, meaning "snow creature" or "wild creature" had made the footprints.

When reports reached the West, the beast was soon given its Western name—the abominable snowman.

In 1951, British mountaineer Eric Shipton published a series of photographs (taken in the Gauri Sankar Range of the Himalayas) of humanoid footprints, 13 inches long and 8 inches wide. Shipton said the tracks were too large to have been made by a bear and too fresh to have enlarged by melting.

Yeti hunting became a popular pastime. Sherpas were happy to enthrall outsiders with stories of these giant creatures of the mountains, and several monasteries in the Himalayas turned up bones, skins and scalps reputed to be those of yetis.

In nearby Russia, stories about a tribe of "wild, hairy men" inhabiting the Vanch mountains of the Pamirs have circulated for as long as anyone can remember. In 1925, a group of Red Army troops supposedly shot down a large, fur-covered creature that tried to attack them. Officers who examined the corpse reported: "Hair covered everything but the face, ears, palms, knees, feet and buttocks. The skin on the hands, knees and feet was coarse and thickly callused. The face was dark, with dark eyes, a heavy, sloping brow, prominent cheekbones, a flattened noise and a massive lower jaw."

For the past three decades, scientists in the United States have combed the mist-shrouded wilds of the Pacific Northwest in search of an elusive creature that witnesses say bears an uncanny resemblance to the abominable snowman of the Himalayas. Thousands of sightings have been reported, many of them by reliable witnesses. Hundreds of footprints have been found and examined, and numerous tales flourish about dramatic encounters with these giant beasts of legend.

Professor Grover Krantz, a Washington State University anthropologist, passionately believes that between 200 and 2,000 such monsters inhabit the rugged high country of northern California, Oregon, Washington and British Columbia. Smaller populations probably inhabit the lonely swamps and bayous of several Southern states as well, he thinks, as well as certain sections of New England and the Great Lakes.

Professor Krantz is one of a growing number of respected scientists in the United States and Canada who have concluded that some kind of giant, hairy primate haunts out-of-the-way locations in North America. They are so convinced they have even given the creature a name—*Gigantopithecus blacki*, or Bigfoot.

Over the years, thousands of footprints attributed to the legendary ape-man have been found, but so far not Bigfoot himself. Droppings and traces of hair have been discovered on trees, fences and even on the bumpers of cars—but no bodies or bones.

If a Bigfoot-like creature truly exists, then why haven't any remains been found?

Believers like Professor Krantz suspect that the creatures

bury their dead. Fast-acting acid soils at such depths account for the fact that no fossils have been found, the professor noted, adding that a "natural disposal system" of scavengers, carnivores and insects help to quickly dispose of the remains.

Cryptozoologists fantasize about the day when conclusive evidence can be found proving the existence of these elusive creatures—a bone, a skull, a clump of fur—perhaps even a live specimen. Until such time, Bigfoot and his hairy kin will remain the stuff of legend.

Monsters of the Deep

Legends about terrifying sea monsters have been passed down by generations of fishermen and sailors in almost every corner of the world.

The tragic Greek hero Perseus supposedly battled a watery beast to save Andromeda, while Homeric hymns warned of a vile, multi-headed sea creature capable of snatching humans from their "dark-prowed ships."

Herodotus, the "father of history," wrote about a one-eyed maritime creature that was part fish and part lion, a symbol that long endured on ancient sea charts.

Ancient Babylonians believed that a golden sea monster named Oannes, which had the body of a monstrous fish but the head and feet of a man, crawled out of the Erythrean Sea (now the Gulf of Persia) and taught barbaric tribes how to read, write and build cities. Oannes went by other names, including Dagon, the fish-god of the Phoenicians, a maritime people who both feared and worshiped serpents of the deep.

The Egyptians also worshipped mythical sea creatures, as did ancient Africans, Polynesians and Romans. The Chinese had their "sea dragons," while the Hebrews of the Bible recalled Old Testament references to "Leviathan...the twisting serpent, a creature without fear" that "makes the Deep boil like a pot..."

During the Middle Ages, a mysterious Christian priest named Prester John supposedly ruled a vast kingdom guarded by huge, terrifying sea monsters. Seafaring nations far to the north—Norway, Denmark and Sweden—had their own myths, legends and traditions about sea monsters, including the kraken, a horrible creature of gigantic proportions that stalked the misty swells of the Northern Atlantic.

Before he set sail in 1492, Christopher Columbus had been warned about ravenous sea beasts lurking far beyond the horizon. Vasco da Gama, the Portuguese navigator, heard similar stories during his long voyage around the world, which ended in 1499.

In the pre-Columbian New World, Indians living along the Gulf coast and eastern seaboard worshiped a variety of ocean-going serpents that occasionally required human sacrifices. Spanish, Portuguese, French and English sailors told of hair-raising encounters with maritime monsters that "belched fire and smoke," gobbled up wayward ships and menaced coastal regions into Colonial times.

Modern scientists generally dismiss such claims as superstitious nonsense, contending that what the observers actually saw were sharks, whales, squid, manta rays and drifting strands of seaweed. Some sightings were attributed to large snakes swimming from island to island—true sea serpents—or large eels.

Monster sightings along American seashores reached an all-time high in the 19th century. Between 1817 and 1847—the so-called heyday of American monster sightings—hundreds of people said they saw sea serpents cavorting off Massachusetts, Maine, Halifax (Nova Scotia), Charleston, S.C., and in the Gulf of Mexico.

The sightings were so plentiful that researcher Bernhard Heuvelman wrote: "Mass reports from the East Coast of the United States agree so well as to be almost monotonous."

From the North Sea to the Mediterranean, the Chinese Sea to the Indian Ocean, new sightings and occasional encounters with sea serpents were becoming increasingly common. In 1666, the burgermeister of Potom said he saw a sea serpent as thick around as a wine barrel and of "10 loopings." In 1687, villagers in Dramsfiorden, Norway, spotted another large sea monster. Erik Pontoppidan, a Danish bishop, reported that "a great sea serpent" was spotted several times that year."

Meanwhile, the South Pacific was heating up with tales about a massive sea monster with "huge tentacles" capable of encircling ships and dragging them down into the depths. These stories were similar to Celtic legends about a multi-tentacled creature said to be more than a mile in length.

But no monster has been better authenticated than the mysterious behemoth said to inhabit the warm waters off Brazil. A Portuguese captain described it as "an enormous serpent, with a head shaped much like a horse's, only bigger, and a mouth full of sharp fangs."

Legends about the creature continued to grow as more Europeans migrated to the region. Frequent sightings were reported during Colonial times and even continued into the modern era. The most reliable accounts came in 1905, when two members of the British Royal Zoological Society traveling on a steamship said they saw an enormous serpentine creature cavorting in the waves.

On Feb. 14, 1872, the crew of the *St. Olaf*, a Norwegian vessel, was approaching the Texas coast near Galveston when they saw an "immense serpent" gliding toward them. In a sworn statement, Capt. Alfred Hassel said the creature was about 70 feet long and 7 feet in diameter, making it one of the largest sea serpents ever reported.

The so-called Galveston Monster sported four fins on its back and appeared yellowish-green in color, according to Captain Hassel. Waves "pushed out loudly" from its undulating motion.

Like most sightings, skeptics dismissed the Galveston monster as nothing more than a long string of seaweed. But some experts theorize that the Galveston Monster might have been a serpent after all—a giant boa constrictor, perhaps, or some other kind of large snake that might have drifted across the Gulf of Mexico from Central America.

But 70 feet long? The longest serpent ever known in the New World—the anaconda—rarely exceeds 20 feet in length, though 40-footers have been reported.

Is it possible that what the crew of the *Saint Olaf* saw was a large snake with strands of seaweed gathered about its body? Such an occurrence would have made the serpent appear much longer and a more exotic and terrible sight to behold.

Merfolk

For as long as sailors have gone to sea, stories have been told about merfolk—mysterious, beguiling creatures that haunt the lonely waves, forever singing their enchanting songs that can calm the fiercest storm or lure mariners to their doom, depending on their mood.

Usually described as beautiful young women with voices like angels, these water-dwelling nymphs were once thought to be daughters of the god Neptune, king of the sea.

Tradition holds that merfolk are descended from the lost world of Atlantis. According to some legends, survivors of the doomed continent escaped by swimming into the sea where they grew scales and fins and became mermaids and mermen.

They go by many names. Coastal inhabitants of England and France sometime refer to them as Dracs, while people of the Scottish Highlands call them Fuaths. Merfolk in Irish legends are called merrows.

These water people were sometimes described as having webbed hands and green hair and eyes. Mermen had long red noses and short arms. The women were always beautiful and famous for their wonderful singing voices.

The Philistines and Babylonians actually worshiped merfolk-like gods. Some ancient Mesopotamian groups believed their ancestors were creatures with fins and scales that emerged from the sea long ago and colonized the land.

While exploring the bottom of the sea in a glass globe, Alexander the Great is said to have had several adventures with beautiful sea maidens. The Roman writer Pliny recounts how an officer of Augustus Caesar saw many mermaids "cast upon the sands and lying dead" on a beach in faraway Gaul.

"The mermaid," opined an Irish priest in the sixth century, "is a much-accursed creature, both foul and tempting. She has no soul."

According to folk tradition, the only way a mermaid could gain a soul was by renouncing the sea. Few did so, however, since terrestrial life was a bit challenging for fish-tailed beings.

Confined to the watery domain, mermaids have been depicted as lonely creatures, occasionally taking human form to participate in village fun or occasional relationships with humans. One story held that a mermaid could be prevented from returning to the sea by stealing a magic cap or pelt. Such action, however, usually resulted in disaster for the thief or thieves.

In 1403, Dutch fishermen were said to have befriended a beautiful mermaid who was stranded on mud flats. According to a 17th century historian, the creature also was befriended by village women who "cleansed her of the sea-mosse, which did stick about her."

The mermaid, so the story goes, never learned to speak, but lived 15 years among the villagers. When she died, the "poor creature" was given a Christian burial in the local churchyard.

Along the rugged Outer Hebridean coast of Benbecula, folks still talk about the "little sea maiden" who swam ashore and was stoned to death by their terrified ancestors.

The tragedy is said to have occurred more than 160 years ago, on a clear spring morning in 1830 when a group of women cutting seaweed by the shore spotted a small woman-like creature splashing in the surf and called for help. A mob of townsfolk came running, pitchforks and axes in hand.

For more than an hour the awe-struck islanders watched the strange little woman cavorting in the waves. One witness described the girl as "pretty and pixie-like," with "long blond hair entwined with seaweed."

Another said she was "about the size of a child of three or four years of age...and she had an abnormally developed breast."

But it was the sea maiden's lower body that drew the most attention.

"The lower part of the body was like a salmon, but without scales," said Alexander Carmichael, author of *Carmina Gadelica*, a four-volume encyclopedia of Gaelic folklore published in the late 1800s. "It was clear for everyone to see that this marvelous little creature belonged to the mermaid race."

After their shock passed, several men waded into the surf and tried to capture the friendly, frolicking creature. Each time they got close, however, she swam farther away.

Then some boys started throwing rocks. One struck the creature in the back, apparently scoring a fatal blow.

A few days later the maiden's lifeless body washed ashore a few miles away at Cuile Nunton. According to Carmichael, "Crowds of people, some from long distances, came to see this strange animal, and all were unanimous in the opinion that they had gazed on the mermaid at last."

Duncan Shaw, the local sheriff, ordered a coffin and shroud made for the little mermaid.

"This was done," wrote Carmichael, "and the body was buried in the presence of many people, a short distance above the shore where it was found."

Scientists theorize that what the villagers saw—and killed—was either a seal or sea-cow. But Dr. Karl Shukar, a British zoologist who has written several books about mermaids and other mythological water creatures, finds that explanation ridiculous.

"Is it really plausible that a hearty seafaring people like

those of the Outer Hebrides, well acquainted with seals and other marine creatures, could genuinely be fooled by the dead body of any such animal into believing that they were looking at the corpse of a mermaid? It seems most unlikely," he wrote.

After all, he reminded, "How many dead seals or whales have been ceremoniously laid to rest in a coffin and shroud, with a solemn crowd in attendance? Its body must have been decidedly humanoid to have elicited such a remarkable response."

If the story about the "Benebecula Mermaid" is true, something strange and of immense zoological importance must have been buried on that lonely Hebridean coastline more than 160 years ago.

Says Dr. Shukar: "No doubt its remains have long since been washed away, reclaimed by the waves and returned to the undersea world from where it had emerged, all unsuspecting of its tragic fate, on that long-vanished day."

Let us hope that if any of the creature's relatives do the same in the future, they will be treated more humanely by our own kind.

Winged Terrors

On an island far beyond the horizon of the known world, there once lived a creature so big and fearsome that even the bravest seafarers avoided its rocky realm. This was the legendary land of the Rukh, or Roc, the giant bird that attacked Sinbad on his fabled second and fifth voyages.

But centuries before Sinbad or the *Arabian Nights*, the Greek historian Herodotus wrote of a gigantic race of birds that lived "beyond the sources of the Nile." Even Marco Polo, the celebrated traveler, reportedly saw such a monster and provided a hair-raising account of the confrontation.

The bird was "so large and strong," he said, "as to seize an elephant with its talons and to lift it into the air, in order to drop it to the ground and in this way to kill it. When dead, the bird feasts upon the carcass."

He added that the bird was so big the wings measured "sixteen paces in extent, from point to point...and the feathers are eight paces in length and thick in proportion."

On the island of Madagascar off the African coast, stories were often told about gigantic birds that frequently attacked humans. Islanders reportedly lived in constant fear of these horrid creatures that swooped down upon them without warning and carried them off to nests on distant summits.

European visitors to Madagascar in the 17th century wrote of seeing a feathered monstrosity that ate large pythons "as ordinary birds eat worms." The creature's egg alone supposedly measured 50 paces around, and in flight it "darkened the sky like a huge cloud."

Exploring the island in 1832, a French naturalist named Sganzin said he saw a group of natives using a "very large half-eggshell as a bowl." Eight years later, Jules Verraeux, a French ornithologist, found the remains of similar eggs and gave them to a Paris museum. One egg was so large it reportedly held 13 quarts of wine, while others were said to hold the equivalent of 2 gallons each—which would have made them about six times the size of average ostrich eggs.

While many of these reports can be attributed to mistaken observations and over-active imaginations, some researchers suspect a kernel of truth might lurk in the background.

It is known, for example, that millions of years ago, giant birds with wingspans of more than 30 feet ruled the skies. These formidable creatures—teratorns—supposedly became extinct, along with the dinosaurs, after some global disaster about 65 million years ago.

But scientists in Argentina and in other parts of the world have found fossilized evidence suggesting that some of these prehistoric winged terrors might have survived until fairly recent times. These discoveries, along with ancient legends about aerial monsters, have convinced some experts that tera-torn-like creatures might have been around as recently as 10,000 years ago.

In the spring of 1890, two Arizona cowboys roaming the desert near Tombstone came across a "monstrous, bird-like creature" floundering in the sand. According to an article that appeared in the April 26, 1890 edition of the *Tombstone Epitaph*, the big bird—which was apparently injured and couldn't fly—had an alligator-shaped head, a "long, snake-like body mounted with unbelievably long wings," two bony claws that extended in front of its wings.

In 1959, a story about a similar creature appeared in the pages of *Popular Science* magazine. According to an article written by Everett H. Ortner, some kind of "giant, flesh-eating flying dragon" apparently inhabits a remote swampy region of Zimbabwe. Information for the story was gleaned from hundreds of interviews with natives who told his associate, Frank H. Melland, about a "giant, fierce, featherless bird" with a 7-foot wingspan, sharp teeth and "smooth, bare skin."

On Feb. 9, 1856, the *London Illustrated News* reported that railroad workers digging a tunnel in the south of France found a cave containing a live pterodactyl—a giant, flesh-eating flying dragon known only to paleontologists and supposedly extinct for tens of millions of years. The report said the creature "has a very long neck, and a mouth filled with sharp teeth. It stands on four legs…and is armed with four claws terminated by long and crooked talons."

Is there a connection between the winged horrors found in Arizona, Zimbabwe, France, Madagascar and elsewhere? The answer is yes, say a few researchers who are convinced that some species of prehistoric animals such as pterodactyls might have somehow survived the fate of their dinosaur cousins millions of years ago.

They point to mythological monsters of old—American thunderbirds, the Egyptian phoenix, the Greek draconta, the bastilisk, the griffin—as proof that ancient man was all too aware of these formidable and fierce creatures from the skies.

The late British zoologist Ivan Sanderson wrote numerous books advancing the notion that prehistoric creatures somehow survived the mass extinction period to figure prominently in legends and myth. He based his belief on a lifetime of research, interviews and personal encounters.

In 1932, while exploring the Assumbo Mountains of Cameroon, his expedition was attacked by a "monstrous bird" with bat-like wings and sharp teeth. Known locally as the olitiau, the creature that buzzed Dr. Sanderson was similar to dozens of other strange birds said to still inhabit remote corners of Africa.

The Kaonde people of western Zambia say the Jiunda swamp conceals a terrifying "lizard bird" called the kongamato. They liken it to a long-tailed lizard or crocodile with bat-like wings and a beak filled with razor-sharp teeth.

In his book, *Ashanti and Beyond*, British traveler Sir Allan Cardinall related how villagers were afraid of "devil flyers," huge birds that attacked their villages at night and killed sleeping women and children.

Identical beasts have also been reported from Angola, Mount Kenya, Zaire, Tanzania and Zimbabwe. Even eminent South African zoologist J.L. Smith, co-discoverer in 1938 of the prehistoric fish known as the coelacanth, believed it possible that unknown, fabulous creatures exist in wild parts of the world.

The Little People

Once upon a time, long before towns and highways, fairies and elves ruled the gloomy forests and mist-shrouded crags of old Europe. Humans wisely avoided these haunted domains, especially as twilight floated and danced among the hidden glens and remote moors.

But as time passed and civilization pressed deeper into the fairy kingdom, people forgot about the Little People. Like the dragons and witches of old, fairies and elves remained alive only in myth and song.

Then, in 1917, the world was shocked when two young English girls reported that they had "discovered" a troop of friendly sprites living in the woods near their home in the Yorkshire village of Cottingley. One of the girls, 15-year-old Elsie Wright, even took photographs of the "Little People" to prove their existence.

The photographs, along with the girls' accounts of the discovery, made the front page of newspapers in London, New York, Frankfurt and elsewhere. None other than Sir Arthur Conan Doyle, creator of the supremely rational detective Sherlock Holmes, accepted the story.

Sir Arthur speculated at length on how certain people could tune in on a "race of beings constructed in material which threw out shorter or longer vibrations."

In a 1922 book, *The Coming of the Fairies*, Sir Arthur wrote that the fairy population was "as numerous as the human race, and is only separated from ourselves by some difference of these vibrations."

Five years before the Cottingley incident, the prestigious *Yale Review* published an article that claimed to substantiate the existence of fairies and elves. Titled *The Historical Existence of Fairies*, the paper correlated the legends of fairies in oral tradition with ethnological evidence and archaeological artifacts.

The report concluded that "Fairies...represent the last traditional memories of an historical race..."

Some scholars suggest that fairy stories originated as old wives tales—a way for frustrated women to surreptitiously rebel against the constraints placed on them by their restrictive society. Most of the earliest tales from France and Germany were dark and gruesome, not intended for children at all.

These so-called "women's stories" were passed down orally by mothers and grandmothers who worked long and hard at boring, thankless tasks like sewing, spinning, maintaining the hearth and child-rearing. It was a way to pass the time and, at the same time, transfer gossip and wisdom at the same time.

Eventually, these darkly brooding tales about man-eating fairy-folk, seductive sprites of the forest and other frightening themes were discovered by writers and artists. The Grimm Brothers, Charles Perrault and Hans Christian Anderson and other literary figures saw social benefit in the old tales. After carefully toning them down to suit younger audiences, they put them down on paper—and became rich.

Fairies—also known as green men, good folk, elves, pixies or gnomes—remain one of the most fanciful races in mythology and literature. They are featured in myths from the early Norsemen, Celts, Romans as well as in Medieval French, English, Irish and Scottish tales. Chaucer and Shakespeare wrote about these shimmering creatures of the forest, as did many other literary figures.

Who—or what—were the fairies? How was it that so many people accepted their existence for so long?

Stories about fairies, elves, dwarfs, sprites and other Little People were common in earlier times, especially in the remote wilds of Western Europe and the British Isles. These "wee folk" were believed to inhabit the meadows and shadowy woodlands of the countryside, occasionally cavorting with mortals.

Folklorists and anthropologists theorize the original fairies were members of conquered races who took to the hills and forests to escape persecution by humans. It has also been suggested that fairies were remnants of the old gods and spirits displaced by Christianity. Some writers have opined that the fairy faith is all that remains of an ancient cult of the dead, pointing to stories that the dead sometime appear in the company of fairies.

Robert Kirk, author of *The Secret Common-Wealth* (1691), said fairies lived in a "middle kingdom" between men and angels, with bodies "somewhat of the nature of a condensed cloud." Mortals with "second sight" can sometimes see these elusive creatures, Kirk explained.

Some investigators claim that the fairies of old were actually aliens in disguise. One popular British writer of the paranormal has reported claims of fairy abductions that are remarkably similar to UFO abduction tales.

Another new theory links elves and fairies with a rare genetic anomaly known as Williams' Syndrome. First described in 1961, this rare disorder produces cardiovascular problems such as heart murmurs, sub-normal intelligence and an acute sensitivity to sound. The most striking feature, however, is the physical appearance of victims—stunted, with child-like faces, small, upturned noses, oval ears and broad mouths with full lips and a small chin. In short, they look like the traditional depiction of elves.

The word elf has become a generic term for diverse groups of Little People that have actually been separated into species, families and genera. There are pixies, hobgoblins, sidhe, red caps, fees, sprites, church grims, wood trolls and lutins, to name a few.

According to researcher Carrol B. Fleming, classifications of Little People are made in terms of their relationships to mortals.

"Little elves are good-natured and helpful, while the dark elves are ill-tempered, live underground and cause continual trouble. A large unpredictable group called dusky elves falls in between," Fleming said.

All Little People possess magical powers, including the ability to become invisible. They vary from ant or thumb-size to about four feet in height. Many prefer to wear red and green—the colors of magic.

Mischievous Little People have been blamed for everything from storms and illnesses to the souring of milk. Whenever a person went missing, it was usually the work of lamias—horrible, fire-breathing monsters that could assume human form to trick and seduce unwary travelers.

While few modern scholars embrace the existence of fairies and their twilight kin, W.Y. Evans-Wentz, author of *The Fairy-Faith in Celtic Countries*, is an exception. The British scientist spent most of his life documenting oral traditions of the fairy realm, ranging from the Far East to the Americas.

"We can postulate scientifically, on the showing of the data of psychical research, the existence of true fairies," Dr. Evans-Wentz concluded.

And what about Elsie Wright's amazing fairy photos? Controversy continued to swirl until 1983 when cousin Frances Griffiths fessed up. The winged sprites in the photographs that had been taken with her father's box camera were nothing more than cleverly disguised paper cutouts, stuck in place by hatpins.

Although the photos were fakes, Ms. Griffiths insisted that the fairies she and her cousin Elsie played with in the garden that day in 1917 were very real.

"Here There be Dragons"

One of the most popular tourist attractions in the Austrian city of Klangenfurt is an imposing stone monument that depicts a naked warrior slaying a winged, fire-breathing monster.

Built in 1590, the monument was inspired by the finding of a "dragon skull" in a nearby cave. The skull was displayed in the town hall until modern scientists identified it as a wooly rhinoceros.

But legends die hard in this remote region of the Alps. According to tradition, horrible, flame-throwing dragons once lurked among the gloomy crags and bogs, guarding treasures and terrorizing the local population. Even today, there are those who believe dragons still roam the world.

"Dragons are more than just legendary creatures of old," says Dr. Joachim Dietrich, a professor of anthropology at the

University of Innsbruck. "Too many clues have been found suggesting that they might still exist in certain protected areas of Europe, Africa and Asia."

Since earliest times, dragons have figured prominently in folklore. The ancient Mesopotamians were the first to tell stories about "water dragons." Five-thousand years ago, the Sumerians spoke of a dragon god named Zu. Another early dragon was Tiamat, said by the Babylonians to have the head and front legs of a lion, wings and hind legs of an eagle and tail of a snake. Similar creatures were known to the Canaanites, Hittites and Egyptians.

Horrible, dragon-like creatures called krakons supposedly ran amok on lonely Greek islands more than 2,000 years ago. In order to capture the golden fleece, Jason the Argonaut had to first slay a seven-headed dragon. Hercules faced—and conquered—many dragons, including multi-headed Hydra.

The first century Roman natural historian Pliny wrote frequently about dragons, believing them to be giant serpents from India. While Westerners perceived dragons as fierce, bloodthirsty creatures to be tracked down and killed, the Chinese generally saw them as good, and—in some cases—actually worshiped these scaly, fire-snorting beasts.

By the Middle Ages, winged, fire-belching dragons with forked tails and curving claws were terrorizing castles and villages from Germany to Wales. To rid the realm of these fearsome monsters, heroic young knights like St. George were routinely commissioned by royal families to attack with flaming swords and golden spears.

In time, the dragons of old were wiped out.

Or were they?

Legend has it that some of the reptilian beasts survived by burrowing deep into caves and taking to bottomless lakes and rivers.

From the dark jungles of Africa to remote swamplands in the South Pacific, rumors continue to surface about dragon-like creatures that breath fire and occasionally take to the air on leathery wings. Some scientists say these reports might be based on sightings of true-life dinosaurs that somehow survived the natural calamity that wiped out other dinosaurs millions of years ago.

For example, expeditions to the Peoples' Republic of the Congo (formerly French Congo) have uncovered striking evidence that a family of giant, water-dwelling sauropods still inhabits the Likouala swamplands. Pygmies call this creature *mokele-mbembe*—"one that stops the flow of rivers."

Mokele-mbembe has been described as about 32 feet in length with smooth, reddish-brown skin. Eyewitnesses say it has a burly, elephant-size body, short, thick, legs, a lengthy tail and an elongated neck terminating in a small, reptilian head.

Cryptozoologists—scientists who study weird animals—say such descriptions are similar to the famous long-necked diplodocus or apatosaurus, long-necked sauropods that romped through these swamps millions of years ago. There may be others lurking elsewhere in dense tropical regions of Africa and the South Pacific, they say.

Take New Guinea, for example. The vine-choked swamplands of this South Pacific island are home to some of the world's strangest and most dangerous creatures—giant snakes, blood-sucking leeches, saltwater crocodiles, head-hunting cannibals and venom-spitting insects.

But the most terrifying is a legendary beast the natives of Papua call *artrellia*, a gigantic, dragon-like monster that supposedly dwells in the trees and feeds on human flesh. Witnesses claim that the creature, said to be more than 30 feet long, swoops down from overhanging branches onto unsuspecting travelers and devours them.

Understandably, native Papuans refuse to enter the creature's habitat.

"Their fear of this creature is very real," concluded one British research team. "They have been taught to believe that they are true dragons, and to come upon one in the wild means certain death."

During World War II, British and American soldiers stationed in Papua reported seeing "giant, lizard-like creatures" prowling the brush. In 1960, David Marsh—the district commissioner of Port Moresby, Papua's capital— announced that he had made two similar sightings during the early 1940s. The same year, residents of Kairuka gave two administration agricultural officers, Lindsay Green and Fred Kleckhan, the skin and jawbone of what they called a "dragon."

"They (the artrellia) will lie in the dark, sheltered canopies of tall trees and wait on unwary passersby, be it wild animals or humans, it matters not, to prey upon," the two officials were told. "They devour everything—flesh, bones, even the skull, so as to not leave a trace of the victim for the scavengers."

So far no one has captured a 30-foot artrellia, but sightings continue. Some cryptozoologists think it is only a matter of time before a giant specimen is found.

For centuries, dragon simply meant "giant snake." Where, then, did the dragon get its legs and wings and the ability to breathe fire and the habit of living in caves?

A 16th century Swiss naturalist, Conrad Gesner, is usually credited for the changes. In a book on the history of serpents, he wrote: "They (the dragons) hide themselves in trees, covering their head and letting the other part hang downe like a rope. In those trees they watch until (prey) comes to eate...then suddenly leaps into his face and digs out his eyes."

Some experts suspect dragon legends were inspired by the discovery of giant Komodo dragons in the East Indies. This creature—the largest living lizard—inhabits parts of Indonesia and grows more than 12 feet long. Discovered in 1912, these colossal carnivores devour large animals such as deer, pigs and—on occasion—humans.

Nosferatu:
Curse of the Undead

Shortly after helping arrange for her husband to become Holy Roman Emperor, Empress Maria Theresa, queen of Hungary and Bohemia, passed a series of new laws aimed at ending an outbreak of vampirism that had gripped Eastern Europe for more than two decades.

The laws specifically sought to prohibit the opening of graves and desecration of bodies while generally trying to disprove the existence of legendary creatures known as nosferatu—the undead.

These bloodsucking creatures—known in Western Europe as vampires—roamed the countryside in search of warm flesh and fresh blood. No one was safe from these unholy man-beasts whose lust for human blood was said to be insatiable.

In 1746, Dom Augustine Calmet, a respected French theologian and scholar, had caused a sensation when he published a book claiming that vampires were real. He described them as "hellish fiends" that rose from dank tombs at night to attack humans and domestic cattle. The only way to kill these creatures, he said, was to drive a wooden stake through their hearts.

After a brief investigation, however, Maria Theresa determined the claims were false. Vampires did not exist, she said, and warned her subjects to stop digging up suspicious graves. While many in power applauded their empress's bold action, ordinary people—peasants mostly, living in remote mountain villages from Bavaria to Transylvania—continued to seek out and destroy the undead with a vengeance.

Legends about the undead go back thousands of years and occur in almost every culture in the world, from Greece and Rome to Japan and the Philippines. Eastern Europeans probably first heard about vampires from travelers returning from the Far East during the ninth and 10th centuries. Over time, these old stories took new forms in places like Russia, Bulgaria, Romania, Serbia, Hungary, Austria and Germany.

Very little was known in Britain about vampires prior to the 18th century. In 1732, however, the same vampire scare that was sweeping through the Balkans got the attention of Parliament, which passed laws aimed at protecting citizens from nosferatu.

Thousands of cases were reported in England, France, Germany and Italy, as well as in the Baltic countries. One sensational story involved a 62-year-old man who supposedly returned from the grave to beg for food. When neighbors started dying from loss of blood, people naturally suspected Peter Plogojowitz, a poor farmer thought to have been bitten by a vampire himself shortly before dying of a stroke.

Persons destined to become vampires usually include certain noticeable characteristics—long teeth, reddish eyes, a tail and a caul. Victims of suicide or sudden, unnatural deaths also run the risk of becoming a vampire, as do those who die before they are baptized or who are bitten by another vampire.

It is likely that these stories and others about vampires influenced British author Bram Stoker who, in 1897, immortalized the semi-legendary monster known as Dracula in his classic novel. At the time, few people realized that Mr. Stoker's story was based on a real-life person who lived in Eastern Europe 500 years ago.

Prince Vlad Dracula was his name, born around 1430 in the Romanian province of Wallachia in the Transylvanian Alps. During his brief but bloody reign, the prince—also known as Vlad Tepes—was responsible for the murder of more than 100,000 people. His methods of execution were many, but always brutal—burning, boiling, decapitation, skinning, strangulation and, his personal favorite, impaling prisoners and criminals on long wooden stakes.

Vlad was particularly fond of mass executions. In order to get the most out of these events, he frequently ordered a banquet table set up in front of his victims so that he could enjoy the sights and sounds of the dying.

On one occasion, he invited a large crowd of thieves and beggars to a royal feast at his court in Tirgoviste. As soon as the ragged mob was seated and had begun eating, he ordered the hall boarded up and set the place on fire. No one escaped the flames.

Defenders of Dracula—which means "Son of the Devil" or "Son of Dracul (the Dragon)"—say historians have given the prince a bad rap, that his actions were greatly exaggerated or fabricated by political enemies. These people usually point to Dracula's valiant campaign to save his homeland from invading Turks and his unwavering support of peasants in their struggle against ruthless feudal lords of Eastern Europe as proof of his heroic spirit.

At least one biographer cites the prince's generous donations to charity as further proof of his compassionate nature. Another maintains that he should be honored rather than scorned because he helped restore order to a land torn apart by foreign invasion and civil strife.

Most historians, however, conclude that Vlad Dracula was a monster of cruelty, even in an age that bred such men as Cesare Borgia and Ivan the Terrible. Dracula supposedly met a violent end in 1476, but there is no historical account of what happened. He may have been assassinated by political rivals or killed by Turks.

What is known is that his severed head was impaled on a stake for public display—a common fate for tyrants in those days. He was entombed on an island in a lake in Romania.

Not long after his death, reports of vampirism became commonplace among rural villagers in Transylvania. Some said the dead prince himself rose from his tomb at night to feed on the blood of the living.

While bloodsucking nosferatu are figments of fantasy, some researchers believe there might be something more to the old vampire legend than black capes and long fangs. In

1982, a Canadian professor suggested that some people claiming to be vampires are actually victims of iron-deficiency condition known as porphyria. Victims of this disease— dubbed "Dracula's Disease"—rarely go outside because of a skin disorder that makes sunlight painful.

Shape-Shifters and Were-Creatures

The notion that people can turn into beasts is not a new one. Prehistoric hunters donned animal skins and howled at the moon in order to acquire the stamina of powerful beasts of prey. Shamans crowned with stag horns ventured deep inside caves to commune with dream-world spirits that guided men on the hunt.

Mystical rituals such as these were thought necessary in order to insure a successful chase. Without transforming— without "becoming" one with the animal world—hunters might fail in their quest for quarry, thus jeopardize the tribe's survival.

Some anthropologists think legends about werewolves, were-bears, were-lions and other "shape-shifters" originated more than 30,000 years ago when Stone Age hunters and shamans "transformed" into wolves, bears, lions and elk.

Ever since, stories have persisted about monstrous, shape-shifting creatures that come out on full-moon nights to attack and slaughter unsuspecting humans and domestic animals. These tales about shaggy, were-creatures became ingrained in the folklore and mythology of nearly every culture in the world.

During the Middle Ages, anybody with pointed ears, prominent teeth, and bushy eyebrows that met over the nose was suspect. Sharp, curvy fingernails and extra body hair were also dead giveaways, as was a long third finger.

While prehistoric people thought they could "transform" into werewolves simply by putting on a pelt, tradition holds that there are many ways to become one of these drooling demons of the night. Most often, the victim is bitten by another shape-shifter or is cursed by a priest. Some become werewolves after tasting human blood, while others are simply born that way—usually the seventh son of a seventh son. Another way to become a werewolf is to be born on Christmas Eve.

Transformation takes place on full moon nights. Some accounts say that werewolves morph into vampires at death unless special precautions are taken, such as exorcism or decapitation.

As with vampirism, cases of werewolf activity have been documented since Classical times. In the fifth century B.C., Herodotus, the "father of history," wrote: "Each Neurian changes himself once a year into the form of a wolf and he continues in that form for several days, after which he resumes his former shape."

Controversial religious texts dating back 2,000 years tell how Christ ordered his followers to stone a pitiful beggar. They obeyed, and as their stones fell upon the wretch, he "slowly changed into a hideous beast with fiery red eyes, having been the devil in disguise."

The universal concept of *lycanthropy*—men turning into animals—played a role in the development of religions around the world. The Scandinavian god Odin turned into an eagle; Jupiter, the Roman god, became a bull; Aetaeon was changed into a stag by the Greek goddess Artemis.

It is said that Saint Patrick once encountered a race of hairy creatures that howled at him like wolves. These people supposedly lived in the woods where they took their food like wolves and turned into shape-shifters every seventh year. Norse folktales contain references to *beserkers*, fierce warriors who wore wolf-skins into battle and drank the blood of slaughtered enemies.

In India there are were-tigers and were-cobras, while

Africa has were-lions, were-hyenas and were-crocodiles. Were-bears once ravaged the Russian countryside, while Mexican legends tell of the dreaded nahual or Nuahualli. Italians feared the lupo manaro while the French avoided areas said to be haunted by loup garoux.

The best way to avoid becoming a werewolf was to avoid being bitten. Short of that, superstitious peasants in Argentina, Portugal, France, Germany and elsewhere placed garlic on their doors. Sometimes a silver-bladed knife or pair of silver scissors would offer protection.

Many medieval scholars thought werewolves were minor demons. It was also commonly believed that witches could change into werewolves at will or cause others to transform by casting spells

For almost a quarter of a century Peter Stubb is said to have terrorized the countryside of 16th century Germany by donning a magical belt made of wolf-skin given to him by the devil and transforming himself into a giant wolf. In 1598, a whole family of werewolves supposedly wreaked havoc in rural western France. These "Werewolves of St. Claude" attacked and killed several people before they were set upon by a mob of villagers and torn apart.

Perhaps the most famous cases of alleged *lycanthropy* occurred in 17th century France. According to well-documented accounts, a "man-beast " killed dozens of children until it was finally tracked down and slain with silver bullets.

From 1520 to 1630, 30,000 werewolf trials were held in France alone. One recent theory suggests that hallucinogenic reactions to moldy bread might have caused some victims to believe they were werewolves.

Stories about shape-shifting were-creatures continue to be whispered in remote parts of the world. In Mexico, isolated villagers often hire shamans and warlocks to protect them from these cunning man-killers. In Portugal, people avoid dark forests for fear of running into a lobis-homems, a particularly horrible shape-shifter that bears the mark of the Devil.

Into
The
Unknown

Amelia Earhart's Ride Into Oblivion

More than six decades after her strange disappearance over the Pacific Ocean, the world still wonders what happened to Amelia Earhart, the "perky young gal" who was trying to make history by flying around the globe. Most investigators theorize that her small plane ran out of gas and crashed into the ocean, but other views continue to hold the public's imagination.

Some say she was captured and executed by Japanese soldiers. Others believe Earhart and her navigator, Fred Noonan, crashed on a remote island and were cannibalized by headhunters. Theories have also been raised that the pair of flyers survived and escaped to Europe, where they lived as lovers.

Thomas E. Devine, who served on the Japanese-held island of Saipan shortly before World War II, said he and other American soldiers saw Earhart's Lockheed Electra 10E airplane at the Aslito Airfield before it was burned by the Navy. In his book, Eyewitness: the Amelia Earhart Incident, Devine says an Okinawan woman showed him two graves that supposedly contained the remains of a white man and woman who "fell from the sky" and were executed by Japanese troops.

Stories like these have convinced Devine and many other investigators that the U.S. government knows more about the Earhart case than it will admit. The Navy's stance, he says, is "patently false and without merit…The facts surrounding the Earhart mystery will never be officially acknowledged by the U.S. government."

The latest detective work, conducted by the International Group for Historic Aircraft Recovery, has led to a document in London describing a lost collection of weather-beaten bone fragments.

The bones were found in 1940 by a British colonial official visiting Nikumaroro Island (then called Gardner Island), an uninhabited atoll in the Phoenix group, about 600 miles north of Samoa and about 400 miles southeast of Howland Island—the destination Earhart never reached. The bones—including part of a skull and several long fragments—have long vanished, but it's commonly believed they were buried or thrown into the sea or even sent to a medical museum in Fiji.

D.W. Hoodless of the Central Medical School in Suva, Fiji, measured them in 1941 before they disappeared, and members of the aircraft recovery group found the late British doctor's record of his measurements in 1998 while searching government archives in London. While Dr. Hoodless's work needs to be treated with caution, two American forensic scientists who examined his papers acknowledge that the bones might be those of Earhart.

Not everybody shares that view, however, including Earhart's niece, Amy Kleppner, an 11th-grade teacher in Montgomery County, Md.

"I've read everything written and reported about my aunt," Mrs. Kleppner said in a newspaper interview, "and I'm convinced that she and Fred simply ran out of gas within 100 miles of Howland Island."

Amelia Earhart's flight into the unknown began early on the morning of July 1, 1937, when she and Noonan, a tall, lanky Irishman, climbed aboard her twin-engine Lockheed Elektra for what was to be the last leg of their headline-making flight around the world. From Lae, New Guinea, the flight was to take the pair to Howland Island, a tiny Pacific atoll 2,750 miles away. There they were to establish contact with a U.S. Coast Guard ship that would guide them the rest of the way on their global journey, which they would break up in a series of short, leisurely hops.

The next day, July 2, the Coast Guard ship received the following message from Earhart: "Gas is running low." An hour later, she gave a final location report, and then disappeared. It was assumed that their plane had simply run out of fuel and crashed into the ocean.

After days of combing the ocean and hundreds of small islands in the area, a massive air-sea rescue ordered by President Franklin D. Roosevelt was called off. In its official report, the Navy declared that "at about 2300 {July 3} the plane landed on the sea to the northwest of Howland Island, within 120 miles of the island."

As far as the government was concerned, the case was closed. But others didn't want to give up. The plot thickened when rumors began to surface that the U.S. government had sent "America's Sweetheart" to the Pacific to spy on Japanese facilities.

Unwilling to accept the loss of its heroine, the nation held out hope she would be found. Stories circulated for weeks about sightings on lonely atolls and faint radio messages. One message reportedly from Earhart said: "On coral southwest of unknown island."

Richard Gillespie, executive director of the international recovery group, recently recovered airplane fragments that might match Earhart's twin-engine airplane. Gillespie plans to lead a full-scale expedition to Nikumaroro in 2000 to comb the four-mile-long atoll and its lagoon for artifacts and bone fragments.

Dr. Tom Crouch, senior curator of the Smithsonian Institution's Air and Space Museum, doubts anything will be found.

"The odds are 100 to 1 that Amelia and Fred came to rest on the ocean floor," he was quoted as saying.

Ironically, Amelia Earhart's round-the-world flight was to be her last. Before departing Los Angeles on May 21, 1937, she told a friend: "I have a feeling that there is just about one more good flight left in my system and I hope this trip is it. Anyway, when I have finished this job, I mean to give up long distance 'stunt' flying."

Cannibals, Crocodiles and Rockefeller

Dutch New Guinea was a wild and remote place in the autumn of 1961 when Michael Clark Rockefeller, newly graduated from Harvard University with a degree in banking, arrived to film a documentary on native lifestyles.

The 1,500-mile-long island contained vast unexplored areas occupied by hundreds of ever-warring tribes, many of them cannibalistic and untouched by civilization.

But primitive adventure was nothing new to the 23-year-old son of New York Governor (and later vice president) Nelson Rockefeller. While in school, the romantic young heir to one of America's greatest fortunes had spent months working on his father's farm in Venezuela before going to Dutch New Guinea to help tape native chants.

It was the island's simple, timeless beauty that brought the romantic young banker back a second time in 1961.

"I see myself in the jungle," he told a friend before setting out with his camera to explore the untamed wilderness.

Shortly after his arrival, however, he disappeared when his catamaran overturned at the mouth of the muddy Eilenden River near a place the natives call the "land of the lapping death"—a reference to an area of mangrove swamps, murky rivers and crocodile-infested tidal flats.

Today, almost four decades after the tragedy, the world still wonders what happened to the young billionaire. Did sharks or ferocious saltwater crocodiles devour him as some investigators allege? Or did he survive the four-to-seven-mile swim to shore, only to be killed and eaten by headhunters?

Michael Rockefeller's tragic story began shortly after he graduated from Harvard University and joined an expedition to study little-known tribes in New Guinea's Baliem Valley, then under Dutch control. It was rumored that the indigenous people of this valley practiced ritual warfare as well as headhunting and cannibalism.

Young Rockefeller paid several visits to the Asmat coast, where he became enamored of the magnificent woodcarvings and fantastically decorated human trophy heads. Thinking they would make great collections for his father's Museum of Primitive Art in New York, Rockefeller swapped chocolates, silver and photographs for several of the unusual artifacts.

The second week of November, Rockefeller hired Rene Wassing, a 34-year-old Dutch ethnologist and expert on primitive art, to go with him on an expedition up the coast. Local officials tried to warn him that such a trip could be dangerous. Two coastal tribes in the region—the Otsjanep and the Omadesep—were particularly unfriendly. In 1958, Dutch patrolmen had killed several members of their tribes, and they held a "blood-grudge" against all white people.

Ignoring the warnings, Rockefeller bought provisions and a 40-foot catamaran from a local Dutchman, then hired a couple of native guides to accompany him and Wassing. On Nov. 18, 1961, the four set sail in the overloaded craft for a village 25 miles down the coast from the mission outpost of Agats.

At about 2 p.m., a giant wave swamped their overburdened boat. As the catamaran drifted out to sea, the guides, being sturdy swimmers and familiar with the currents, volunteered to swim ashore and get help. Rockefeller and his Dutch companion agreed to remain with the boat, rather than risk the harrowing swim through shark-infested waters.

But no help came.

Rockefeller and Wassing spent an uncomfortable night being tossed about by the waves. One big wave finally capsized the boat, forcing them to cling to the sides for their lives. At first light they thought they saw land and tried to paddle towards it. It was then that Rockefeller—an excellent swimmer—decided he wanted to swim to shore.

Wassing, who couldn't swim, begged him to stay. "Don't try it," he said. "Help will come soon."

"Nothing to worry about," Rockefeller replied. "I'll be fine."

He stripped down to his underwear, improvised a flotation device and swam away. He was never seen again.

Wassing was rescued the next day.

In the late 1970s, a documentary filmmaker reported that he had talked with a chieftain who claimed that Rockefeller had barely stumbled ashore before he was killed, cooked and eaten by natives. Milt Machlin, author of *The Search for Michael Rockefeller*, says a group of Otsjanep speared Rockefeller like a fish, dragged him to shore, killed and ate him.

Then they threw what was left of his body into the swamp. The only reminder of Rockefeller they kept were his glasses, which several people reported seeing in the village. They, too, disappeared a few years later.

Judge Crater's Strange Disappearance

Joseph Force Crater lived the kind of life most men can only dream of. Young, handsome and rich, the 41-year-old New York lawyer enjoyed the pleasures the world had to offer—yachts, travel, fast cars, private retreats and beautiful women.

As president of the prestigious Democratic Party Club of Manhattan, he was also very powerful—so powerful, in fact, that in April of 1930 he was appointed to the New York State Supreme Court.

In those days, Judge Crater was the most popular man in New York City. Ambitious, hard working and gifted with persuasive charm, he possessed an uncanny knack for being in the right place at the right time. He quickly became the darling of the New York media—hardly a day went by without his name and picture in the news.

A bright political career obviously lay before this tall, dapper ladies' man who parted his iron-gray hair neatly down the middle. All he had to do was stay out of trouble and remember his friends down at Tammany Hall.

On the evening of Aug. 6, 1930, less than four months after his appointment to the bench, Judge Crater disappeared. One minute he was laughing and talking with friends outside a posh Manhattan restaurant, the next he waved goodbye, stepped into a cab, and was never seen or heard from again.

Judge Crater's ride into oblivion prompted one of the most massive manhunts in New York history. After years of investigative efforts costing millions of dollars and covering several states, the fate of Joseph Force Crater remains an unsolved mystery.

To understand the story, it is necessary to go back to that summer in 1930 when Judge Crater and his family were vacationing in their cottage in Belgrade Lakes, Maine. On Aug. 3, he told his wife he had to go back to New York for a few days, but he didn't explain why.

Three days later, he spent several hours at his courthouse chamber desk going through some old files. That afternoon he instructed his assistant, Joseph Mara, to cash two checks for him in the amount of $5,150.

Later that evening, Judge Crater had dinner with two friends—a lawyer and a showgirl—at a restaurant on West 45th Street. Nothing unusual happened that night, according to the lawyer's testimony, and at exactly 9:10 p.m., Judge Crater, dressed in a double-breasted brown suit, gray spats and a fashionable high collar, waved goodbye to his companions and climbed inside a waiting taxi.

That was the last anybody ever saw of him.

When the judge failed to return to the cottage, Mrs. Crater became worried. She contacted his office, and on Aug. 25, the day his court cases were due to come up, even his law partners suspected something was wrong.

At first a private search was conducted to keep the affair out of the newspapers. Nothing turned up, however, and on Aug. 26 the disappearance became front page news.

A police investigation revealed the judge's bank deposit box was empty, as was a private safe, and two personal briefcases were missing. Foul play was immediately suspected, though rumors were flying around town that the judge had simply skipped out, perhaps with a girlfriend he had reportedly been seen with in recent months.

A grand jury was quickly convened to get to the bottom of the case. After 95 witnesses had testified and 975 pages of testimony had been amassed, the foreman concluded: "The evidence is insufficient to warrant any expression of opinion as to whether Crater is alive or dead, or as to whether he has absented himself voluntarily, or is a sufferer from disease in the nature of amnesia, or is the victim of crime."

In other words, Judge Crater had simply vanished, and it would be fruitless to continue the investigation.

The judge's distraught widow suspected otherwise. She went on record as saying her husband had been murdered "because of a sinister something that was connected with politics."

Her main suspect was Tammany Hall itself. It was her opinion that forces within that organization had killed her husband because he refused to pay them back for helping with his nomination to the bench. Other theories linked the judge's fate to organized crime. Some investigators believed he was killed after a hotel deal he helped organize went sour.

The most likely explanation, according to some, was that the judge was murdered in a showgirl's blackmail scheme— killed by a gangster friend of the girl when he refused to pay more money.

On June 6, 1939, almost nine years after he went missing, Judge Crater was declared legally dead. The case was never officially closed, and reports about his reappearance continue to pop up more than six decades later.

D.B.Cooper,
Where are you?

One stormy night in 1971, a frail, friendly man dressed in a dark business suit and wearing prescription sunglasses boarded Northwest-Orient Airlines Flight 305 at the Portland International Airport in Oregon.

Minutes after takeoff, he calmly handed cabin attendant Flo Schaffner a note saying he had a dynamite bomb in his briefcase. The passenger, who used filthy language, drank bourbon and chain-smoked Raleigh filter-tipped cigarettes, appeared to be about six feet tall and in his mid-40s. He demanded $200,000 in used $20 bills.

"No funny stuff," he warned the stewardess, cracking his briefcase open so she could see a couple red cylinders, wires and a battery.

It was Thanksgiving eve. Most of the 36 passengers aboard the Boeing 727 were going home after having spent the holidays in Portland. As the plane bucked and rumbled through the storm, the last thing on anybody's mind was a skyjacking.

The clean-cut man with the bomb identified himself as Dan Cooper. At least that's the name that appeared on the passenger list. Investigators are unsure who he really was, where he came from or what happened to him.

That's because, only minutes after taking off from the Seattle-Tacoma International Airport where they had stopped briefly to pick up the ransom money and release the passengers, Mr. Cooper bailed out of the plane and vanished.

The plane's crew was stunned: Only a lunatic would parachute into a freezing rainstorm at 10,000 feet in the middle of the night. Clad only in a business suit, white shirt and loafers, the man surely died either on the way down or once he landed in the rugged wilds of southwestern Washington.

"It was obviously not well thought out," commented

Ralph Himmelsbach, a retired FBI agent who has spent decades investigating the crime. "It was stupid."

If the skyjacker didn't freeze to death on his way down, he probably died when he hit the ground wearing a faulty parachute provided by authorities in Seattle, said Himmelsbach.

"And he came down right smack dab in the middle of the woods in really rugged country," he added. "If the cold didn't kill him, if he withstood the powerful turbulence, Cooper was still parachuting into a dense forest at night, at the onset of winter, with no food or survival gear."

What kind of man would do such a thing? According to Himmelsbach and others who have investigated the case, D.B. Cooper was either the bravest criminal in American history—or the dumbest.

"This was a desperate act you wouldn't expect from a normal man in his mid-40s," Himmelsbach theorized. Jumping from a plane flying at 200 MPH in a howling storm over a snow-covered wilderness "was something you would expect from somebody who had nothing to lose."

Jerry Thomas, a retired Army survival instructor who has investigated the case for years, thinks the hapless skyjacker landed hard—"splattered"—and was swallowed by the dense expanse of firs and ravines north of the Columbia River, about 12 miles east of Vancouver.

But there are those who insist that Cooper was not a lunatic, nor was he killed during the jump. In fact, some of the air pirate's legions of fans insist the escapade was brilliantly planned to throw investigators off the trail. A few even argue that he took part in at least one other skyjacking three years later.

To be sure, Cooper's Thanksgiving crime was the most spectacular skyjacking in American history. It also was the only time the skyjacker of a domestic aircraft has eluded capture.

Dan Cooper, or D.B. Cooper as a reporter called him in error, became a Northwestern folk hero almost overnight. In an age of anti-Vietnam protests, Nixon, and hippies, many saw him as a loner, a sympathetic anti-establishment figure who beat the odds and managed not to hurt anyone in the process.

Tales circulated about the mysterious skyjacker and how he survived the ordeal, assumed a new identity, married, and today, leads a quiet life somewhere on the East Coast.

In 1980, an 8-year-old boy playing along the muddy banks of the Columbia River near Portland discovered a bundle of crumbling $20 bills. The serial numbers of the bills matched those given to Dan Cooper in Seattle nine years earlier. But those were the only bills of the air pirate's 10,000 twenties to show up.

Agent Himmelsbach speculated that Cooper either landed in the Columbia River and drowned or died in the mountains and the money was washed out.

Cooper believers are unfazed. Each Thanksgiving, crowds gather at taverns in the Northwest to celebrate the anniversary of their hero's famous skyjacking. At one bar in Ariel, Wash., for example, some locals believe Cooper himself once made an appearance at a party in his honor.

One woman, identified only as Clara, claimed Cooper lived with her until his death from illness in 1982. Another woman living in Florida said her late husband confessed on his deathbed in 1995 that he was the real Cooper.

Perhaps the best clue to Cooper's fate came to light in 1974 when an escaped convict named Richard Floyd McCoy was gunned down in a shootout with FBI agents in Pennsylvania. A former Sunday school teacher and Green Beret helicopter pilot, McCoy had been serving a 45-year sentence for skyjacking a United Airline jet for $500,000.

Investigators say that McCoy's technique had been virtually identical to Cooper's, down to the phrase "No funny stuff" in his note and parachuting out of an airplane. When captured, McCoy refused to confess to being the vanished Cooper.

Will the truth ever be known about America's most celebrated crime caper?

"It's still a pending investigation," says Seattle-based FBI agent Ray Lauer, who says the agency maintains a 60-volume file on the Cooper incident. He added the case will "probably stay open forever."

Paul Redfern's Final Flight

One sweltering August morning in 1927, thousands of anxious spectators gathered on a windy beach at Sea Island, Ga., to watch a young Georgia pilot set out to make aviation history.

Paul Redfern had dreamed of being the first person to fly nonstop from the United States to South America. Charles Lindbergh's famous flight from New York to Paris three months earlier had made the young Georgian more determined than ever.

Twenty-five years old and outfitted in a modern, well-stocked monoplane christened *Port of Brunswick*, the aviator's dream was about to come true.

Or so he hoped that morning as he taxied down the beach runway, waving to the cheering onlookers. Among the spectators were his pregnant wife and several investors in his bid to make history.

After a ceremonial dip of the wings, the brightly-colored plane took off into the clouds, never to be seen or heard from again.

"It was as if he simply disappeared," a newspaper reported, "swallowed up by the Great Unknown like so many brave explorers before him."

A massive land-sea rescue operation involving hundreds of ships and planes was launched. One party was led by swashbuckling movie idol Errol Flynn.

After months of probing jungles and mountaintops in the Caribbean and parts of South America, however, the searchers called the effort off.

Some believed Redfern had simply crashed into the sea. Others thought he might have died in a crash landing on some nameless island. A few said he probably made it as far as Brazil before his plane went down in a remote jungle.

Redfern's destination was Rio de Janeiro, about 4,600 miles from Sea Island, almost twice the distance of Lindbergh's 2,500-mile trans-Atlantic voyage. His flight plan was to take him from Georgia to the Bahamas, across the Caribbean and then over Puerto Rico. He would continue past the tropical islands of Grenada, Tobago, and Trinidad, cross the coast of British Guiana (now Guyana), Dutch Guiana (now Suriname) and northern Brazil to Macupa on the north bank of the Amazon.

Aboard his Stinson-Detroiter airplane, loaded down with about 550 gallons of fuel, he carried a 2-gallon container of drinking water, food to last 20 days and survival equipment for ocean or jungle—including a pneumatic air raft, a small distilling outfit, mosquito netting, quinine and a collapsible rifle and ammunition.

Since radio instrumentation was not yet available, pilots in Redfern's day were alone among the clouds.

Over the years, numerous theories emerged to account for his disappearance, some of them quite fanciful. One had him crashing into a jungle and becoming head of a tribe of Brazilian Indians. Another said Redfern was captured by a hostile tribe that used spears to discourage rescuers from reaching him.

One modern adventurer claims to know where the plane went down but says it would cost a fortune to reach the spot and retrieve the wreckage.

"We're talking about true dinosaur country," said retired commercial airline pilot Robert Carlisle, who has spent years researching the Redfern story. "Steel wool jungle, pristine. Not even any Indian trails."

Seven years after her husband's disappeared, his widow finally gave up hope and had him officially declared dead.

"If anyone had seen my husband and had been with him, as some of these people say, I would think he would have given them something to prove his identity," she said.

The mystery of Paul Redfern's final flight would soon be overshadowed by that of another ill-fated pilot—Amelia Earhart, who disappeared in 1937 while on a record-breaking round-the-world voyage.

The Fearless Colonel Fawcett

In the spring of 1925, famed explorer Col. Percy Harrison Fawcett embarked on his seventh and final expedition into the wilds of Brazil. His mission: find the lost city of "Z," said to have been built by survivors of Atlantis, the legendary kingdom that supposedly sank in the Atlantic Ocean thousands of years ago.

For more than a decade, the British adventurer had blazed paths all over the Brazilian countryside while doing survey work for the Royal Geographical Society. Battles with giant snakes, flesh-eating piranha, and savage headhunters had not diminished his desire to explore.

Now he had more reason than ever to push off into the bush. Recently discovered documents at the National Library in Rio de Janeiro had convinced the colonel that the fabled city was located in the Mato Grosso, a wild and dangerous realm in the heart of the Brazilian wilderness. According to old Portuguese accounts, the Atlantean refugees had used gold brought from their doomed homeland to build temples, palaces and a magnificent wall around the city.

Whoever found the lost city stood to profit handsomely.

Thinking a small expedition might be less threatening to hostile Indians in the region, he hired only his son, Jack, an

18-year-old friend of Jack's named Raleigh Rimell, and two Mufuquas Indians as guides. Before leaving, the colonel left instructions that no rescue party should come after him should he fail to return.

"It's too dangerous," he told friends and supporters.

Several days into the journey, the frightened guides ran away. It was a moment of truth for the 58-year-old colonel: should he turn back or remain on course? Never before had he beheld a wilderness so "wild and untrammeled" and thoroughly unexplored as that which he was now about to enter. He and his two young companions decided to press on.

On May 29, 1925, he sent a message back to his wife. "You have no fear of failure," he wrote.

That was the last anyone heard from the colonel. His disappearance shocked and saddened millions around the world who were cheering his attempt to find "Z," the name he had given the lost city.

A military engineer by trade, Fawcett had sought lost cities in the jungles of Ceylon as well as South America. He never tired of the hardships and dangers, preferring the company of savages to "civilized bores."

"The forest in these solitudes is always full of voices, the soft whisperings of those who came before," he once wrote about South America.

Like other adventurer-explorers of his day, Fawcett believed in the legend of Atlantis. It seemed likely to him that survivors of this doomed continent reached South America, where they built cities and temples in an attempt to re-create their destroyed civilization.

Earlier that year, an attempt to find the lost city had almost ended in disaster when Fawcett was swept over a waterfall into a pool infested with piranha and alligators. A little later, on a trip down the Chocolatal River, his boat pilot was riddled with 45 arrows shot by hostile Indians. Wild bulls had attacked his group, before they were chased away by gunfire.

But his most harrowing encounter occurred when a giant

anaconda attacked them while crossing a river. In his diary, he wrote: "We were drifting easily along the sluggish current not far below the confluence of the Rio Negro when almost under the bow of the igarit'e (boat) there appeared a triangular head and several feet of undulating body. It was a giant anaconda. I sprang for my rifle as the creature began to make its way up the bank, and hardly waiting to aim, smashed a .44 soft-nosed bullet into its spine, ten feet below the wicked head."

Fawcett estimated the snake to be 62 feet in length and 12 inches in diameter. Such dimensions, if accurate, would make it the largest anaconda on record.

With food and supplies running low, the expedition turned back. Weary of snakes, blood-sucking bats, exotic diseases, swarms of insects and tangled undergrowth, Fawcett decided to regroup and resume his search later.

Finding reliable companions for his dangerous trips had always been a problem. By 1925, however, Jack—a strapping teenager who shared his father's love for adventure—was eager to explore. The lure of "Z" fascinated young Jack as well as his father and ultimately led to their doom.

Three years later, in the summer of 1928, a search party found a small trunk believed to belong to the missing explorers but nothing else. They were told that hostile natives had killed the three white men soon after they entered the heavy forest. Indians drove the rescuers out of the region before they could confirm the stories.

The fate of Colonel Fawcett and his tiny expedition remained one of the most talked about mysteries of the time.

In 1929, a Swiss trapper, Stefan Rattin, reported that he had come upon an old Englishman living as a well-cared-for prisoner for a group of Indians. Although the man had not given his name, Rattin's description and the man's circumstances raised hopes that Colonel Fawcett had at last been found.

But when Rattin returned to rescue the putative Colonel

Fawcett, he and two partners also disappeared.

For decades afterward, Mato Grosso travelers reported meeting gaunt, English-speaking oldsters along the jungle paths. But no real trace of the British explorer or his two companions was ever found.

In all probability, the fate of the dauntless explorers will forever remain a mystery.

Heavenly Fires, Hellish Fates

Spontaneous Human Combustion

Glenn Denney was a quiet man, but when neighbors didn't see him for several days, they began to worry. Finally someone detected a strange smell coming from his Algiers, La., house and called the police.

Officers and firemen broke down the door and made a grisly discovery. Heaped between two chairs in the middle of the living room were the charred remains of the 46-year-old foundry worker. Flames so hot firemen had to don protective clothing to smother the blaze still engulfed the blackened corpse.

Nothing else in the room was damaged by smoke or fire. Except for the smell, the only physical sign of the conflagration was the body.

An investigation was launched to determine the cause of death. If it was suicide, as some authorities initially suspected, the victim must have used a lot of kerosene or gasoline to create such an intense fire. But no drop of combustible fuel was found in the house, not even a match, lighter or cigarette.

It appeared that Denney had simply died, "struck down by a fire from heaven," in the words of one writer.

That was in 1951. But for centuries, scientists have been intrigued by the curious phenomenon known as "spontaneous human combustion," or SHC, the ability of the human body to catch fire for no apparent reason. Hundreds of such cases have been reported, most of them still unsolved. Some victims were simply sitting in chairs or lying in bed; others were walking down the street or riding in cars. An English woman caught fire and burned alive while dancing at a nightclub.

One of the most spectacular cases occurred on July 2, 1951, when Mary Hardy Reeser, a 67-year-old widow, was visiting her son in St. Petersburg, Fla. Dr. Wilton M. Krogman, a physical anthropologist and expert on the effects of fire on the human body, called the Reeser case "the most amazing thing I've ever seen. Were I living in the Middle Ages, I'd mutter something about black magic."

The ordeal began when a neighbor summoned police to investigate smoke coming from beneath the door of Mrs. Reeser's apartment. When officers entered, they found smoke but no signs of fire—except for the remains of a burned chair in the corner.

Within that blackened area, roughly four feet in diameter, they also found the remains of a human body—a charred liver attached to a piece of spine, a shrunken skull, one foot wearing a black satin slipper, and a small pile of ashes. The slipper belonged to Mrs. Reeser, as did apparently the foot protruding from the pile of ashes.

The FBI was called in to investigate. It was determined that it would have taken an enormous white-hot fire at least 3,000 degrees Fahrenheit—the same temperature range used by modern crematoriums—to have incinerated Mrs. Reeser's body so thoroughly.

But what could have caused so hot a fire in such a confined space? Why didn't the fire spread? Why wasn't any other furniture in the room at least scorched from the heat?

Theories were advanced, ranging from lightning to falling asleep while smoking. Murder and suicide were also speculated, but no answer seemed satisfactory. Mrs. Reeser's bizarre death was simply baffling. How could a human body be so thoroughly incinerated, yet one portion—a foot—remain untouched?

"This is a mystery we'll never know the answer to," Dr. Krogman concluded.

Some scientists believe that—under the right circumstances—gases inside a person's body can ignite. Several books have touched on this particular phenomenon, including Mark Twain's Life on the Mississippi and Charles Dickens' Bleak House. Dozens of TV shows and movies have featured it as well.

While most medical scientists stop short of accepting SHC as a real condition, Larry Arnold, director of ParaScience International, and a few like-minded investigators suspect there may be something to the phenomenon. It's possible, they say, that some unknown agent inside the body—a gas, perhaps—might be responsible for triggering these internal infernos.

Arnold said the body's electrical systems "appear to go haywire," sometimes resulting in internal fires that barely singe the skin or any other object around the room. Sometimes these internal fires can explode, or become so intense the victim is actually cremated, leaving the body in a pile of ashes.

Researchers have found references to this phenomenon in the Bible, as well as medieval records. It wasn't until the 17th century, however, that compelling cases of SHC begin to appear in the medical records.

One of the earliest cases, recorded in 1673, involved a woman who caught fire on a Paris street and exploded in full view of witnesses. Some observers said she had been drinking—a common link to many cases, leading some investigators to theorize that alcohol might play a role in SHC.

Static electricity has also been mentioned as a cause. Some people have been known to generate up to 30,000 volts, which is ordinarily discharged through the hair. In certain circumstances, however, these highly-charged individuals have been known to spark explosions, especially when working around combustible materials.

A number of other physical causes have been suggested, including fireballs, lightning, internal atomic explosions, laser beams, microwave radiation, high-frequency sound and geo-magnetic flux.

Solving the mystery of "fire from heaven" has become a quest for many researchers, but might take a lot longer than they'd like.

The Restless Skies

On Feb. 11, 1859, John Lewis was strolling across his field near Mountain Ash in the valley of Aberdare, Wales, when thousands of fish started raining from the skies. One slipped down the neck of his shirt. Several got caught in his hat brim. The fall went on for about two minutes, then stopped. Ten minutes later it started again, this time lasting a full five minutes. Incredibly, in full view of Mr. Lewis, his wife and several neighbors, the fish were not only fresh, they were "very lively."

Samples were sent to the British Museum for examination, where authorities determined that there were two types, minnows and sticklebacks. Later, the surviving fish were exhibited at the Zoological Garden in Regent's Park—perhaps the only famous minnows in history.

Scientists at the British Museum were inclined to dismiss the Mountain Ash incident as some sort of joke. They suggested that someone had thrown a bucketful of fish over Mr. Lewis with or without his knowledge.

To his dying day, Mr. Lewis insisted that the fish had fallen on him from the sky. Friends and relatives who witnessed the sky fall supported Mr. Lewis's bizarre claim, saying he was a "God-fearing gentleman" incapable of distorting the truth.

The Wales "fish fall" was similar to thousands of others reported around the world. The March 1972 issue of *Australian Natural History* lists 54 separate falls of fish—and a few frogs—recorded in Australia between 1879 and 1971.

According to the *Australian Museum Magazine*, hundreds of little fish called gudgeons were found in the streets after a rain at Gulargambone, New South Wales.

The 20th century brought fresh reports of strange skyfalls. In June 1901, hundreds of small catfish, trout and perch suddenly rained down on a cotton field belonging to Charles Raley of South Carolina.

On Oct. 23, 1947, the town of Marksville, La., was deluged by fish—largemouth bass, sunfish, hickory shad and minnows. The fish were described as "absolutely fresh and fit for human consumption." According to a local newspaper, the town threw a big fish-fry that lasted all week.

Perhaps more bizarre than fish falls are the "snake falls" occasionally reported. One such "snake fall" is said to have occurred in a small Alabama town in 1925. There, thousands of squirming reptiles suddenly dropped from the sky into the streets, causing mass panic.

Another incident involving snakes occurred one hot Sunday afternoon in 1887 in Memphis, Tenn. Many citizens just out of church services reported being inundated with thousands of rattlesnakes and copperheads that fell from the sky.

Pedestrians watched in horror as the wriggling masses of venomous serpents slithered away in all directions. Some stayed where they landed, coiled and hissing. One bewildered rider jumped from his horse after a snake draped around the animal's neck.

No one was bitten or seriously hurt.

Smelly fish and squirming snakes falling mysteriously from the sky—what exactly is going on?

Since ancient times, there have been reports of strange objects falling mysteriously from the heavens, ranging from small creatures and food to more dangerous objects like stones and hot bricks. The Old Testament tells how "hot stones" rained down on Amorite warriors. In the sixth century, a "fall of stones" destroyed an Abyssianian army laying siege to Mecca.

Skyfalls consisting of fiery globs of oil, lumps of flaming sulfur and other burning objects have been reported from India to South America. Sometimes it's ice and mounds of jelly. A foul-smelling substance, the consistency of butter, supposedly fell over large areas of southern Ireland in the winter and spring of 1696. A fibrous substance resembling blue silk fell in great quantities at Nauamburg, Germany on March 23, 1665.

In 1961, construction workers in Shreveport, La., were deluged with green peaches. Investigators credited that oddity with a crate of produce that somehow fell from an airplane. But when objects fall out of a clear sky with no wind or aircraft around, people begin to wonder. The Memphis snake fall, for example, was attributed to a whirlwind that supposedly had swept through a nearby swamp. No one bothered to explain how or why such a whirlwind bothered to pick up only snakes—and poisonous ones at that—and not rabbits, squirrels, turtles and other small creatures.

Others theorize that earthquake activity might have something to do with this strange phenomenon, but so far no one has been able to explain how.

Toward the Light

The old woman was dying. She lay quietly on her deathbed, surrounded by grieving friends and family members, trying to ignore the pain of the cancerous tumor eating at her emaciated body.

Suddenly, she sat up and stared at the foot of the bed. "Mama," she cried, "is it really you?"

Those in attendance saw no one. But when they tried to comfort the dying woman she said, "She's right there— Mama. So white and bright and full of radiant glory."

The old woman described the "dazzling white light" that flooded the room, music that came to her from far away, "beautiful gardens" beyond the light and a "wondrous feeling of joy" that came over when she saw her mother, who had been dead for more than four decades.

Then she lay back and died, a peaceful smile on her face.

Each year, thousands of people the world over experience similar deathbed visions. These visions usually include passing through a dark tunnel into a bright light, the sensation of floating out of one's body, a warped sense of time and space, and a reluctance to return to the earthly plane.

Such experiences are usually attributed to drugs, fever, disease-induced hallucinations, oxygen deprivation to the brain or wish-fulfillment.

But specialists who have studied the phenomenon of NDE—Near Death Experiences—maintain that medical factors do not necessarily generate true deathbed experiences. According to some researchers, such visions are sometimes shared by those near the dying person.

"As the person dies," says Rosemary Ellen Guiley, an author and journalist who has studied the subject, "clouds of silvery energy are sometimes reported floating over the body. In some cases, the energy is seen to clearly form into the astral body of the dying one, connected by a silvery cord which severs at the moment of death."

Studies show that deathbed visions are found in all cultures throughout history. They typically occur to individuals who die gradually, such as from terminal illness, rather than those who die suddenly from heart attacks, car crashes or other traumatic deaths. The majority of visions are of apparitions of the dead, usually described as "glowing" and dressed in white.

Sometimes mythical and religious beings are perceived, including angels, Jesus, the Virgin Mary, Krishna, Yama (Hindu god of death) or similar figures. Apparitions invariably are close family members, such as parents, children, siblings or spouses.

One report suggested that the purpose of these apparitions is to beckon or command the dying to accompany them—to assist in the transition to death. Descriptions most frequently given include gardens of great beauty, golden gates, bridges, rivers, boats and other symbols of transition.

Other visions include tunnels of light, sweet music and white-robed angels or messengers that guide them along their journey.

One man recalled meeting a "being of light" who forgave

him for a lifetime of violence. Another survivor said she traveled down a long tunnel to "a place filled with love and a beautiful bright white light" where Elvis Presley took her gently by the hand.

Some scientists who study these near-death-experiences theorize they may be "peep-holes" into a world beyond. Bruce Greyson, a psychiatrist at the University of Virginia Medical School, says that those who have such experiences "become enamored with the spiritual part of life, and less so with possessions, power and prestige."

Nancy Evans, president emeritus of the International Society for Near-Death Experiences, said, "Most near-death experience survivors say they don't think there is a God... They know."

Such revelatory experiences are nothing new. Writing in *The Republic*, Plato told the story of how a wounded soldier journeyed toward "a straight, light-like pillar, most nearly resembling a rainbow, but brighter and purer."

Art and literature of the Middle Ages is replete with the borderland between life and death. One 13th-century monk recounted tales of people who supposedly returned from the edge and reported "corridors of fire" and "icy" paths to the afterlife.

P.M.H. Atwater, author *Coming Back to Life: The After Effects of the Near-Death Experience*, insists that NDEs occur practically all the time.

"It's been shown that 40 percent of all resuscitated patients have near-death experiences," said Ms. Atwater, a Charlottesville, Va., writer who claims to be an NDE survivor herself.

Even though skeptics link such experiences to natural causes—hallucinations, sleep deprivation, etc.—the medical community's perception of these reports began to change in 1975 when Raymond Moody published *Life After Life*, a book that coined the term "near-death experience" to describe this phenomenon.

If NDEs are so common, then why isn't more known about them—and why don't more survivors come forth to talk about them?

"Old-fashioned fear of ridicule," noted survivor Bob Smith of Austin, Texas. "That, plus the fact that most NDEs occur in hospital environments and medication somehow prevents most patients from remembering what happened to them."

Dance of the Doppelganger

During World War II, a young infantry sergeant named Alex Griffith was leading a patrol through enemy territory in France when a strange feeling came over him, warning him to turn back.

A battle-hardened veteran, Griffith fought off the sensation and continued until he came upon an eerie sight. Less than 20 yards ahead, another American soldier stepped out of nowhere, waving for him to retreat.

No words came from the soldier's mouth, though Griffith seemed to understand exactly what he was saying: *Turn back! Turn back!*

The oddest thing about this soldier, however, was that he looked exactly like Griffith, down to his sergeant's rank, the same beard growth, dirty uniform—even the same Band-Aid covering a small cut on his face.

Instinctively, Griffith turned and ordered his men off the road. When he looked again, his mirror-image was gone.

A few seconds later an American jeep came roaring past him heading straight up the road. Momentarily he heard machinegun fire, followed by an explosion. The jeep had driven into a German ambush. Had Griffith not ordered his men to turn back, they would have walked directly into the trap and been slaughtered.

None of the men in his patrol had seen the mysterious soldier.

Twenty years later, while on vacation in Canada, Griffith and his wife and two children were hiking down a rugged mountain trail when a storm blew up. The situation grew steadily more dangerous as lightning popped and cracked around them and huge branches and debris whipped through the air.

Then Griffith saw a strange sight—a man dressed in a World War II combat uniform. The soldier was identical to the one he had seen 20 years earlier in war-torn France, the same soldier who had warned him to turn back!

Once again, the soldier seemed to be warning him of danger. And even though no words came out of his mouth, the message was clear: *Turn back! Turn back!*

As before, Griffith responded by turning around and heading his family in a different direction. Several seconds later, he heard a loud crackling noise, followed by what sounded like a tremendous explosion.

The strong wind had apparently been too much for a massive old tree that toppled over the spot where Griffith and his family would have been standing had they continued their journey up the trail.

As before, no one had seen the silent soldier but Griffith.

Who was the mysterious uniformed stranger who twice saved Alex Griffith's life?

Years later, Griffith became convinced that what he had seen was a doppelganger—a spirit that is the exact double of the person who sees it. Tradition holds that a doppelganger—a German word that means "double spirit" or "double walker"—usually appears to warn of impending danger.

The phenomenon is generally described as a malicious shadow-self that accompanies every human. Although flesh-and-blood—not semi-transparent in form like a ghost—the doppelganger is invisible to everyone except the owner.

"Very often it appears as a pale bloodless version of yourself, almost like looking at yourself as a corpse," says Douglas Colligan, an author who has spent two decades researching doppelgangers.

No one knows how or when doppelganger stories got started, but the ancient Egyptians, Greeks and Romans told of "shadow creatures" that stalked their human counterparts. During the Middle Ages, it was commonly believed that to see one's doppelganger meant death or disaster.

Animals—especially cats—were said to have the power to perceive these invisible phantoms.

"If this is dying, It ain't so bad"

On a clear, cold night in the spring of 1944, British Royal Air Force Sgt. Nicholas Alkemade climbed into the tiny "gunner bubble" at the rear of the Lancaster bomber and settled back for the long, dangerous flight to Berlin.

He was a nervous, since this was his 13th bombing raid over Germany.

As he hunkered down behind the pair of Browning machineguns, he couldn't help thinking that this was the loneliest, most dangerous job in Bomber Command. With any luck, the mission would be over in a few hours. Then it was back to England, where the 21-year-old airman was looking forward to spending a much-needed leave with his girlfriend, Pearl.

Everything was fine until a German Junker 88 aircraft raced up to meet them over Frankfurt. There was a loud explosion followed by a blinding flash, then screams from the front of the plane.

The Lancaster was on fire and going down.

"Bail out! Bail out!" the captain shouted.

But the young flight sergeant couldn't bail out. His parachute, which was stowed outside the gunner's turret in the fuselage, was in flaming shreds.

"My stomach seemed to drop out of my body when I realized my parachute was useless," Sgt. Alkemade recalled.

His choices were clear—stay inside the plane and die—or jump and take his chances on surviving a fall of more than 18,000 feet.

Thinking it was better to die a quick, clean death than to fry, he jumped.

"It was perfectly quiet and cool, like resting on a cloud," he recalled. "It was as though I was lowered onto a super-soft mattress. There was no sensation of falling…I thought, 'Well, if this is dying, it ain't so bad.'"

Indeed, he felt so peaceful that he was able to calculate that from 18,000 feet it would take him 90 seconds to reach the ground.

Then he blacked out.

Three hours later, Sgt. Alkemade awoke. Staring up at the stars, he wondered what he was doing still alive.

"It was a miracle," he said. "I was in one piece—hardly hurt, in fact."

Somehow, trees had broken his fall. Eighteen inches of fresh-fallen snow made a final cushion that saved his life. The only damage were a couple of cuts on his face and a badly twisted right knee.

A few minutes later German soldiers arrived and took him to a hospital. There he tried to explain what had happened—but nobody believed him.

"They thought I was a spy who parachuted in," he said. "They couldn't believe that someone could fall from a plane without a parachute and survive."

Then news reached the hospital that a Lancaster had crashed nearby during the night. When investigators sifting through the ruins of the downed bomber found items in the gunner bubble that belonged to the young airman—including the remains of his shredded parachute—they were convinced he was telling the truth.

Sgt. Alkemade survived his 13th bombing mission and continued to live a "charmed" life, working in a chemical factory. Once a steel girder fell on him. Hauled out for dead, he walked away with a bruised scalp.

He narrowly escaped death several years later when he was drenched with sulfuric acid. He also survived an electric shock that threw him into a hole, where he lay breathing chlorine gas for 15 minutes.

His luck finally ran out in 1988, when he died of a heart attack at the age of 65.

Spectral Incursions

Angels in Blue and Gray

The American Civil War was a long and bloody ordeal, with incredible heroism on both sides, North and South. Nowhere was that gallantry and devotion to cause given a greater test than at Gettysburg, a quiet little community on the Pennsylvania-Maryland border where more than 30,000 men perished in two days of bloody fighting.

The tragic loss of so many lives in such a short time soon gave rise to stories that the battlefield was haunted by spirits of the slain soldiers. Visitors and local planters frequently reported seeing "ghostly soldiers" in blue and gray marching across the field or charging into battle, sometimes shouting the rebel yell.

Late one night in October 1966, a group of Union re-enactors camped near Devil's Den—site of one of the bloodiest battles of the campaign—were awakened by strange music floating through the dark woods. Thinking another group of re-enactors was approaching, they got up to investigate.

No one was there—only the sound of drums and fifes drawing closer in the dark.

"I tell you, a chill went down my spine as that music continued to move toward us," recalled John Rushoe, a Union re-enactor from Pennsylvania who recognized the Civil War tune. "The music seemed to be coming right out of the air."

Next day, as they marched to a nearby hill called Little Round Top, the Union boys were in for another spectral shock. Several said they noticed a "gray luminescent mist" possessing a vaguely human form gliding among the trees toward the hill's stony summit.

"It wasn't ground fog, I can tell you that," Rushoe said. "The shape was over 5 feet tall and about a foot wide and had sort of a human shape. I'd never seen a ghost before, but I knew I was looking at one now."

Some men who saw the ghost believes the phantom might have been the spirit of a Union soldier from the 20th Maine, a regiment that courageously defended the hill. Others speculated it might have been the ghost of a Confederate soldier.

Rushoe and his comrades are among thousands who are convinced the battlefield is haunted. In fact, say some paranormal researchers, the Civil War town and surrounding battleground is the most haunted place in America, with a long list of ghost sightings and poltergeist activity.

Spectral phenomena associated with the Civil War have been reported at other battlefields, towns, encampments and hospitals as well. One of the most famous reportedly took place in October 1863 near Lewisburg, Va., in rural Greenbriar County.

It was the height of the war, and the South was still reeling from bloody defeats at Vicksburg and Gettysburg. The Confederacy was demoralized and many leaders thought that only a miracle could save them now.

Then it happened. At about 3 p.m., while battles raged all around the once-tranquil valley, a mysterious army of phantom soldiers suddenly appeared in the sky, marching in a westerly direction. Hundreds of eyewitnesses supposedly watched the eerie procession as it continued across the hazy blue sky, finally vanished in a puff of green-tinged smoke beyond the low line of hills.

Moses Dwyer, a local planter, was sitting on his front porch when he saw them—"thousands upon thousands" of strange aerial beings floating into view.

"They were traveling in the same direction," Dwyer said in one interview. "They were marching double-quick, some 30 or 40 men in depth as they crossed the valley and ascended the almost insurmountable hills opposite."

Dwyer and other thunderstruck observers said the eerie army of cloud-borne marchers "seemed to stoop as if carrying a heavy load up a steep mountain."

Another witness noted: "The men were of great variety and size. Some were extremely large while others were very small in stature. As they marched, their arms, heads and legs could be seen distinctly moving. They observed military discipline with no stragglers breaking ranks."

Some witnesses claimed that a multitude of other objects also appeared to be edged in a light-blue glow.

"All of the soldiers wore a uniform outfit," commented another stunned witness. "White shirts with white pants."

Although most observers described the marchers as militaristic, one gave the following account: "They were not armed with guns, swords or anything that would give the indication of men marching off to war. They continued through the valley, over a steep road, up the hills and finally in approximately an hour, disappeared from sight."

News of the apparition traveled fast. Newspaper reporters, artists and photographers came from all over to interview witnesses. The sightings in Greenbriar County coincided with several similar but less spectacular visions in nearby counties.

Two weeks later, on October 14, a remarkably similar vision was observed by Confederate pickets at nearby Runger's Mill. A number of locals confirmed the second spectacle, claiming that it tasted more than an hour.

Several attempts were made to explain the pair of phenomena, none to the satisfaction of eyewitnesses or the legions of others who have studied the incidents. One editorial writer said they were "angelic armies" sent into battle on the side of the South.

Another witness disagreed, claiming instead that the ghostly soldiers were Northern reinforcements sent down from a "tear-stained Heaven."

Eventually, the bloody business of war diverted attention from the bizarre incident. For years, however, folks in the region continued to talk about the day the angels came to Virginia.

The President From Beyond the Grave

On the night of May 27, 1955, President Harry S. Truman went on national television to reveal a shocking secret. While an estimated 50 million Americans looked on, the president told interviewer Edward R. Murrow that a ghost stalked the drafty corridors of the White House.

It was no ordinary ghost, either.

"I think it's the ghost of Abraham Lincoln walking around," the president said calmly into the camera. "Perhaps he's here to warn me about something."

Ever since his arrival at the White House eight years earlier, Truman said he had been bothered by a strange tapping noise on the other side of the presidential bedroom door. The sound, described as "unusually sad and melancholy," usually came to him late at night or early in the morning.

Most often it happened around 3 a.m. while the rest of the White House slept. As the president told it, he'd be awakened by the knocking sound beyond the door. He'd crawl out of bed, fling open the doors and peer down both sides of the hallway.

The results would always be the same—nothing.

"There was no one there," he explained. "So I'd go back to bed."

In bed he'd think about all the old legends about how the spirit of Lincoln, who was 55 when he was struck down by an assassin's bullet, prowled the dark halls of the White House, moving from room to room, a tormented look in his eyes and a plaid shawl draped around his craggy shoulders.

According to old reports, Lincoln had seen his own death in a dream at least twice. He also had visions about other unworldly events, a gift supposedly handed down to him by his psychic mother. Night after night, disturbing and significant symbols and premonitions came to him in his sleep, and he found that he was greatly troubled by his conscience.

Among the things Lincoln claimed to have seen was "the knowledge of and...the power to change the future." As a youth growing up in a backwoods log cabin near Hodgen's Mill in what is now Larue County, Ky., Lincoln felt it wiser to keep his psychic powers to himself.

But just about everybody who knew him was aware of the ill-fated president's amazing ability to "see" into the future and predict events without knowing how.

Edwin Stanton, a close friend and member of Lincoln's cabinet, once confided: "I have known that the president is not like other men, and that he believes that the future can be seen now and that the afterlife is for repentance. It would not surprise me if, when he dies, his spirit refused to leave the White House and that it remains there, restless and troubled, until it feels that the last of these ësins' has been paid for."

Far-fetched and fanciful though this seemed, it began to make sense to Harry Truman some 90 years later as he pondered the mysterious spectral visitor outside the presidential bedroom door. The more he read about Lincoln's alleged psychic abilities and the series of ghostly visions the late president claimed to have had while in the White House, the more convinced Truman became that Lincoln's tormented spirit still haunted the White House.

"It's possible," he said. "Anything's possible."

Many other visitors to the White House claimed to have encounters with a ghost matching Lincoln's description, including Eleanor Roosevelt who often sensed the dead president's presence, usually at night while she was writing. The Roosevelts' dog, Fala, would bark excitedly for no apparent reason.

The first sighting was made in the 1920s by Grace Coolidge, wife of Calvin Coolidge. She reportedly saw the president's spirit standing by an Oval Office window looking across the Potomac.

One of the most chilling encounters occurred late one

night in the 1930s while Queen Wilhelmina of Holland was sleeping in the White House stateroom. According to press reports, the queen was awakened by a soft knocking at her bedroom door and went to investigate.

When she opened the door, she found herself facing the ephemeral figure of a tall, bearded stranger in black frock coat and stovepipe hat. The startled queen had seen enough pictures of Abraham Lincoln to know it was the long-dead American president whose ghost stood before her.

She fainted.

Harry Truman thought Lincoln's ghost was trying to warn him about something. The fact that the hauntings occurred at the height of the Cold War suggested to him that the phantom president who had fought so hard to preserve the Union in another time was concerned about deteriorating East-West relations and the nuclear threat to world peace.

To the end of his days in 1972, Truman believed that whoever was president and whoever lived in the White House would also hear the discreet rapping on the bedroom door and perhaps would someday have the opportunity to communicate directly with Lincoln's ghost.

Except for the Reagans, no other administration has admitted to any encounters with the famous ghost.

Man in Gray

Few sights are more chilling to residents along the South Carolina coast than an appearance by the so-called Gray Man, a silent, solemn specter said to materialize shortly before the arrival of a hurricane.

Hundreds have reportedly seen the ghost, usually described as a somber little man dressed in an old-fashioned hat and long, gray coat. Many witnesses swear the sightings came within days or even hours of a major storm.

"He's real," said Matt Rodgers, a Boston insurance executive who vacations at Pawleys Island near Charleston. "I've seen him several times with my own eyes. So have other members of my family."

Rodgers said he first saw the Gray Man in 1971, the first year he rented a beachfront house.

"It was early one morning," Rodgers said. "I was alone on the beach, watching the waves and birds. Suddenly I looked behind me, and there he was. He was a little man, about 5 feet tall, standing about 30 yards up the beach. He was dressed in a quaint, old-fashioned suit, complete with long tails, hat and tie. Then he vanished, right before my eyes."

The startled Bostonian never told anyone about the apparition. In fact, he forgot about it until the late 1980s, right before Hurricane Hugo struck.

"My brother was down from Charlotte, and we were out walking the beach, looking for shark's teeth," Rodgers explained. "We happened to turn around and saw him at the same time, the same little gray man I had seen some 15 years earlier. Then he vanished again, just like he did before.

It wasn't until after Hugo slammed into the Carolina coast a few weeks later that Rodgers heard about the "curse of the Gray Man." According to legend, those fortunate enough to see him are spared from the storm.

Just how the legend got started is unclear, but some researchers think it originated in the early 1800s when a young man sailing down from New England to meet his bride near Charleston drowned after his ship sank in a storm. The Gray Man is said to be the young man's ghost patrolling the shore to warn others about impending bad weather.

Variations of the story say it is a "Gray Woman" instead of a "Gray Man" who haunts the lonely beaches. Said to be the bride-to-be of the doomed young man, her spirit roams the beaches in search of her dead lover. Like the Gray Man, she sometimes appears to warn mortals that a storm is rolling in.

Other coastal regions have their own versions of the Gray

Man story, but none has received the notoriety of South Carolina's famed specter. Sightings have been made from Myrtle Beach south to Edisto Island and Hilton Head. The apparition is frequently spotted strolling the dunes at Fripp Island.

The most memorable warnings came shortly before powerful storms hit the South Carolina coast in September 1822, October 1893 and October 1954. In each case, several people reported seeing a strange little man dressed in gray clothes walking the stormy beach just hours before the storms struck.

In 1954 an automobile dealer named Bill Collins had an encounter with the Gray Man near his beachfront home at Pawleys Island.

"I was looking down from my deck when I saw a strangely dressed little man looking right up at me," Collins said. "I knew in my heart I was having a genuine out-of-this-world experience."

A few days later Hurricane Hazel blew in from the south, washing away scores of beachfront houses. But Collins' house was spared—indisputable proof, he believes, that the man in gray had come to warn him.

The Surrency Haunting

Hauntings and other paranormal happenings were popular media events in the late 1800s, as evidenced by the phenomenal success and notoriety of mediums like the Fox Sisters and other celebrated psychics and "spirit advisers."

None, however, received more international attention than the so-called Surrency Ghost, a particularly frightful specter seen and heard by tens of thousands of people, from newspaper reporters and clergymen to scientists and psychic mediums. The ghost brought considerable fame to the hamlet of Surrency in deep South Georgia's Appling County, but caused suffering and pain to the town's founder, a middle-aged sawmill operator named Allen Powell Surrency.

The hauntings began in the early 1870s, shortly after Surrency decided to turn his rambling, two-story home into a rest haven for travelers. Surrency was little more than a village perched on the edge of a vast pine wilderness. Its main connection with the outside world was the Macon-Brunswick railroad line, which ran through the heart of the hamlet.

On Oct. 23, 1872, the *Savannah Morning News* published a letter sent by Surrency describing a series of strange happenings at his house.

"Please allow me a small place in your paper to publish a strange freak of nature," he wrote. "On Thursday last, I returned from (Hazlehurst) to my residence...where I have lived for twenty years unmolested. On my arrival at home about 7 o'clock, I found my family and some of my neighbors...my brother and several others whom I consider men of truth, very much excited.

"A few minutes after my arrival I saw the glass tumblers begin to slide off the slab and the crockery to fall upon the floor and break. The books began to tumble from their shelves to the floor, while brickbats, billets of wood, smoothing irons, biscuits, potatoes, tin pans, water buckets, pitchers, etc., began to fall in different parts of my house. Nearly all of my crockery and glasses have been broken."

Surrency added: "There have been many other strange occurrences about my house. These facts can be established by 75 or 100 witnesses."

Soon after the letter ran, the first of what would become an army of journalists descended on the Surrency home to see the "ghost" for themselves. The media frenzy was on. Before long, reporters and curiosity-seekers from as far away as Canada and England arrived.

Visitors were rarely disappointed, as the ghost almost always made its presence known. Untouched dishes would fly off shelves, doors would open and close on their own, clocks would strike thirteen and, most amazing, hot bricks would fall onto the roof and in the yard.

Until his death a few years ago, Herschel Tillman, a retired postal carrier whose home was in Surrency, used to talk about his many visits to the Surrency house to see the ghosts. His first trip came when he was 8 years old.

"It was on a Sunday, right after church," he recalled in an interview shortly before his death. "My daddy drove us out to the old Surrency house in an old buggy. We went inside and saw and heard things not of this world."

Tillman said he never got over all the things he saw and heard there—unearthly screams, clocks that spun backwards, boots that clopped across the floor by themselves, hot bricks falling from the sky.

"That place was possessed by something evil," said Tillman. "There's no two ways about it. There must have been at least a dozen ghosts inside the Surrency house."

After watching several ink bottles leap from a table and listening to disembodied voices inside a bedroom, a reporter from the *Savannah Morning News* wrote: "The whole house is clothed in darkness…and bears the spirit of the supernatural."

That same reporter said he watched the hands of a clock "move around with exceeding rapid motion…It would pause and strike oddly, and this went on for 17 minutes."

A reporter from the *Atlanta Constitution* said logs kept rolling out of the fireplace and that books mysteriously fell off shelves. The reporter fled the house when several hogs and chickens suddenly appeared in the living room from out of nowhere.

By the turn of the century, stories about the Surrency haunting had appeared in newspapers as far away as Russia and Greece. Dozens of books were written about it, and hundreds of articles appeared in newspapers all over the world.

The late Rev. Henry Tillman said his father often described how objects in the house would dance on the table at mealtimes, bedcovers would roll up and down at night, and glowing red eyes would hover over the railroad tracks directly in front of the house.

Eager to rid their home of their unnatural guest, the Surrency family sought the help of scientists, ministers, mediums and psychics. But efforts to drive away the ghost—or ghosts—were unsuccessful. If anything, they seemed to make matters worse.

Tradition has it that a murder was behind the Surrency haunting. One story says a railroad worker was killed outside the home and that his spirit plagued the house and its occupants until the place went up in flames in 1925.

Another version holds that Allen Surrency was in league with the devil. One witness recounted how Surrency once demonstrated his arcane powers by running a stick completely through his hand without spilling a drop of blood.

According to tradition, the ghost—or ghosts—continued to torment the Surrency family long after the house burned and they moved to another home on the other side of the county.

"That thing haunted Old Man Surrency until the day he died," said one old-timer. "But when he was buried, the haunting stopped.

The Gray Lady of Sherwood Forest

The old house sprawls in stately splendor beneath the outstretched arms of centuries-old oaks, a stone's throw away from the muddy banks of Virginia's historic James River. Known locally as Sherwood Forest, the house has been home to two presidents—William Henry Harrison and John Tyler.

For 150 years, it has also been home to one of the Tidewater's most famous specters—the legendary Gray Lady.

The present owners, descendants of President Tyler, are convinced something haunts their 44-room mansion.

"It's here, no question about it," said Payne Tyler, whose husband, Harrison, is a descendent of the 10th American president. "Everyone who has ever lived here has heard it."

Legend holds the ghost is the spirit of an elderly woman who cared for a sick baby in the plantation nursery. According to one version of the story, the baby died sometime before 1842.

Some say she was named Gray, while others contend the spirit is known as the Gray Lady because of the color of the cloak seen about the apparition. She is said to walk over the creaking floorboards in the hallways, rock in nonexistent rocking chairs and spends time in the corner of the master bedroom.

Payne Tyler learned about the Gray Lady from reading old letters found inside the house when the family restored the plantation in the 1970s. It was during the restoration period that she experienced her first visit from the ghost.

"She disturbed me two times," Mrs. Tyler noted. "I heard her in the next room, but I was not about to open the door. I told her, very politely, that we were going to stay here, she was going to stay here, so we might as well be friends. Then she left me alone."

But she became a firm believer one night in the late 1980s as she slept in the house. Around midnight, she awoke to the sound of someone entering the locked bedroom.

"Someone walked across my room and piddled around in the corner," she said. "You could hear them moving and shuffling things, and I thought it was a burglar. Then they walked over to the foot of the bed and stood there for quite a while and then they went out."

Mrs. Tyler added: "I know all of this really sounds crazy. I would have never believed in a ghost or spirit until I came to live in a house with one. If you live in a house where there's a ghost in it, you believe in it."

Borley Rectory

Borley Rectory, a gloomy, twin-gabled Victorian mansion atop a muddy hill overlooking the Stour River in England's Essex County, was once described as one of the ugliest houses in England. Before it mysteriously burned to the ground 60 years ago—precisely at the stroke of midnight—some said the red-brick monstrosity located 60 miles northeast of London was also one of the most haunted.

For more than a century, the 135-year-old house was the scene of strange noises, phantom coaches that came and went at midnight, mysterious cold spots and unending poltergeist activity. Locals said it was cursed as well as haunted and refused to go anywhere near the place, especially after dark.

The most commonly reported apparition was that of a young nun strangled on the grounds more than 300 years ago. The nun was reportedly seen at all hours of the day and night, a gray, diaphanous form gliding along a dark path dubbed "nun's walk."

Other phenomena included heavy footsteps tramping stairways late at night, objects appearing and disappearing, bells ringing and writing on walls. Organ music was often heard coming from nearby Borley Church, along with weird monastic chantings.

In 1945, *The Times of London* called Borley Rectory "the most haunted house in England." Built in 1863 for the Rev. Henry Dawson Ellis Bull, the brooding old building was supposedly situated on the site of a medieval monastery. Ghostly encounters began almost as soon as the rector and his family moved in.

"We heard strange footsteps almost every night," the rector wrote in his diary. "Bells rang constantly. Voices whispered to us in the dark."

One daughter was awakened by a slap in the face. Another saw the dark figure of an old man in a tall hat by her bed. One frequent visitor saw a nun several times.

No one was harmed, but the experiences were unnerving. The vicar's son, Harry Bull, took over the rectory in 1892 and stayed until 1927. In that period a headless man was seen in the bushes; a phantom coach appeared almost every night; a cook reported that a locked door was open every morning; and four of the Rev. Bull's sisters together saw a young nun who disappeared in full view.

Edwin Whitehouse, who later became a Benedictine monk, visited the rectory with his aunt and uncle during 1931. On one occasion a fire started in the baseboard of an unused room. As the flames were put out, a flint the size of a hen's egg fell to the floor. Later, while the vicar conducted a service of exorcism in his room, Edwin and his aunt were hit by falling stones.

In 1937 Harry Price, flamboyant founder of Britain's National Laboratory of Psychical Research, advertised in *The Times* for people "of leisure and intelligence" who were intrepid, critical and unbiased to join a group of observers who planned the spend the night in the house. From more than 200 people who applied, he chose 40.

Ellice Howe, an Oxford graduate who accepted Mr. Price's challenge, swore he saw objects move. Others reported unexplained noises. Commander A.B. Campbell of the BBC "Brains Trust" team, was hit by a piece of soap in a sealed room. Dr. C.E.M. Joad, the philosopher, another member of the team, reported that a thermometer recorded a sudden and inexplicable drop of 10 degrees.

Price's investigation was sharply criticized by the media, noting that the celebrated author and para-psychologist had a reputation for showmanship. After his death in 1948, allegations of fraud were made, but none were proved.

Precisely at midnight on the night of Feb. 27, 1939, Borley Rectory caught fire and burned. Some observers claimed they heard screams of anguish emanating from the flames, though no one was in the house.

In 1943, four years after the rectory was destroyed, excavators digging a trench found fragments of a woman's skull and pendants bearing religious symbols. The woman's identity was never revealed, but some investigators suspect foul play was involved and linked her ghost to some of the supernatural manifestations at Borley Rectory.

Strange things continued to happen on the property, even as late as 1961 when torches, car headlights and camera flashes all failed during an investigation of the site.

In 1953 and again in 1954, newspapers reported sightings of ghosts in the vicinity of the rectory. Bricks taken from the Borley ruins and buried under a school playground at Wellingborough were connected with the alleged appearance of a ghost. The burning of a Borley village chicken house was also linked to the rectory's haunted history.

Symphonic Spirits

Robert Schumann, the great German composer, was having a bad day. Twice in one morning he had tried to commit suicide—once with an open blade, the second time by throwing himself into the Rhine River near Bonn. The first attempt was thwarted by a nurse at the asylum where he was confined.

"Why don't you let me die in peace?" he reportedly shrieked at a pair of fishermen who plucked him out of the river after his second attempt failed.

He wanted to do die, he said, to escape "evil inner voices" that had tormented him since childhood.

In the beginning, the voices had been kind to the gifted young musician born in Saxony in 1810. He was only 12 when they came to him, whispering in a language not of this earth. As an adult, he called them "spirits of the voice," but as a child they were always giving him advice and warning him of impending danger.

The voices helped him publish his first composition at the

age of 12, a simple accompaniment to the 150th Psalm. They also helped him write and publish plays, poems and translations of classical verse.

At first he was afraid of the strange murmuring. They came to him at night, when he sat alone at the piano, struggling to find the right note. He described them as "soft sounds, gentle whisperings that ran fingers deep within my brain."

Soon, the voices seemed to take control of his music. They urged him to write more, play more, perform more. At the same time they warned him never to ignore them, never forget that they were in total command of his spirit as well as his music.

By the time he was 30, Schumann, the son of a working class bookseller, was a famous—though not necessarily rich—man. When friends like Chopin and Brahms inquired as to the origins of his music, the deeply sensitive composer and poet always claimed that "the angels in my head" provided themes and melodies.

In 1840, Schumann married Clara Wieck, the beautiful young daughter of his piano teacher, who would go on to become a famous pianist in her own right. The artistic couple had stormy moments, yet managed to produce eight children.

The next few years were productive, as the Schumann's traveled to Russia and Austria, where Schumann received critical acclaim for his First Symphony in B-flat. During this busy period he helped many talented friends, including Mendelssohn and Brahms, by giving them favorable reviews in a musical magazine he published.

It was also during this time that he composed many of the solo songs, or *lieder*, on which his reputation was built. Friends referred to that year—1840—as the Year of the Song because Schumann wrote more than 100 songs.

Again, the inspiration was attributed to his inner voices—the "angels" in his head that whispered to him sweet tunes and melodies at night.

In 1844, Schumann suffered a nervous breakdown. He

found that he could no longer focus on music. The voices were growing too loud, getting out of control, seemingly wanting to take over his life.

Suddenly, the voices went away. He moved to Dresden, a thriving musical center, and began working furiously. The next year, still living in Dresden, Schumann penned his famous Symphony Number Two in C Major. He was overjoyed at the thunderous reception he received!

Then the hallucinations returned—more painful than ever—and he sank into a deep depression. In constant pain and fear of his sanity, the great artist was unable to work for months. To make matters worse, his old friend, Brahms, had moved into his house and—some say—began a torrid love affair with his wife.

By 1852, he was complaining of "strange afflictions of hearing"—a repetition, apparently, of nonstop tonal sounds. As his mental condition worsened, Schumann sought solace in seances. In vain he tried to communicate with the spirit world, to try to better understand his supernatural torment.

In 1853, the Schumann's participated in a "table rapping" session—a phenomenon that was all the rage in Europe. According to notes left in his diary, Schumann was convinced that tables could "move" and "rap out" rhythms to songs. "I said, 'Dear table, play the opening theme to my C minor symphony,' and it tapped it out..."

The tide of music began to drown him. No longer soft and gentle, the sounds in his brain became bitter, threatening. Then one day the "sweet voices" of the angels returned, softly urging him back to work.

Schumann told a friend that the music inside his head was "fully formed and complete." The sound, he said, "is like distant brasses, underscored by the most magnificent harmonies. This must be how it is in another life, after we've cast off our mortal coil."

One night Schumann told his wife that the angels were calling out to him to enter their world. Then, without further warning, those same warm entities became "terrifying demons" that beckoned him to join them in hell.

In 1855, Schumann checked himself into an asylum at Bonn, a medieval village on the Rhine River. The next year, the day after a visit from his wife—her only visit to see him in the asylum, in fact—he choked on some food and finally passed over into the realm of the angels.

Ghost of Flight 401

Eastern Airlines Flight 401 was making its final approach to Miami International Airport on the night of Dec. 19, 1972, when a panel light suddenly came on, indicating trouble with the landing gear.

The pilot and flight engineer went to work trying to correct the problem. In their haste, they failed to notice the aircraft's steady descent over the Florida Everglades until it was too late.

Seconds later, the L-1011 jumbo jet crashed, killing 100 passengers and crew members, including the pilot, Captain Bob Loft, and Flight Engineer Dan Repo.

An official investigation concluded that equipment failure and pilot error caused the crash..

The tragic story might have ended there had Eastern not decided to salvage parts of the downed plane and install them on other company aircraft. Soon after parts were incorporated into Flight 318, strange things started happening.

A flight attendant making her way down the aisle of Flight 318 fainted when she saw the ghost of Captain Loft standing at the rear of the plane. Other attendants claimed to see the dead captain's reflection in windows and in the galley stove's glass door. One crewman said he saw the captain's ghost sitting in a passenger seat staring out the window, while another said he heard the dead captain's voice over the public address system warning passengers to put on their seatbelts.

"I knew it was the captain immediately," one frightened attendant said when she heard the ghostly voice. Later she saw what appeared to be the dead captain standing in the aisle near the back of the plane. "He turned around and looked at me and smiled then vanished."

Witnesses also reported experiencing abnormally cold sensations and an invisible presence aboard other L-011s that contained parts from Flight 401's wreckage. There were other manifestations of supernatural activity, including tools that suddenly appeared in the hands of mechanics and power consoles that suddenly flashed on and off.

Repo's uniformed ghost also appeared frequently, usually seen sitting in a plane's first-class section or crew compartment. He was also seen sitting in the cockpit as well. Flight officers said Repo always seemed calm and relaxed, but "very concerned" about the safety and operation of the plane.

Whenever the dead flight engineer's ghost appeared, "It often made suggestions or gave warnings to crew members who only realized he was an apparition after he had vanished," said John Fuller, author of *The Ghost of Flight 401*.

On numerous occasions, the ghosts appeared in the cockpit where they warned crew members about equipment problems and impending danger. "But we will not let it happen," they reportedly told pilots.

The sightings persisted for several months, then started tapering off after Eastern complained that they were hurting business. Management threatened to fire workers who continued talking about their ghostly experiences.

Eyewitness reports continued, however, until Eastern finally removed the parts associated with Flight 401.

In supernatural lore, ghosts frequently haunt airplanes, ships, trains, buses, carriages and other vehicles of mass transit. But paranormal investigators say the haunting associated with Flight 401 was most unusual because of the large number of sightings and reluctance on the part of the specters to leave.

Angels,
Aliens and
Abductions

Flying Saucer Mania

Flying saucer mania was at its peak in the fall of 1953 when the Central Intelligence Agency convened a panel of top scientists, government officials and military leaders to discuss what should be done to calm the public's nerves.

For six years, starting with Kenneth Arnold's famous sighting of several "disk-shaped" objects skipping through the skies over Washington State, thousands of Americans had rushed forward to lay claim to similar sightings. Some even said they had been kidnapped and taken aboard spacecraft, where they had been subjected to painful medical experiments.

While most people laughed at such reports, the CIA embarked on a mission to uncover the truth.

After months of study, the Robertson Committee concluded UFOs were no threat to earthlings, but that UFO reports were. In the words of one panelist: "If an enemy attacked our country, the report might be ignored as just another UFO sighting until it was too late."

In the interest of national security, the CIA sought to repress sightings of UFOs. It concocted a bewildering array of explanations and launched a public relations campaign to convince the world that UFOs were not real and to smear the reputations of those who said otherwise.

The Robertson Committee was not the first attempt to stifle public interest in UFOs. Project Sign, launched in 1947 shortly after the Arnold sightings, was the first official government investigation. A six-month study found that 20 percent of all UFO sightings could not be explained.

Project Sign was replaced by Project Grudge. Investigators were given strict instructions to find "logical explanations" for each sighting. "From this point on," writes Janet Riehecky in *UFOs*, the "official government position has been that the idea of UFOs is ridiculous and people who believe in them are either misled or crazy."

In its first year, Project Grudge couldn't explain 23 percent of its cases. Two years later the investigation was upgraded and given a new name, Project Blue Book.

Project Blue Book's purpose was to prove that UFOs were ordinary things that were misunderstood. Project leaders refused to release information about sightings unless they had been explained. Military personnel who spoke to the press could be fined up to $10,000 and sentenced up to 10 years in jail.

The Condon Study, launched in 1966, was another government attempt to quell public concern about UFOs. After investigating thousands of reports in a two-year period, committee members were unable to account for 22 percent of the cases, but Project Blue Book was officially closed.

After that, a number of citizen groups began investigating UFOs on their own. One of the most important was founded by Dr. J. Allen Hynek, an astronomer who had been a consultant to Project Blue Book. A skeptic initially, Dr. Hynek eventually became convinced that UFOs deserved further study and formed the Center for UFO Studies.

Some serious private groups, including APRO (the Aerial Phenomena Research Organization) and NICAP (the National Investigations Committee on Aerial Phenomena) said the government knew more than it was telling the public.

Even today, many investigators say the Air Force and other government agencies are deliberately withholding the truth about UFOs.

Circles of the Gods

When John Scull woke one morning and saw a series of strange circles carved in his 6-acre wheat field near Westbury, England, his first thought was that vandals had sneaked onto his property during the night and caused the damage. After an exhaustive search yielded no footprints or other signs of trespassing, however, the perplexed farmer concluded that alien spaceships were somehow behind the mystery.

So did a lot of other people.

On Oct.15, 1980, a few days after the mysterious "crop circles" appeared on Scull's property, the *Wiltshire Times* reported that they had been "made by some kind of energy field of unknown origin." Another paper, the *Daily Express*, suggested that the circles—all within sight of the famous White Horse chalk carving—might be related to dozens of similar pictograms that had popped up in British fields in recent years.

The presence of so many circles had spawned nationwide interest in the markings and led many in the media and scientific community to believe visitors from other words were indeed responsible.

At the time, "crop circle fever' was sweeping the British Isles. New Age investigators, journalists and scientists armed with recorders and infrared vision scopes descended in droves, marking, mapping and measuring the circles. Many fully expected to find proof that visitors from outer space had paid a call and left behind these cryptic calling cards.

The British press dubbed it the "silly season."

Although crop circle reports go back many centuries, the first known example in the modern era appeared on a cane farm in Queensland, Australia in January 1966. Tractor driver George Pedley was driving through a cane patch when he saw a "large, bluish-gray" spaceship take off from a nearby swamp. On the ground where the strange craft had been parked, the astonished farmer found a curious, 30-foot-circle of dead reeds.

"The whole place was burned black and lay about flat in a huge circle," Pedley said.

His weird story about the Australian circle brought hundreds of reporters and curiosity-seekers to Queensland. Other witnesses stepped forward to say they, too, had seen spaceships and found enigmatic crop circles in their fields.

It wasn't long before elaborately constructed pictograms started turning up in England. The first ones, found in the mid-1970s, were small and crudely rendered but sometimes stretched hundreds of feet in diameter. By the early 1990s, immense geometrical figures, some the size of football fields, appeared from Cornwall to Kent. The phenomenon eventually spread to the United States, Canada, Bulgaria, Hungary, Japan and the Netherlands.

Each year brought new and increasingly dramatic and complex markings. Since most circles were showing up in southern England near Stonehenge, Avebury, Silbury Hill and other ancient sites associated with mysticism, some investigators conjectured they were somehow connected to the supernatural. A few investigators who ventured close to the rings complained of giddiness and nausea, while others told of religious and mystical experiences.

Today crop circles have become one of the most famous and visually recognizable enigma of all time. The study of these baffling markings even has its own name—cereology. The variety of circles seems almost endless, from the simplest crude circles that appear to have been flattened out, to complex geometric designs covering several acres. Sometimes the main circle is surrounded by a cascading series of smaller, though no less intricate, formations.

While some investigators claimed the circles had been produced by natural phenomena—whirlwinds, ball lightning, rutting hedgehogs or "elastic plasma fireballs," for example—many others insisted they were the work of UFOs. Several argued that the circles were mathematical and geometric attempts by aliens to communicate with earthlings.

Such designs have been found all over the world, in nearly every culture, ancient and modern. The earliest report of a crop circle came from the village of Assen in Holland in 1590. In the 17th century an English scientist, Robert Plot, suggested that circular patterns in fields might be caused by rapidly descending blasts of air. Another said they were the work of "mowing devils."

In their book, *Circular Evidence*, authors Pat Delgado and Colin Andrews suggest that these circular pictograms were created by some higher cosmic intelligence and were recognized by primitive tribes as well as more modern people.

The late astronomer Carl Sagan stopped short of embracing the authenticity of crop circles, but admitted that at least one of his colleagues believed that "extremely sophisticated mathematics" were hidden in the enigmatic figures.

By the mid-1990s, it began to look as if whoever—or whatever—was creating the circles took pleasure in taunting investigators.

"When believers in the whirlwind theory pointed out that the swirling had so far been clockwise," wrote Colin Wilson, another author who has investigated the mystery, "a counter-clockwise circle promptly appeared. When it was suggested that a hoaxer might be making the circles with the aid of a helicopter, a crop circle was found directly beneath a power line."

Then, in 1991, Doug Bower and Dave Chorley of Southampton announced they had been fabricating crop circles for more than a decade. Other hoaxers also stepped forward to claim credit, including Fred Day who announced he had been making them "all my life."

For every admitted prankster, however, a dozen other believers have stepped forward to insist the circles are the real thing. Some predict it's only a matter of time before the true meaning of the crop circles is revealed.

Captain Mantell's Last Mission

"It appears to be a metallic object...tremendous in size...directly ahead and slightly above...I am trying to close in for a better look." Moments after uttering those strange words on the afternoon of Jan. 7, 1948, Air National Guard pilot Capt. Thomas Mantell aimed his P-51 Army fighter into the Kentucky sky and flew off into oblivion.

What strange thing did Capt. Mantell, an experienced combat pilot and decorated World War II hero, see that afternoon that led him to his doom? That question continues to haunt investigators, more than 50 years after the tragedy. The government claims Capt. Mantell saw a new type of weather balloon. Others, however, insist he accidentally came upon a top secret experimental aircraft and was killed because of his discovery.

Not so, say a growing number of researchers who suspect Capt. Mantell's airplane was shot down by a spacecraft from another world and accuse the U.S. government of covering up the incident.

Capt. Mantell's story began shortly after he and three other airplanes under his command took off from Goodman Field—now Fort Knox—in Kentucky on a routine training exercise. A few minutes into the flight, the control tower informed him that an unidentified flying object was in the area and told him to check it out.

About an hour later, Capt. Mantell radioed that he had made contact with the rapidly moving object and was in pursuit. He described the object as strange looking, resembling "an ice cream cone topped with red."

Unable to keep up with the swiftly flying object and unequipped with oxygen, the other three P-51 pilots dropped out of the chase, leaving Capt. Mantell alone. A few minutes later he told the tower he was going to 20,000 feet—an extremely dangerous altitude.

"If I get no closer I'll abandon the chase," he informed the tower.

Those were his last words. Minutes later, witnesses reportedly saw his aircraft explode and crash. Capt. Mantell, a veteran of the Normandy invasion and holder of the Distinguished Flying Cross, had now achieved the dubious distinction of becoming the world's first "UFO martyr."

Officials downplayed reports that Captain Mantell had

been chasing a flying saucer when his plane went down. They said he probably blacked out from lack of oxygen and his plane simply ran out of fuel and plowed back down to earth in a fiery spiral.

Others aren't so sure.

One retired Air Force officer who helped investigate the crash said that Capt. Mantell, an experienced pilot all too aware of the dangers of anoxia (oxygen starvation) above 15,000 feet, was drawn into the clouds against his will.

James F. Duesler, a former captain in the U.S. Army Air Corps now living in England, was stationed at Godman Field at the time of the crash. His primary duty was to investigate air crashes, though he sometimes worked in the control tower. When Capt. Mantell's plane went down, he was called in to assist with the investigation.

There were a number of things wrong with the official account of the crash, Duesler said in an interview with an international magazine. "The damage pattern was not consistent with an aircraft of this type crashing onto the ground," he said. "The official report said that Mantell had blacked out due to lack of oxygen. This may well have been the case, but the aircraft came down in a strange way."

Although the government continues to deny it, Duesler said there had been other reports of "glowing, orange, cigar-shaped" objects in the area the same day Capt. Mantell's plane went down. One report put the second UFO over Wright-Patterson Air Force Base in Ohio, while another described an object coming in from St. Louis.

There were other mysteries as well. For example, Duesler accused the government of faking his signature on a document issued by the State Department shortly after the crash. He said he never signed the document and doesn't know why the government would fix his name on the report without his approval.

Most incredible of all, Duesler said that when he arrived at the still-smoking wreckage, he found no trace of blood in the cockpit or anywhere else on the plane.

Capt. Mantell's body had already been taken away, but Duesler was informed by others at the scene that "nowhere on the body had the skin been punctured or penetrated, yet all the bones had been crushed and pulverized."

Corel E. Lorenzen, author of numerous books about UFOs, spent years investigating the Mantell case and says: "I am not prepared to dismiss this theory (that Mantell died chasing a weather balloon) except to say that no balloon flight for that particular area had been discovered in military archives. As far as I'm concerned, the Mantell case should be listed as 'unknown' until the 'object' can be positively identified."

More than five decades later, the official investigation of the crash remains top secret. If he was killed in a mere training accident as the government alleges, why are the official transcripts between Capt. Mantell and the control tower still classified?

Interlude on a Lonely Road

On the night of Sept. 19, 1961, Betty and Barney Hill were returning from a Canadian vacation to their home in Portsmouth, N.H., when they spotted a strange light hovering over the dark woods along U.S. Route 3. Intrigued, they stopped the car to investigate. For several minutes they watched the object, described as a "glowing mass of Christmas decorations," as it moved erratically just above the dark tree line.

"It was big," Hill later told reporters, "but it was so quiet as it hung there, like it was watching us or something."

They finally drove on, convinced the strange object was a weather balloon or some kind of experimental aircraft. Still, they couldn't shake the eerie feeling that the thing was watching them as they drove.

Every now and then, they'd stop to check on the moving,

soundless light. As they neared the White Mountains, the object—now appearing much larger—seemed to be moving parallel to their car. Near Indian Head it suddenly swooped down directly in front of them.

"I've had enough of this," Hill told his wife.

He stopped the car and hopped out, determined to find out once and for all what the thing was that was following them. Using binoculars, he saw a double row of windows surrounding the object, then noticed "five or 11 figures" moving around inside.

"I don't believe it!" he shouted to his wife, who stood on the opposite side of the car but could not see the humanoid figures. "This is ridiculous!"

Hill later said the creatures were dressed in shiny black uniforms that looked like leather and wore caps with visors. He added, "They had red hair and round faces and moved with odd military precision."

When the UFO descended to within 70 feet overhead, Hill dashed back to the car, yelling, "Get inside! They're going to capture us!"

They jumped into the car, locked the doors and sped away. Hill remembers pressing his foot down on the gas pedal so hard his toes ached.

Several minutes later they heard a strange beeping noise. It appeared to be coming from above the car. Hill was convinced the object was still following them.

"Who are they?" Mrs. Hill shouted hysterically. "What do they want? What are they?"

Suddenly they both felt very drowsy.

"It was as if someone had switched off the lights inside our heads," Mrs. Hill later remarked.

Two hours later, the couple found themselves driving in the vicinity of Ashland, some 35 miles south of Indian Head. They drove home, feeling puzzled and uneasy about the missing two hours. Where had they been? What happened to the strange object chasing them?

The next day they reported their experience to officials at Pease Air Force Base. A few days later Mrs. Hill called the National Investigations Committee on Aerial Phenomena (NICAP) in Washington, D.C. A special investigator was sent to document their story.

In the days that followed, Mrs. Hill experienced recurring nightmares in which strange men dressed in matching uniforms and "military" caps would halt them in the middle of the road. Each time the "leader" would assure the couple they would not be harmed. Then the Hills would be led aboard a disk-shaped craft and examined. Samples of hair, fingernails and scrapings of skin would be taken from Mrs. Hill. In addition, a long needle was inserted into her navel.

Afterward, the couple would be returned to their car and allowed to drive home.

In the weeks following their ordeal, the Hills began to experience "unbearable" feelings of anxiety and dread. Eventually they were put in touch with Benjamin Simon, a prominent Boston psychiatrist who specialized in treating personality disorders and amnesia through hypnotherapy.

Starting in January 1964, Dr. Simon treated the Hills for six months. During this period, under time-regression hypnosis, some amazing details were revealed about their experience.

One of the most fascinating aspects of the case concerns a strange "star map" the leader showed Mrs. Hill when she asked him where he was from. The map was drawn by Mrs. Hill under deep hypnotic suggestion—years before astronomers would discover a cluster of stars near two stars called Zeta Reticuli that is amazingly close in configuration to the "map" sketched by Mrs. Hill.

What happened to the Hills on that dark night in 1961? Did they actually encounter a UFO—and were they taken aboard and examined by humanoid-like creatures from another world?

Or—as is the opinion of Dr. Simon—was the couple's

account of their abduction by UFOnauts nothing more than fantasy?

Dr. Allen Hynek, an internationally respected scientist, former member of the Air Force's Project Blue Book and head of NICAP at the time, thought otherwise. In published reports, he stated his belief that something extraordinary had happened to Betty and Barney Hill on that lonely New Hampshire road.

Hoaxes and *Outlandish* Claims

Mask of Agamemnon

"I have gazed upon the face of Agamemnon," German archaeologist Heinrich Schliemann wired a newspaper in November 1876.

The lofty announcement came only days after the businessman-turned-archaeologist claimed to have excavated one of the world's greatest archaeological treasures —a golden mask said to a portrait of the mythological Mycenaen king who led a Greek army against Troy.

Schliemann, whose discovery of ancient Troy five years earlier had made him an international celebrity, boasted to King George of Greece: "With great joy I announce to your Majesty that I have discovered the tomb proclaimed to be the grave of Agamemnon."

The mask, which he described as being in a "perfect state of preservation," was one of several unearthed in shallow graves at Mycenae. Scholars hailed it as the most important, however, because it supposedly portrayed the likeness of the fabled Bronze Age leader.

But was it real? For years, some classical historians have been troubled by a number of discrepancies associated with the find, as well as Schliemann's renowned penchant for dishonesty, exaggeration and self-glorification.

Some experts have called the glittering artifact a fake, deliberately planted by Schliemann to boost his reputation and standing in the scientific community. Recent scholarship suggests the critics might be right.

Three decades ago, William M. Calder III, a professor of classics at the University of Illinois at Urbana-Champaign, fired the first salvo in the debate when he questioned the veracity of several claims in Schliemann's autobiographical writings. Dr. Calder, an award-winning author and editor of numerous books on 19th century classical studies, accused the German archaeologist of faking several important so-called discoveries, such as a bust of Cleopatra he claimed to have found in a trench at Alexandria in 1888.

Most grating of all was Schliemann's bold assertion that he had found the ultimate archaeological treasure of all time — the "masterful" Mask of Agamemnon.

"I've learned to doubt everything Schliemann said unless there is independent confirmation," Dr. Calder said.

Other scholars agree. Gunter Kopeke of New York University's Institute of Fine Arts insists that the mask is stylistically different from all other Mycenaean masks, right down to its distinctive eyebrows, ears, beard and mustache. Dr. Kopcke asserts that the mask is the work of an innovative and highly talented modern goldsmith.

Why would Schliemann lie? Scholars point to several reasons that might have motivated him to manufacture, bury, then excavate the mask.

"He wanted to close the excavations with a bang," noted one critic. "He also desperately needed a *Herrscherbild*, a portrait of a leader. The other masks he had found were not worthy of a great king."

Critics of Schliemann have long contended that he often exaggerated accounts detailing his work in the field. They also say he deliberately lied about other aspects of his professional and personal life.

Schliemann reportedly made bogus claims of heroic acts during the burning of San Francisco; lied that he had gained American citizenship on July 4, 1850; misrepresented his wife, Sophia, as an enthusiastic archaeologist; faked the discovery of ancient Greek inscriptions in his backyard; and lied about his unearthing of an enormous cache of gold and silver objects at Troy, known as Priam's Treasure.

Once universally accepted as truth, art collectors, archaeologists and ancient historians the world over now know that these and many of Schliemann's other accomplishments and claims fall short of the truth.

Ernst Curtius, director of the excavations at Olympia and

professor of ancient history at Berlin, called Schliemann a "swindler and con man."

Anthony Snodgrass of Cambridge University called him "profoundly dishonest."

Supporters, however, noted that Schliemann's work at Mycenae was carried out under the watchful eye of the Greek Archaeological Society and its director of antiquities, Panaagiotis Stamatakis, a respected scholar. They say it would have been impossible for Schliemann to have faked discoveries under such scientific scrutiny.

Piltdown Man

In 1856, the fossilized remains of a prehistoric skull was unearthed in Germany's Neander Valley, heralding the possibility that human beings had been on Earth a lot longer than previously believed.

For the next half century, as the great nations of Europe competed for political and economic dominance, the race was on to see who could find the next "Original Man." Such a find would go far in establishing European primacy—the notion that humankind had originated in the Western world rather than in Asia, Africa or some other dreary corner of the globe.

The bombshell came two weeks before Christmas in 1912. Two amateur archaeologists went before London's prestigious Geographical Society and announced they had found the "Earliest Man," a creature believed to be vastly older than Germany's Neanderthal Man.

Charles Lawson, a lawyer by trade, and Arthur Smith Woodward, a geologist at the British Museum, said they had found *Eoanthropus dawsoni* in a shallow gravel pit near the village of Piltdown in the county of Sussex.

At first they called the creature "Sussex Man," then "Dawn

Man," before finally settling on Piltdown Man, the name that stuck.

Newspapers around the world touted Piltdown Man as "the greatest find in the history of mankind." Many saw the fossilized remains, which consisted of skull fragments, an unusually large jawbone and several huge molars, as the most newsworthy event since Christopher Columbus's voyage to the New World. It also proved—as many Englishmen already knew—that mankind had originated in England, which seemed important in an age of expanding nationalism.

For years, scientists who followed the teachings of naturalist Charles Darwin had confidently predicted that a "missing link" would someday be found to connect modern man with primitive beasts. Now that the "link" had been found, history books would have to be rewritten.

But there were some troubling questions. For example, skeptics wanted to know more about the precise location where the fossils were found. They were also unsure about the fossil's age and fretted that too many pieces were still missing to determine whether they actually belonged together. Other details were omitted and unclear.

Some came to see the whole thing as a sham. Particularly disturbing was the fact that the fossil pieces were kept securely locked in the British Museum and placed off limits to outside investigators. How could reputable scientists make a determination if they weren't allowed to see the specimen with their own eyes, touch it with their own hands?

Suspicions lingered, but the overwhelming acceptance of Piltdown Man by the general public as a whole soon quieted down the skeptics.

It wasn't until many years later—the 1950s, in fact—that modern technology proved the skeptics had been right all along. Using a newly discovered fluoride dating method, paleontologists and anatomists at the British Museum and Oxford University found compelling evidence that Piltdown Man was not nearly as old as claimed.

In fact, they said, it was a fake.

Among the jolting revelations: the jawbone was from a modern orangutan. Some of the teeth had been filed flat to make them appear more human. As for the skull bones, chemical analysis indicated it was from a fairly modern human—between 520 and 720 years old. Some of the bones had been stained with chemicals, others with ordinary paint, to make them look extremely old.

On Nov. 20, 1953, Oxford anthropologist Joseph Weiner and paleontologist Kenneth Oakley presented their findings to the Natural History Museum. The Piltdown Man was "a most elaborate and carefully prepared hoax," they wrote. "The faking of the mandible (jawbone)—is so extraordinarily skillful and the perpetration of the hoax appears to have been so entirely unscrupulous and inexplicable as to find no parallel in the history of paleontological discovery."

The news was shocking: "Piltdown Man Hoax is Exposed," announced *The New York Times*. "Part of the skull of the Piltdown Man, one of the most famous fossil skulls in the world, has been declared a hoax by authorities at the British Natural History Museum."

Thus ended more than four decades of rumors and uneasy speculation among the world's leading scientists. In the process, fortunes had been lost, reputations ruined and careers cut short. But science and the search for truth suffered worst of all, as many people now viewed science as fallible and scientists as corrupt.

How was it possible that so many scientists could have been duped for so long—and who was behind history's most elaborate hoax?

All fingers pointed to Piltdown Man's original discoverers, Charles Dawson and Arthur Smith Woodward. Based on his reputation as one of the British Museum's leading paleontologists, Woodward generally escaped blame, as did Father Pierre Teilhard de Chardin, a French Jesuit who had assisted in excavation on several occasions.

Dawson, on the other hand, was an amateur, a mere lawyer, and therefore a prime suspect. Unfortunately, his death 37 years after the event meant he had taken whatever secrets he might have known about the caper to his grave.

Other individuals have been proposed as the hoaxer, either as a co-conspirator with Dawson or working on their own. These include Sir Grafton Elliot Smith, a neuroanatomist; Martin A.C. Hinton, a curator of zoology at the British Museum; W.J. Sollas, a geologist; and Sir Arthur Conan Doyle, the famed mystery writer and creator of Sherlock Holmes.

Many investigators are convinced that Doyle was the perpetrator. The writer lived only 7 miles away from the pit where the fossils were found and knew Dawson and Woodward.

The most compelling evidence linking him to the hoax can be found in one of his books, *The Lost World*, an adventure yarn about ancient men and prehistoric beasts that was published in 1912. According to some researchers, there are numerous passages and clues contained in the book that indicate he was behind the scheme.

As far as motive goes, some have speculated that Doyle had a grudge against mainstream scientists as a whole because they frequently ridiculed his strong personal belief in spiritualism. The Piltdown hoax might have been his way of getting back at them.

Kensington Stone

Late one afternoon in 1898, Olaf Ohman, a successful and respected Minnesota farmer, was pulling up tree stumps on his farm near Kensington when he unearthed a strange stone buried at the base of a poplar tree.

Intrigued, Ohman called his son over to help him pull the stone free from the tangled roots and clean it off. Unable to read the strange, chicken-like scratchings on the stone's surface, they put it away in the barn and forgot about it until several days later when they showed it to a Norwegian neighbor.

The neighbor, Nils Flaten, got excited when he saw the inscriptions on the 200-pound chunk of gray sandstone —so excited he took it to the downtown bank where several scholars were brought in to examine it. When translated, the inscription described a bizarre but heroic tale about a band of eight Swedes and 22 Norwegians who had sailed across the Atlantic Ocean and continued westward across the New World to what is now Minnesota.

According to the inscription, several explorers were killed in a bloody confrontation with Indians in 1362. Written in runes —the alphabetic characters of Northern Europe during the Middle Ages—the inscription appeared to be genuine.

More specialists were called in to study the huge block of stone, which measured almost 3 feet long, 16 inches wide and 6 inches deep.

University of Minnesota historian O.J. Breda was one of the first scholars to examine the stone. He declared it a "genuine artifact" and published the first translation.

"Eight Swedes(Goths) and Twenty-two Norwegians on an exploration journey from Vinland westward. We had our camp by 2 rocky islets one day's journey north of this stone. We were out fishing one day. When we came home we found ten men red with blood and dead. AVM save us from evil. We have ten men by the sea to look after ships, fourteen days' journey from this island. Year 1362."

Professor Breda and others who examined the stone saw it as an historic account of an amazing and true story of courage and survival in the New World by a band of plucky Scandinavians.

Other weren't so sure about the relic. Most scholars who looked at the tombstone-looking slab insisted that the relic was nothing more than a crude forgery. With the exception of a few alleged runes scattered throughout the Midwest, there is no evidence that the Vikings ever set foot in Minnesota.

But the controversy surrounding the so-called Kensington

Stone evoked a rash of stories about Viking landings and new evidence that Scandinavians had preceded Christopher Columbus to America.

Scholars now know that Viking explorers and settlers did reach the shores of North America at least five centuries before Columbus's landfall on San Salvador. Only a few consider it possible that a band of Scandinavian explorers could have journeyed as far as Minnesota, as comforting as that thought might be to the many inhabitants of the state who trace their ancestry to Scandinavia.

Dismayed by the scholarly outcry over his find, Ohman, who denied knowledge of any fabrication or hoax, took the stone home where he used it as an anvil.

The story of the Kensington Stone would probably have ended there—another hoax about pre-Columbian voyagers to the New World—had it not come to the attention of a young Norwegian college student, Hjalmar Holand. In 1907, Holand purchased the stone and spent the rest of his life defending its authenticity.

With the Kensington Stone in his possession, Holand sought the support of academia as he lobbied to prove that the Vikings had made it to Minnesota—and perhaps elsewhere in North America—in the 14th century. He claimed that there was an expedition led by a Paul Knutson to Christianize the Vikings of the West and that this story correlates with the dates given on the stone.

According to Holand, the Vikings expedition led them through Hudson Bay, Lake Winnipeg, and up the Red River to a place near present day Kensington, Minnesota. It is his belief that the stone is a remnant of the Knutson expedition.

His campaign did get the attention of the Smithsonian Institution, which put the stone on exhibit during the 1940s. One museum director, in fact, hailed it as "probably the most important archaeological object yet found in North America."

Other experts disagreed. Some continued to insist that the artifact was a fake and pressed for its removal from the museum.

The uproar over the Kensington Stone did little to dampen Holand's spirits. Until his death in 1963 at the age of 90, he continued to champion its authenticity.

The controversy over the stone did not end with Holand's death. Frederick J. Pohl, one of the more active supporters of the concept of Viking exploration in America, has continued to defend the stone's integrity in several books, as have other scholars.

In a 1982 work, *The Kensington Stone Is Genuine*, Robert Hall, a professor emeritus of linguistics at Cornell University, asserted that the stone is real.

While the controversy continues, the Kensington Stone lies in a modest museum in Alexandria, Minnesota, its secrets guarded by the local chamber of commerce.

Flat Earthers

Astronaut Neil Armstrong thrilled the world on July 20, 1969, when he set foot on the dusty surface of the moon for the first time and proclaimed, "one small step for man, one giant leap for mankind."

Not only was the historic lunar landing an inspiring technological achievement, it also laid aside a number of age-old myths about the shape and size of the Earth and its place in the solar system.

Since ancient times, people had believed that the Earth was flat, not round, as Christopher Columbus and other 15th century explorers would later prove. Even though the Greeks had assumed the world was spherical, many scholars continued to hold the notion that it was flat and that the North Pole lay in the center of the pancake-shaped plane.

Another common assumption was that the Earth was stationary in space and that the sun and stars revolved around it. Since the Earth was home to God's special creation —Adam and Eve—this made perfect biblical sense to so-called Flat-Earthers who continued to deny the existence of a spherical world and even scoffed at the great voyages, claiming most were either elaborate hoaxes or out-and-out lies.

Medieval thinkers pointed to the Bible to prove their theories about a flat Earth. How could the Holy Books speak of the "four corners" of the Earth if the planet was a sphere without corners?

Such thinking kept most ancient mariners close to the shore until fairly modern times. Although a few explorers might have crossed the Atlantic before Columbus—the Vikings being one such group—most never reached the "terrible edge of the Earth" because of what stood in the way—hungry sea serpents, monstrous whirlpools, vine-clogged seas and boiling lakes of fire.

Belief in a flat, stationary Earth did not die out, even after Ferdinand Magellan circumnavigated the globe in 1519 and failed to report any sea serpents, giant whirlpools or tangled, burning seas. Even today, while satellites hurdle around the planet and men walk in space, there are people and organizations that insist that the Earth is actually flat.

One such organization is the International Flat Earth Research Society, founded in 1800 in Great Britain and the United States. According to one president, Charles Johnson, Neil Armstrong never actually walked on the moon.

"It's all one big lie," Johnson explained. "It's nothing more than a piece of clever stage-managed science-fiction trickery."

What about the pictures reputedly taken in space showing the Earth to be a rotating sphere?

"They are just too ludicrous for words," explained Johnson, who believes that the sun circles the Earth instead of the Earth revolving around the sun—a notion that most people have taken for granted since the days of Copernicus.

The society, whose membership is currently estimated to be about 2,000, dismisses much of accepted modern thinking about the shape of the Earth as sheer nonsense and is convinced that the entire human race is being subjected to the greatest hoax in history.

From its headquarters in Lancaster, Calif., the society wages a non-stop war of words through newsletters and pamphlets against the evils of science.

In the 1900s there emerged another group of Flat Earthers who attracted international attention because of its offer to pay $5,000 to anyone who proved Earth to be round. Led by a charismatic, almost fanatical preacher named Wilbur Glenn Voliva, the group settled in Zion, Ill., a few miles north of Chicago, and founded a church to support its unorthodox doctrine.

Rabidly fundamentalist, Voliva ruled Zion with an iron hand. Under his guidance, the town was governed by a notorious set of blue laws that would have made the Salem Puritans proud. For example, anyone caught smoking or wearing shorts on the streets could go to jail. Alcohol was banned, as were gambling, swearing and whistling in public on Sunday.

As the town's virtual dictator, Voliva proclaimed his own special belief that the Earth was shaped like a pancake, with the North Pole in the center and the South Pole distributed around the circumference.

What kept ships from falling off the edge of the Earth? A solid wall of ice, Voliva's Flat Earthers explained, pointing to icebergs.

The self-styled preacher , who denounced other fundamentalists as "liars," also believed stars were small, flat bodies and not very far away. The moon, he said, was lighted from within. He dismissed the notion of the suns great distance from Earth by saying: "The idea of a sun millions of miles in diameter and 91 million miles away is silly.

On the contrary, he said, the sun was only 32 miles across and not more than 3,000 miles from Earth.

"It stands to reason it must be so," he noted. "God made the sun to light the Earth, and therefore must have placed it close to the task it was designed to do. What would you think of a man who built a house in Zion and put the lamp to light it in Kenosha, Wisconsin? Doesn't make sense."

Even though Voliva frequently traveled, often making trips around the world himself, he never came to accept the existence of a spherical planet. A small, comfortable universe, familiarity and what passes for common sense—these were and remain the hallmarks of the Flat Earth appeal.

Cardiff Giant

Legends around the world speak of a long-ago time when giants ruled the Earth—a time before the Great Flood when the sons of God came down from on high and walked among the mortals.

"There were giants on the Earth in those days," the Bible says in Genesis 6:14, "and also afterward, when the sons of God had relations with the daughters of men, who bore children to them."

The ancients accepted these legends as fact. Gigantic warriors—offspring of the gods—were found in almost every culture, from the desert kingdoms of Egypt and Mesopotamia to the verdant hills of Greece and Rome. During the Middle Ages, the unearthed bones of prehistoric beasts were believed to be the bones of this vanished race of giants washed away in the deluge.

By the middle of the 19th century, advances in new sciences like geology, paleontology and archaeology had all but destroyed the old myths. But the gods and giants of yore lived on in the hearts and minds of many people who continued to see every newly excavated dinosaur bone as evidence that gigantic beings once walked the Earth.

In the fall of 1869, newspapers were full of the latest findings of the naturalist Charles Darwin. People everywhere were talking about evolution and "missing links." Some thought it was only a matter of time before some distant ancestor—a pre-Flood giant, perhaps—would be found.

Then, late one October afternoon, workmen digging a well on the outskirts of Cardiff, an obscure little village in upstate New York, were startled when their shovels uncovered what appeared to be the mummified remains of a large human foot.

Digging deeper, the workmen found that the enormous foot was attached to the body of an incredibly large man, measuring more than 10 feet tall and weighing nearly 3,000 pounds. Apparently the giant had been dead thousands of years.

Was it real? Was this the fossilized remains of an antediluvian giant?

As news spread, scientists, clergymen and newspaper reporters came at first, then thousands of curiosity-seekers from across the region who paid 50 cents apiece to gaze upon the face of the gigantic corpse.

William "Stubb" Newell, the farmer on whose land the giant had been found, was stunned by all the publicity and scientific curiosity. But he quickly took advantage of the hoopla and was soon making big bucks.

Among those who came to gawk were fundamentalist preachers and some scientists who were convinced the giant belonged to a long-forgotten race of man. Some called him the "Original Man." One investigator so firmly believed the giant to be real, he announced that any man who declared it to be a hoax "simply declared himself a fool."

Physicians who examined the creature also insisted the giant had once been a living human being. To prove his point, one physician drilled a hole in the giant's enormous skull and claimed that he was able to make out fascinating aspects of its anatomy.

Professor James Drator of the New York State Museum, one of the most distinguished paleontologists of his time, said the specimen was "the most remarkable object yet brought to light in this country."

Some observers called the find a fossil, while others thought it was an ancient statue. It took a famous New York sculptor, Eratus Dow Palmer, to finally break the news—the so-called Cardiff Giant was a fake, nothing more than a big slab of carved gypsum.

Instead of snuffing out interest in the giant, however, Palmer's revelation only created more excitement about the mysterious object nicknamed "Goliath" by the press.

Even when Stubb Newell stepped forward and confessed to having made the whole thing up, business continued to boom, earning him and his partners more than $30,000 by the end of the first week. The Cardiff Giant was so popular, in fact, famed showman P.T. Barnum manufactured his own giant after Newell refused to sell it to him for $36,000.

The Cardiff Giant was actually the brainchild of Newell's cousin, New York cigar manufacturer George Hull. An avowed atheist, Hull had hatched the scheme for the sole purpose of getting even with a fundamentalist preacher with whom he had recently been arguing over the biblical origins of man.

Hull decided to teach the preacher a lesson. He bought a large block of stone in Fort Dodge, Iowa, and then transported it to Chicago where a crew of sculptors—pledged to secrecy—fashioned it into the likeness of a giant human being. To make it look authentic, he had hundreds of large darning needles inserted into a block of wood before hammering it all over the body to stimulate the pores of skin.

Finally, after hosing the giant with sulfuric acid to make it look old, Hull loaded his creation into a bronze box and had it transported it by train and wagon to Newell's farm where it was buried by night to await the great moment of discovery.

Everything went according to plan. Exactly one year later, workers hired by Newell and Hull "discovered" the oddity while digging a well.

Although they made a fortune from their hoax, many reputations were ruined, including those of preachers who had accepted the giant on faith and of numerous scientists who had staked their careers on its authenticity.

In 1947 the Cardiff Giant was acquired by the New York State Historical Association for $30,000 and placed at the Farmer's Museum in Cooperstown, N.Y., where it is on public display.

Fountain of Youth

Before the European conquest of America, Caribbean legends told of a wondrous kingdom far to the north where people could drink from a certain stream and "live like young men" forever.

This "fountain of youth," as the stream was called, was supposedly located somewhere north of Cuba in the mysterious land called Florida—which could have been anywhere from modern-day Texas to the Carolina coast.

The legends were similar to dozens of Old World stories about life-giving rivers, lakes and streams that had been around since the dawn of time. In fact, some researchers suspect the Indian stories might have actually been based on versions they had heard from shipwrecked European mariners who, centuries earlier, had preceded Christopher Columbus to North America.

Myths about "magical fountains" feature prominently in Icelandic literature, so could have been brought over by Viking explorers more than 1,000 years ago. These myths often matched Greek, Germanic, Roman and even Hindu legends about life-giving waters, down to supposedly magical settings.

The River of Immortality offered eternal life for the Semites, and the Pool of Youth provided renewed vigor for the Hindus. Such realms went by a variety of names—the

Land of Apples, King of the Fairies, Oberon, Morgan la Fay, and the Land of Blessedness where old age and disease could be washed away by either bathing in or drinking special waters.

In the late 14th century, Sir John Mandeville wrote that the Fountain of Youth was only "ten days journey...from where St. Thomas' church was to be found," and if one imbibed, "he is hool (cured) of alle manner of sykness...(and if) Drynken often...their semen alle ways young...Sum men clepen (call) it the Welle of Youthe."

And in 1530 Peter Martyr said, "There is an Ilande about three hundred and XXV leagues from Hispaniola...in which is a continual sprynge of runnynge water of such marvelous vertue, that the water thereof being dronk, perhapps with sume dyete maketh owld men young ageyne."

New World explorer Rene Goulaine de Laudonniere claimed that his scouts in Florida had talked with men who had drunk from the Fountain of Youth and were more than two centuries old. And even Edmund Burke, about 1770, is quoted as saying that such a pool would be a good investment.

While many Spanish conquistadors must have heard these stories, only Don Ponce de Leon, the governor of Puerto Rico, apparently resolved to find the legendary fountain.

In about 1512, the governor set sail to explore Florida and Bimini. His convoy, consisting of two caravels—and no priests—sailed northward, finally making landfall near modern-day St. Augustine. He named the place Florida in honor of "Pascua Florida" and the Easter season.

He found no fountain of youth, so turned southward again. Eventually he passed the Florida Keys and worked his way up the west coast to Charlotte Harbor, or perhaps as far as Apalachicola Bay.

At every stop, he heard stories about the fountain—but they always pointed in another direction, on another island, three days journey by sail. The aging conquistador kept going, but in the end, found nothing—no gold, slaves, or fountain of youth.

Disgruntled, he set his sights on the West Indies, hoping to find Bimini—where some accounts placed the magical fountain.

After a full decade of searching, Ponce de Leon finally gave up his quest and went back home.

Much of what we know about his voyages is based on accounts provided by Antonio de Herrera, a highly imaginative Spanish historian of unreliable integrity. Some say Herrera made up the whole thing in order to make his writings more dramatic—thus, enhancing his own reputation.

Some scholars say Ponce de Leon probably had never even heard of a fountain of youth, let alone make it the focus of a decade-long search through the wilds of Florida and the Caribbean. They say the enterprising conquistador was probably doing what everybody else was doing—looking for gold and slaves.

Herrera reportedly had come across a fanciful Indian story about a mysterious stream of water located somewhere north of Cuba that supposedly had the power to restore youth. Indians who drank or bathed in these waters were said to live hundreds of years.

According to Herrera, the governor had heard about the legend from various tribes of Caribbean Indians and decided to investigate. One tribe, the Arawaks, is said to have migrated from Cuba northward because of a "magical river...where life-giving waters flow pure and plenty."

It's a romantic tale, one that has endured for centuries. Books, plays, movies and documentaries have been made on the subject, making the Fountain of Youth one of the most popular legends of all time.

Yet, researchers, mindful of Herrera's zealous pen, say there is nothing in the pages of Ponce de Leon's original patent from Emperor Charles V to suggest anything but a businesslike expedition to explore and perhaps colonize

Florida. Nor are there indications from subsequent records to suggest he had the slightest notion about the curious fountain that would follow his name through the ages.

Where was the fabled fountain? Some historians place it near Silver Springs in northern Florida, while others point to Georgia—in the vicinity of the Okefenokee Swamp, perhaps—or Alabama. Still others claim it was on the island of Guanahani (San Salvador), or on the island of Bimini.

In the event such a wondrous stream ever existed, one can rightfully suspect that it is no longer there—drained away, perhaps, or bulldozed over to make room for another parking lot or theme park.

Enduring
Mysteries

Search for Noah's Ark

In the summer of 1916, Lt. Vladimir Roskovitsky, a Russian pilot, was flying over mountains in northeastern Turkey when he spotted what appeared to be the weathered remains of a huge ship half-buried on the upper slops of Mount Ararat.

Intrigued, he sent a detailed report to Czar Nicholas, along with maps, drawings and charts. Within days, a research team was dispatched to the region to investigate what many thought might be the remains of Noah's Ark.

Researchers dug, drew pictures, photographed artifacts and wrote numerous essays. Newspapers in Moscow and London called it "the greatest discovery in the history of mankind."

Unfortunately, the report was lost during the Russian Revolution.

Some scientists who saw the report before its disappearance were convinced they had seen the real thing —evidence that the ark had existed, just as it was described in the Book of Genesis.

Rumors about the ark's existence have circulated since the third century, when Greek writers said it was "common knowledge" that the ark could still be viewed on Mount Ararat. Descriptions of the vessel usually matched those given in Genesis, a barge-like wooden ship 450 feet long, 75 feet wide, 45 feet high, with three interior decks capable of holding as many as 75,000 animals.

According to the Bible, Noah's boat came to rest on "the mountains of Ararat," a term that probably designated a region (the ancient kingdom of Uratu) and not a specific mountain peak.

The story of Noah and his ark is similar to dozens of others told around the world since prehistoric times. Nearly every major culture, in fact, includes a variation on the basic plot — ancient flood destroys the earth, sparing only a selected few.

The biblical account is the most famous. Genesis tells how "God saw that the wickedness of man was great" and sent a great deluge to purge his creation. It seems likely that the Genesis story was based on an even older story, that of Babylonian King Gilgamesh who met Utnapishtim, survivor of a great flood sent by the gods.

Ancient Greeks and Romans had their own flood legends, as did the Irish whose Queen Cesair sailed for seven years to avoid drowning when the oceans overwhelmed Ireland. European explorers in the New World were startled by Indian legends that sounded similar to the story of Noah. Spanish priests feared the devil had planted such stories in the Indians' minds to confuse them.

Many scholars see a common thread running through most of these old stories, based on some actual, terrifying occurrence. Columbia University geologists William Ryan and Walter Pitman theorize that melting glaciers at the end of the last Ice Age caused major flooding in the eastern Mediterranean, drowning vast areas and forming the basis for the old legends.

While many experts put the location of Noah's ark elsewhere, the majority believe the big boat came to rest on Ararat. Most believe it was buried in glacial ice midway up the mountain—about 10,000 feet—and forgotten about until the 20th century when aerial photos and drawings such as those made by Lt. Roskovitsky and others revealed its image on film.

Acting on those claims, dozens of expeditions have been launched this century, mostly by Christian groups eager to find evidence to support the biblical story.

In the early 1950s, American oil engineer George Jefferson Greene supposedly took photos of a ship-like shape half submerged in a gully on Ararat. Greene was mysteriously murdered in 1962, however, and the photos disappeared.

The most publicized investigation features an extraordinary ship-shaped object of impressive size discovered not on

Ararat, but on a nearby range and immediately below the mountain of al Judi. First reported in the late 1950s during an aerial survey by the Turkish Air Force, the object was the focus of several expeditions in the 1980s and 1990s.

Participants included American shipwreck specialist David Fasold and archaeological researcher Vandyl Jones, who would go on to seek the Ark of the Covenant.

Resembling a ship's hull bounded by a raised ridge, this eye-catching enigma's dimensions correspond fairly well with those given for Noah's Ark in Genesis. Fasold argues that the Ark has become fossilized.

Geologists counter that it is just a syncline—an oddly shaped uplift of the Earth. It has even been suggested that the structure might have inspired the story of Noah's Ark—a thought-provoking reversal of traditional concepts.

In the meantime, however, Fasold and a team of Turkish scientists continue to study Al Judi's ark-shaped anomaly in the hope of confirming that one of the Bible's greatest wonders is more than just a myth.

Shroud of Turin

In a chapel of the cathedral at Turin in northern Italy lies a shroud that millions of Christians revere as the burial cloth in which the crucified body of Christ was wrapped.

On the cloth, which is about 14 feet long and 3 feet, 6 inches wide, the dim, brown image of a dead and disfigured man can be seen—almost like a photographic imprint. At the top can be seen the compelling features of a bearded man so like the commonly accepted face of Christ that those who cherish the shroud are convinced that the resemblance must be more than mere coincidence.

If genuine, the cloth is the most impressive and moving relic to have come down to us from the time of Christ.

But is it real?

For centuries, skeptics have repeatedly proclaimed doubts of its authenticity. Controversy still rages—but 20th century science has, surprisingly, made the voice of the skeptics less strident than it used to be.

Tests by impartial scientists are producing increasingly firm evidence that what is revered by so many is, in fact, the shroud of someone who was crucified in Palestine around the time that Jesus died. Whether the body was that of Christ can probably never be ascertained.

The burial cloth under investigation bears the marks on its left-hand portion of the front, on its right-hand portion of the back, of a man around 35 to 40 years old and about 5 feet, 6 inches tall. There is evidence of a wound in the ribs and of bleeding from the forearms.

Even more striking are bloodstains in the head area—proof, say some, that a crown of thorns had been placed around the victim's head.

One of the most controversial issues, of course, is how the shroud came to bear such clear imprints of the body it covered. Another equally vexing problem arises from the fact that there is no record of its existence before 1357, when it was publicly exhibited at the small French town of Lirey.

At that time the cloth belonged to a noble French family, the de Charnys, who never explained how it had come into their possession. Among the many people both inside and outside the Church who nevertheless had faith in its authenticity wee the powerful dukes of Savoy, to whom the controversial relic was bequeathed in 1453.

At first they kept it in their capital city of Chambery, where it was slightly damaged by fire in 1532. Then, in 1578, they moved their capital to Turin, where the shroud was enshrined in a cathedral chapel built expressly for it. There it has lain since, venerated by many—although the Catholic Church itself has never declared it valid.

Skeptics suggest the figure imprinted on the shroud was

simply painted sometime in the 14th century. One American expert, Walter McCrone, insists that the bloodstains are unnaturally red for 2,000-year-old blood and were probably made by some artificial substance—probably rose madder, a paint pigment favored by medieval artists.

On the other hand, scientific tests have revealed that blood found in the shroud contains the right mixture of calcium, protein and iron.

Textile experts have also concluded that the weave of the linen is of a type common in Palestine 2,000 years ago and that its fibers contain traces of cotton, which does not grow in Europe.

The Devil's Triangle

Christopher Columbus might have been the first to notice something strange about the vast expanse of Atlantic Ocean now known as the Bermuda Triangle. In his log, the Genoese explorer wrote about flaming balls of fire whizzing through the skies and "glowing streaks of white in the surface."

Five centuries later American astronauts orbiting the earth described similar "mysterious patches of light and foam" off Bermuda.

Today, this picturesque, seemingly peaceful stretch of the Atlantic Ocean ranging from Florida and Puerto Rico to Bermuda continues to draw attention because of its alleged link to the disappearance of thousands of people and hundreds of ships and planes.

Some officials—including the U.S. Coast Guard—now regard the Bermuda Triangle area as one of the most dangerous maritime regions in the world.

During the past century, this three-sided area of the Atlantic known also as the Devil's Triangle, Hoodoo Sea, Limbo of the Lost, as well as Bermuda Triangle, has claimed more than 50 ships and 20 aircraft. Such loses have prompted many experts to recommend more study of the region—especially the erratic weather patterns that occasionally baffle meteorologists.

"The seas out there can be just indescribable," says one veteran Coast Guard captain. "The waves break and you get a vertical wall of water from 30 to 40 feet high coming down on you. Unless a boat can take complete submergence in a large, breaking sea, she can not live."

The Coast Guard averages 8,000 distress calls a year in the area. Most problems stem from boats running out of gas or being swamped in storms, but a few "are just plain mysterious," one officer declared.

It wasn't until December 1945 that the world's attention was focused on this mysterious realm covering almost a million square miles of ocean. That's when a squadron of Navy bombers vanished off Florida.

The 27 crewmen of Navy Flight 19, based at the Fort Lauderdale, Fla., Naval Station, were on a routine training mission when the lead pilot, Lt. Charles Carroll Taylor, radioed that he was "lost" and gave the following cryptic message: "Everything is wrong. We can't be sure of any direction. Even the ocean doesn't look as it should."

Shortly after communications broke down with Flight 19, a Martin Mariner rescue plane with a crew of 13 was dispatched to the general area. Inexplicably, the rescue plane vanished, too.

Despite a massive air-sea rescue operation involving 300 planes and hundreds of ships and submarines, no trace of Flight 19—or the rescue plane—was found.

Eighteen months later, an Army Air Corps Superfortress bomber disappeared 100 miles off Bermuda without having signaled any hint of trouble. Again, an immediate search of 100,000 square miles of sea turned up no wreckage.

A few years later, a DC-3 with 36 people aboard apparently "evaporated" within sight of Miami. "We are approaching the field only 50 miles to the south," the pilot told the control tower. "We can see the lights of Miami now. All's well. Will stand by for landing instructions."

The plane vanished from the radar screen a few seconds later. The spot where the aircraft supposedly went down was over the Florida Keys, where clear waters only 20 feet deep should have made the DC-3 visible.

More bizarre evidence was piling up from other pilots. One of the most unusual stories was given by the pilot of a Pan-American DC-3 who said he had to swerve violently to avoid colliding with a "mysterious luminous object" off the coast of Florida.

Speculation abounded about the Bermuda Triangle's alleged connection with extraterrestrials, time warps, Atlantis, mystical rays from the sun, sea monsters, and the supernatural. Some experts suspected undersea earthquakes, tidal waves or magnetic fields might be behind the strange occurrences.

While skeptics point to purely natural causes—human error, mechanical breakdown, Gulf Stream currents, and sudden, violent changes in weather—a growing number of scientists insist that there is probably more to the story than is being told.

Charles Berlitz, who has done more to popularize the Triangle than any other author, puts forward the theory that a giant solar crystal, which once supplied power for the lost continent of Atlantis, lies on the ocean floor. Periodically, he says, passing ships or planes trigger this crystal, which befuddles their instruments and sends them to their doom.

It should be stated that the Bermuda Triangle is one of only two places on Earth where a compass needle points to true rather than magnetic north. The other, called The Devil's Sea, lies in the Pacific, southeast of Japan. Ironically, a group of scientists disappeared while investigating the area in 1955. Nothing has been heard of them since.

Sargasso Sea

Just off the southern tip of the United States lie millions of square miles of weed-choked ocean that for centuries has enflamed the imagination of mariners.

It's the Sargasso Sea, legendary graveyard of ships and men. According to maritime lore, this mysterious, watery realm is the tomb of thousands of unfortunate ocean voyagers who sailed into its fearsome tangles and became trapped forever.

Until recent times, sailors went to great lengths to avoid the cursed "island of the dead." Many familiar with Jules Verne's *Twenty Thousand Leagues Under the Sea* assumed it was inhabited by demons and horrible, long-tentacled monsters.

It was a "darkly tangled" world without wind, wave or storm. Victims who became ensnared in the twisting, treacherous coils of the weed were doomed to drift helplessly upon the unyielding sea for all eternity. Stories circulated at seaport taverns about wayward ships getting caught in the entangling currents, never to be seen or heard from again.

The rotting remains of Chinese junks, Viking warships, Irish curraughs and Spanish galleons were said to float ghost-like upon the still waters, their creaking timbers and the mournful wails of skeletal crews echoing on the night wind.

In July 1884, the *Brittania*, bound for London from Buenos Aires, came across a merchant ship that had apparently been abandoned in the Sargasso. There were a few corpses on board, but most of the crew and passengers were missing.

Nowadays, it is known that the dreaded sea, which covers nearly 3 million square miles between North America and Europe, is actually one of the safest places in the ocean. Warm currents and calm winds prevail over still, glass-smooth waters, and only occasionally does an ocean-going vessel come in contact with the once-feared sargassum weed.

Such was not the case 500 years ago when the man who

discovered America first laid eyes on the mysterious Sargasso Sea. On his maiden voyage to the New World, Christopher Columbus saw what he took to be long strands of seaweed, stretching in every direction as far as the eye could see.

At first the veteran sea captain took heart at the sight, thinking that perhaps his tiny flotilla was nearing land. But his optimism soon turned to terror when he realized just how thick grew the ancient weeds.

More than any other single factor, Columbus' grim account about the perils of the Sargasso Sea helped inspire the terror that would fill the hearts of future generations of seafarers. Fear of the Sargasso and its clutching embrace of death soon became an obsession with sailors and oceangoing travelers everywhere.

The Sargasso is cold and deep, averaging more than three miles in some spots. It is also home to many unusual life forms—including crabs, shrimp, octopus and snakelike eels that migrate here from Europe, the Mediterranean and rivers in the eastern United States each year to mate, spawn and die.

The region got its name from Portuguese explorers who preceded Columbus. They christened it *sargaco*—the Portuguese word for grape—because they thought the thick clusters of seaweed resembled grapes.

The mystery of this haunting region lives on, and despite the testimony of some questionable sources, no evidence exists to suggest that any vessel, ancient or modern, has ever been lost in the Sargasso Sea.

The Lindbergh Tragedy

On the night of March 1, 1932, the infant son of Col. Charles A. Lindbergh was taken from the second-floor nursery of the Lindbergh home in Hopewell, N.J. The kidnapper—or kidnappers—left behind a note saying the 20-month-old Charles

A. Lindbergh Jr. would be returned unharmed in exchange for $50,000.

Eleven days later, despite the Lindbergh's agreement to pay the ransom, a truck driver found the child's badly decomposed body in a shallow grave a few miles from his home. His skull had been shattered.

A 36-year-old German immigrant named Richard Bruno Hauptmann was arrested and convicted of the kidnapping and murder. Four years later, on April 3, 1936, Hauptmann went to the electric chair maintaining his innocence.

Thus ended one of the saddest and most bizarre chapters in American criminal history. The Lindbergh kidnapping, coming so soon after the handsome aviator's celebrated trans-Atlantic flight, sent shock waves around the world.

And while the world mourned, the famous family's tragic loss became the subject of a media feeding frenzy, complete with elaborate hoaxes, confessions and investigations that stained the reputation and careers of many prominent people.

Even today, more than six decades after the ordeal, there are lingering doubts as to Bruno Hauptmann's guilt. Some contend the German hero of World War I might have been set up. Others say the Lindbergh child was not murdered at all, that the body found in the grave was a plant—part of a bizarre scheme hatched by organized crime lord Al Capone to gain freedom from an Atlanta penitentiary.

In 1980, a 52-year-old longshoreman from New York came forward and told police he was the missing Lindbergh heir. Harold Olsen claimed that the body buried in the shallow grave near the Lindbergh home had been put there by operatives working for Capone.

"The body the police found was not that of the Lindbergh baby," Olsen told reporters. "It was badly decomposed, making positive identification a near impossibility. And the whole thing was done very quickly."

The accused kidnapper and killer—Hauptmann—was

"perfectly innocent," Olsen said. "He had nothing to do with the actual killing."

Had police not been in such a hurry to solve the case, Olsen added, they would have noticed numerous physical differences between the real Lindbergh baby and the child found in the grave. For one thing, he said, the dead baby's body was 4 inches too long—"a fact that the police knew but chose to ignore."

Why didn't the grieving parents notice the physical difference?

"Lindy wanted to get the thing over with and to save his wife's sanity," Olsen explained. "He also wanted to shut out Capone's interest."

According to Olsen, the famed Chicago gangster had told Lindbergh that he knew the whereabouts of the missing baby and would organize his release in exchange for freedom. The crime boss was desperate to avoid being sent to Alcatraz, Olsen noted, where he was to serve the remainder of his life sentence.

But "Lindy refused to go along," said Olsen, who described the famous aviator as a "super-patriot and stiff upper lip gentleman of the old school" who so despised the mob that he would rather sacrifice his own son than have Capone released from prison.

But it was still in the interest of the Chicago mob to keep the real Lindbergh child alive, Olsen went on. "As long as they could produce the boy, they didn't have to fear a murder rap. Besides, the mob always plans for the future. The child might be a valuable pawn worth playing at a later date."

A Capone operative arranged for the real Lindbergh baby to be raised by his brother and wife in Connecticut. They changed the child's name and birthdate but could not alter the physical scars and deformities.

Apart from a skull indention over the left eye and deformed toes, a result of rickets, Olsen said that Lindbergh's other son, John, noticed that Olsen had birthmarks that matched those of his brother.

"For what it's now worth, I am the missing Lindbergh baby," Olsen said.

For years following the kidnapping, a number of private investigators stepped forth to cash in on the international hoopla surrounding the case. One such man was Morris Rosner, a former government agent, who declared: "We have established beyond doubt that the baby is alive and will be restored to his parents."

But the cruelest hoax involved John Hughes Curtis, president of the Curtis Boat Building Corporation of Norfolk, Va. Curtis, who claimed to be the "real spokesman" for the kidnap gang, organized a committee of concerned Norfolk citizens to serve as a liaison between Lindbergh and the kidnappers.

Curtis informed Lindbergh that the gang required a "good faith" deposit of $25,000. The money would be held in the hands of the committee until the baby was delivered ësafe and sound, into our hands."

About this time Lindbergh received the baby's sleeping suit—proof that the kidnappers did, in fact, possess the child. As for his part, Curtis was prepared to offer additional evidence that the baby was still alive.

According to Curtis, the boy was being held on a schooner off the coast of Cape May, New Jersey. Lindbergh spent several weary weeks searching the Atlantic waters for his son, but found no trace of the ship supposedly commanded by a "Captain Dynamite."

The discovery of the baby's body resulted in a startling admission by Curtis that he had made the whole story up.

Amid the drama, Violet Sharpe, the maid who had been in charge of the infant at the time he was kidnapped, committed suicide. She had been linked to the kidnapping by sensational newspaper claims that there was an "inside connection."

The affair reached its climax when the short, stocky Bruno Hauptmann, a carpenter by trade, was brought to trial in Flemington, New Jersey. Tens of thousands of spectators shouting "Burn the Dutchman!" surrounded the courthouse, while throngs of curiosity-seekers looking for souvenirs combed the woods where the baby's body was found.

After the trial, the Lindberghs fled to England to escape the notoriety surrounding the case—and to put their lives back together.

The "Wild Boy" of Nuremburg

There was something strange about the sad-eyed boy who limped into the village of Nuremberg, Germany, on the morning of May 26, 1828.

Some people thought he looked wild, like an animal, and stayed clear of him as he made his way slowly through the heart of town, past bread shops and cafes where the aroma of fresh-baked cakes and sausages lingered heavily in the early morning air.

His clothes were old and ragged, and it was clear from the thick calluses on his feet that he was unaccustomed to shoes or boots. He appeared to be about 16 years old—thin, stoop-shouldered and pockmarked. His unwashed hair was long and stringy and full of lice.

He said his name was Kaspar Hauser. But those were all the words he could—or would—utter. He carried no identification, but he did have two unsigned letters in his pocket.

One, dated October 1812 and supposedly written by his mother to someone who was to take care of him, stated that he had been kept isolated from infancy. The second letter was from a "poor laborer" who said the child's name was Kaspar and his father, now dead, had been a cavalry officer.

But Kaspar had no knowledge of his family or where he

came from. When asked by a police officer how he got to town he pointed to his feet, then into the woods.

It was obvious by his manner and smell he had spent a lot of time wandering the forest. A group of concerned citizens took charge of the boy, gave him a bath and food and a place to sleep.

As the days passed, the boy would sit for hours in a corner staring at the wall. He would eat and drink only bread and water. He refused to talk to anyone—except for a kind woman who brought him food and helped him with the bath.

News of the strange boy traveled fast. Newspapers wrote of "the wild boy of Nuremberg" as if Kaspar was half-boy, half-animal. In many ways, it seemed like he had been dropped onto Earth from another world.

The general consensus was that he was some kind of "lost soul of nature...known only to God." One report called him a "child of the forest," perhaps reared by wolves or bears.

When asked about his past, the only thing the boy would say was that he remembered being raised in a dark room so small that he had been unable to stand. He never saw who kept him, he said, never saw a smile or felt the arms of a human being around his neck.

Then one day, he said, he was drugged and taken away. The next thing he knew he was in the woods near Nuremberg. He finally wandered onto a road, which he followed into town where he was found.

It was rumored that Kasper was the illegitimate son of some important person. There was endless speculation as to who that "important" person might be—perhaps some rich noble or famous celebrity, even a member of the royal family.

In the meantime, Kaspar Hauser learned to read, write and draw. But he could never really overcome the dreadful damage done by his years of imprisonment.

Years later, a wealthy Englishman who had befriended Kaspar moved him to the small town of Ansbach, where he again became the center of attention. But here, too, his fame was temporary.

On Dec. 14, 1833, Kaspar Hauser returned from a walk in the park dripping blood. He said a tall man in a black cloak had stabbed him, and he mumbled something about a purse.

In the park, police found a silk purse with an enigmatic note inside, saying the attacker's name was "M.L.O." but not much else. Unfortunately, it had snowed that morning, and the only footprints found at the crime scene were Kaspar's.

The wound proved more serious than first believed. He died three days later. His final words were: "I didn't do it to myself."

When news of his death was published in newspapers, readers angrily demanded a full investigation. But the strange circumstances surrounding Kaspar Hauser's death remains today as mysterious as his own baffling life.

Pied Piper of Hamelin

One of the most popular tourist destinations in northern Germany is the small town of Hamelin, a quaint community of timbered houses, cobblestone squares and Renaissance palaces overlooking the winding Weser River in Lower Saxony.

For centuries its biggest draw has been the so-called Rat-Catcher's House, a brooding, steep-gabled structure in Old Town where the Pied Piper reputedly stayed when he arrived in 1284 to rid the town of rats.

Thanks to the poet Robert Browning and Grimm's Fairy Tales, every schoolchild knows the story—a mysterious young stranger wearing a ragged, multicolored cloak wanders into town one night and, for a fee of 1,000 florins, offers to lure the unwanted pests into the river by playing his pipe. The mayor and town council are only too happy to agree, but refuse to pay up the next day when the rat catcher comes to collect.

"Playing a tune on a flute is not worth 1,000 florins, so get out of Hamelin!" the mayor is said to have shouted.

Enraged, the piper returned the following Sunday while the grownups were at church and began to play a different tune. This time it was the children who ran into the street, charmed by the notes.

They danced away with the piper to nearby Koppelberg Mountain, where an enormous cavern opened and swallowed them. They were never seen again. Until the 19th century, two crosses stood on the mountain to mark the spot where the 130 children were last seen.

Some researchers believe the story of the Pied Piper, immortalized in song and literature by Browning and the brothers' Grimm, might be more than a fairy tale. Rats were a big problem in medieval Europe, just as the legend suggests—and something terrible did happen to the children of Hamelin, a wealthy trade center that traces its origins back to 851 when it was built as a Benedictine Monastery.

Just what that was, no one can say. But for centuries it was commonly believed that the children disappeared into the side of the mountains, just as the old legends allege. Others thought they joined a group of Crusaders marching off to the Holy Land and never returned.

One modern theory holds that they were slaughtered at the battle of Sedemunde, a local feud, in 1260. Yet another seriously considered possibility suggests that the children died of bubonic plague—the Black Death that raged across Europe during the 12th and 13th centuries.

Memories of another sickness may also be buried in the legend. The children in the story are described as dancing away to their deaths. According to some, this might well be a symbolic description of victims of Saint Vitus' dance (chorea), a disorder of the nervous system characterized by irregular, jerking movements.

Music played on a pipe was believed to calm the uncontrollable muscle spasms the victims of the disease endured. It is ironic that, in the story, only two children are left behind—both crippled and unable to keep up with the others.

The legend of the Pied Piper of Hamelin—the Haemelschen Kinder, as the Germans say—is certainly not the first, nor is it the only one of its kind. Remarkably similar tales of pipers who spirit away children figure in folklore of Europe and the Middle East.

In the northern German region of Brandenburg, it was a fiddler who stole children. A bagpiper was the culprit in the Hartz Mountains, while another piper led a group of laughing, dancing children away from Lorch, a village on the Rhine, in the 13th century.

Unlike most of the tales, however, the Hamelin tragedy gives precise dates, names and places.

Were the doomed children lured away by promises of new toys and riches? Some historians suggest that the rat catcher of yore had been actually hired by some foreign sovereign to recruit settlers for new colonies in Eastern Europe. One popular version of the story, for example, has the charmed children walking through a tunnel all the way to Transylvania.

Most recently, Prof. Jurgen Udolph, a linguist from Gottingen, has gathered evidence that he thinks supports the colonization theory. By comparing place names and personal names of different regions, he claims that the youngsters were brought to the regions of Priegnitz and Uckermark, now located in the state of Brandenburg, northeast of Berlin.

Other modern scholars say the children were taken to Moravia, the eastern part of the modern Czech Republic.

The most likely explanation, then, is that the tale of the Pied Piper is a strange amalgam of truth and myth. The original Pied Piper story must have taken on increased significance for the people of Hamelin as more children were lost to the Black Plague, the Crusades, forced colonization or some other cause.

"Not even God can sink this mighty ship"

She was the greatest ship ever built—and supposedly the safest, according to William Pirrie, president of Harland and Wolff, the Belfast firm that constructed the colossal, 11-story luxury liner known to history as the *RMS Titanic*.

A double-bottomed hull and 16 watertight compartments made the floating palace virtually unsinkable, its builders promised.

"Not even God can sink this mighty ship," Pirrie boasted only days before the *Titanic*, crowded with 2,220 passengers— including 325 of the world's richest people—set sail from Southampton, England, to New York City on her maiden voyage.

But shortly before midnight on April 14, 1912, the "Unsinkable Ships of Dreams"—the largest movable object ever made by man—struck an iceberg some 400 miles south of Newfoundland and sank, taking 1,513 passengers and crew with her to the bottom of the freezing sea.

Ever since, experts have been trying to figure out what caused the greatest maritime disaster in world history. All evidence points to human error: the ship was simply traveling too fast in the dark through iceberg-choked waters. At least seven messages had been sent, warning the *Titanic* about the danger of icebergs.

By the time icebergs were spotted, it was too late to take evasive action. The doomed ship slammed side-first into a massive mountain of ice, splitting her open like a tin can and allowing millions of gallons of Atlantic Ocean to come pouring in below deck.

Groaning and heaving, the massive, $7.5 million vessel— nicknamed "The Millionaire's Special"—sank within three hours. Hundreds of passengers and crewmen fortunate to find a lifeboat froze to death awaiting rescue.

Ironically, less than 20 miles away, a would-be rescue ship named the *Californian* was steaming through the dark. Had her radio operator not been asleep—or had the *Titanic* been able to send up proper flares—crewmen on the *Californian* might have been able to rush to her aid.

Only the arrival of the Cunard liner *Carpathia* 1 hour and 20 minutes after the *Titanic* went down prevented further loss of life in the icy waters.

As news of the tragedy swept around the world, legends sprang up around the night's events, those who lived and those who died. Newspaper stories told of heroes and heroines—like Molly Brown—the gallant way in which many gave up places on the limited number of lifeboats so that others could survive.

Stories were also told about how second and third-class steerage passengers crammed below deck drowned like rats because the ship's crew neglected to help them escape.

John Jacob Astor—worth more than $100 million and the richest man on board—supposedly asked permission to go in a lifeboat with his wife. He was told, "No men are allowed in the boats until the women are loaded first." The boat left only two-thirds full.

Another legend—probably false—told how the ship's band kept playing until the ship vanished beneath the waves. One man identified as Ben Guggenheim supposedly exchanged his life belt for a sweater, proclaiming, "If I am to die, I wish to die like a gentleman!"

The memory of that horrible night lives on in the dreams and nightmares of those who survived. One woman—Eva Hart—said: "The sound of people drowning is something I cannot describe to you and neither can anyone else. It is the most dreadful sound, and then there is dreadful silence that follows it."

Watching the ship go down, one male passenger described it as a "surrealistic death glide," while another—Second Officer Lightoller—said: "Slowly she reared up on end until at last she was absolutely perpendicular. Then quite quietly but quicker and quicker, she seemed to slide away...and disappear."

Could the disaster have been avoided? Some investigators say yes—had authorities heeded a flood of paranormal premonitions that surfaced before the tragedy. Acclaimed English director John Black was one of many people who warned about the danger after several dreams in which he saw "a large ship sinking and hundreds of people being drowned."

Ian Stevenson, a well-known professor of parapsychology at the University of Virginia, said the sinking of the *Titanic* was accompanied by more paranormal experiences than any other sea disaster on record. He doesn't know why, but he theorizes that the "shock" of the event itself might have been a contributing factor.

The ghostly remains of the *Titanic*, forever shrouded in drifting clouds of sediment and icy currents, now lies serenely in her watery tomb 4,000 feet below the surface where she vanished almost nine decades ago.

Hindenburg Disaster

A rusty iron weathervane fluttering high above a sea of scrubby weeds and cracked asphalt marks the spot where one of the most famous disasters in aviation history occurred more than six decades ago.

It was here, on the evening of May 6, 1937, that thousands of excited spectators had gathered on a grassy airfield outside Lakehurst Naval Air Station, N.J., to watch the arrival of an airborne legend—the German airship *Hindenburg*.

The monstrous aircraft, built by Germany's Zeppelin Company, was the biggest in the world, more than three football fields long and only a few yards shorter than Cunard's great ocean-liner, the *Queen Mary*. Powered by several massive engines and kept aloft by millions of cubic feet of highly flammable hydrogen, the *Hindenburg* was supposed to be the safest—and most luxurious—airship in the world.

More than 50 passengers were crowded aboard the silver leviathan that afternoon as the huge ship floated slowly into view, plunging the airfield below into deep shadow. Many on the ground could make out the faces of men and women leaning out windows, smiling and waving handkerchiefs.

Two-hundred feet below, they marveled at the giant airship, which boasted a dining room 50 feet long, mirrored lounges, a writing room, bar and a hydrogen-proof smoking room.

The *Hindenburg* was not only luxurious, it was fast. With a range of 11,000 miles and a cruising speed of 84 miles an hour, it had broken a Trans-Atlantic record the previous year.

At precisely 7 p.m., ground crewmen rushed forward to grab mooring lines. Amid the roar of engines and cheering spectators, photographers and reporters shoved through the crowd for a close view of the slowly descending aircraft. Twenty-five minutes later, as cameras clicked and rolled, someone noticed a spark near the tail-fin.

"It looked like a mushroom-shaped flower bursting speedily into bloom," commented one officer on the ground.

The flames spread quickly, devouring the giant red swastika painted on the rear of the plane. Within seconds, the beautiful airship burst into flames and crashed, killing 36 passengers and crew. Miraculously, 61 people aboard the doomed aircraft survived by jumping to the ground.

Broadcaster Herb Morrison was on hand to capture the fiery moment of infamy: "It's burst into flames... It is burning...and is falling on the mooring mast and all the folks we...this is one of the worst catastrophes in the world! Oh, it's four or five hundred feet into the sky, it's a terrific crash, ladies and gentlemen...oh, the humanity and all the passengers!"

Investigators, including the Federal Bureau of Investigation, and the German Gestapo, quickly agreed that hydrogen was the culprit. Hydrogen was the flammable lifting gas used by all the world's airships except those of the United States, the only nation with large natural reserves of helium, a nonflammable gas.

Other people, however, weren't so sure. A few suspected sabotage, stemming from the international crisis brought on by Adolf Hitler's phenomenal rise to power only a few years before.

But, to most people, the *Hindenburg* disaster seemed simple enough: the ship was filled with more than 7 million cubic feet of hydrogen. It also carried a heavy load of diesel fuel, and some kind of ignition converted all that into an inferno.

But a recent study by two American experts has disclosed that hydrogen may not have been the primary cause of the fire.

Addison Bain, former head of NASA's hydrogen program, and former space shuttle contractor Richard G. Van, reached a surprising conclusion: The outer fabric stretched over the *Hindenburg's* frame, and especially the lacquer dope used to smooth and waterproof it, may have been a far more dangerous fire hazard than the hydrogen inside the ship's rubberized internal gas cells.

"In fact," Bain said, "the recipe for airship dope was about as flammable as you can get."

The scientists believe that a static electrical discharge ignited the ship's canvas cover. The skin, Bain said, burned as fast and as violently as one of NASA's rockets, freeing the hydrogen inside to burn.

Files examined at the Zeppelin Archive in Friedrichshafen, Germany, seem to corroborate the American scientists' theory. A note written by an electrical engineer on June 28, 1937, said: "The actual cause of the fire was the extreme flammability of the covering material brought about by discharges of an electrostatic nature."

The moment observers on the ground saw the tongue of flame licking the tail fin, they knew the mighty ship was doomed. As it fell, crashing tail-first onto the field, it splintered, then exploded into a huge fireball. Miraculously, many survived the initial impact to crawl and run screaming from the inferno, some on fire.

Those who witnessed the horrifying spectacle were amazed that more people—on board and on the ground—did not perish.

Curse of the Hope Diamond

Deep within a carefully-guarded vault inside the Smithsonian Institution lies the Hope Diamond, a glittering, heart-shaped stone whose impassive beauty has been linked to madness, despair and the deaths of more than 20 people.

For more than three centuries, kings, paupers, thieves and courtesans have gazed upon the stone's shimmering opulence and been driven to doom.

According to legend, the diamond's ill-fated history began when it was stolen from the forehead of an Indian idol worshiped by followers of Rama Sita. The god supposedly placed a curse on the stone, ensuring that tragedy would befall anyone who owned or wore it.

Its first victim was the Hindu priest who stole it—tortured to death by temple authorities. In 1642, the cursed stole fell into the hands of a French trader-smuggler, Jean Baptiste Tafernier, who made enough money from selling it to buy a title and estate.

Tafernier was later forced to sell his estate and everything he owned to pay his son's gambling debts. The distraught trader then headed back to India to remake his fortune—and was torn to death by a pack of wild dogs.

The gem reappeared in the possession of the French King Louis XIV, who had it cut from its original 112.4 carats down to 67.5 carats. Nicholas Fouquet, a government official who "borrowed" it for a state ball, was convicted in 1665 of embezzlement and imprisoned for the rest of his life.

Ignorant of the curse that they had added to their crown jewels, several more members of the French royal family were to die. The Princess de Lamballe, who wore it regularly, was beaten to death by a mob. The countess de Barry—one of Louis XV's mistresses—supposedly wore the stone shortly before she was executed.

Louis XVI and his queen, Marie Antoinette, who had inherited the glittering heirloom, died on the guillotine. Then, in 1792, while post-revolutionary Paris was still in turmoil, the diamond vanished again—this time for 40 years. The gap left plenty of room for speculation.

A French jeweler, Jacques Celot, is said to have gloated over its beauty—until he went insane and killed himself. A Russian prince, Ivan Kanitovski, gave it to his Parisian mistress, a Folies-Bergere dancer named Mademoiselle Ladrue, then shot her dead, and was later murdered himself.

Even Catherine the Great of Russia is believed to have worn the stone before she died of apoplexy. Later, a Dutch diamond cutter sheared the stone down to its present weight of 44.5 carats. When the cutter's son stole it from him, the cutter committed suicide.

The stone continued to bounce from hand to bloody hand across Europe, finally landing in the hands of Henry Thomas Hope, a wealthy Irish banker who bought it for $150,000 and gave the diamond its modern name. His grandson later died penniless.

In 1901, a jeweler bought the diamond, then went bankrupt. Another jeweler then purchased it, but he is said to have gone mad before killing himself.

The diamond's next owner was a dissolute Russian nobleman who shot his showgirl lover while she was onstage and was reportedly stabbed to death by a group of Russian revolutionaries.

The next owner was a Greek jeweler who fell off a cliff. In 1908, the Turkish sultan Abdul Hammid bought the stone for

$400,000. He gave it to his wife Subaya, then stabbed her. A year later he lost his throne.

The jinxed jewel moved on to the United States where it was bought for $154,000 by business tycoon Edward B. McLean in 1911. Shortly after purchasing the diamond, McLean's mother died. So did two of the servants in the McLean household.

Edward McLean himself seems to have been rather wary of the gem, but wife Evelyn McLean loved it and haughtily dismissed all notion of a curse.

But tragedy continued to stalk the McLean family. The couple's 10-year-old son, Vincent, was struck down by a car and killed. The couple later divorced, then Mr. McLean set sail on the *Titanic*—never to return.

Only American jeweler Harry Winston, who bought the blue stone from the heirs of the McLean family, escaped the rays of doom, perhaps by giving it away to the Smithsonian.

In 1990, socialite Georgette Mosbacher wore the fabulous Hope Diamond to publicize a $1 million gift to the Smithsonian museum where it is frequently displayed. Mrs. Mosbacher was the first person to wear the glittering, walnut-size diamond and its diamond-studded necklace—valued at more than $100 million—publicly since its bequest in 1958 by Winston.

The rare, deep-blue diamond—believed to have been formed deep below the earth's crust a billion years ago—was mined in India more than three centuries ago. Today it is kept in a museum vault behind inch-thick glass, guarded around the clock by police, dogs and sophisticated electronic devices.

In spite of the stone's bloody history, Paul E. Desaultes, retired curator in charge of the National Collection of Gems at the museum, has declared that the curse is nothing more than a "carefully nurtured fairy tale."

Tens of thousands of visitors brave the curse each year to come to the museum and see the legendary stone with their own eyes—proof, say some, of the Hope Diamond's mystical power.

Tunguska Explosion

Early on the morning of June 30, 1908, a mysterious explosion split the dark skies over a remote region of central Siberia.

The blast—centered near Tunguska, about 2,200 miles east of Moscow—could be heard more than 600 miles away, shattering windows and roofs and sparking forest fires that raged for weeks. Seismographs as far away as Washington State picked up the impact.

Investigators say the blast was a thousand times stronger than the atomic bomb dropped over Hiroshima and much more powerful than the Mt. St. Helens eruption in 1980.

Resulting shock waves leveled thousands of acres of trees and wiped out vast herds of reindeer. Farmers and herders asleep in their huts were blown into the air and knocked unconscious.

Because the object apparently exploded in the atmosphere instead of hitting the ground, it left no crater. Directly below the blast, tree branches were stripped, leaving skeletal-like trunks standing straight up. Fanning out beyond three miles, however, trees were blown over like matchsticks, their charred tops pointed away from the blast.

Witnesses in the town of Kirensk and other nearby cities said they saw a "pillar of fire" arcing across the sky moments before the explosion occurred.

"I saw a flying star," one villager reported, "It's tail disappeared into the air." Another said: "A ball of fire came down obliquely. A few minutes later we heard a deafening crash like peals of thunder...followed by eight loud bangs like gunshots."

A second eyewitness told interviewers: "The whole northern part of the sky appeared covered with fire. I felt a great heat, as if my shirt had caught fire. At that moment there was a bang in the sky, and a mighty crash. The crash was followed by a noise like stones falling from the sky, or guns firing..."

Another witness said: "I saw the sky in the north open to the ground and fire poured out. The fire was brighter than the sun. We were terrified, but the sky closed again and immediately afterward, bangs like gunshots were heard."

More than 90 years later, the world still wonders what powerful force struck Siberia that fateful morning, charring vast regions of wilderness and incinerating wildlife for miles around. Was it a meteorite or part of a flaming comet that plowed into the Stony Tunguska River region north of Lake Baikal—or was it something else?

Some investigators have theorized that only an impact with a black hole or mass of anti-matter could have caused damage on such a colossal scale. Serious suggestions have been made that a damaged spaceship might have crashed into Siberia, triggering some kind of nuclear explosion.

American physicists Thomas Ahrens and John O'Keefe think the culprit was an ice-rich comet—in essence, a giant snowball that did the damage. Their comet hypothesis seems reasonable to many researchers, but not all. Leonard Kulik, a Russian astronomer, thinks it was a large meteorite that lighted the skies over Siberia before exploding into fragments that rained down on earth from about 200 miles.

Since no large solid object was found in the ground, nor has an impact crater been located, Dr. Kulik theorized that the meteorite was destroyed upon contact with the atmosphere.

Scientists know that space is filled with huge chunks of rock—asteroid fragments left from the birth of the solar system billions of years ago. These frozen rocks continue to circle the sun in elliptical orbits, but occasionally stray off course and intersect with other heavenly bodies, including Earth.

One such strike occurred in Arizona about 20,000 years ago, leaving the 2-mile-wide "Arizona Meteor Crater." Another giant asteroid is believed to have hit earth around 65 million years, ending the reign of the dinosaurs. As recently as 1972, a 1,000-ton object barely missed the earth on a trajectory that skipped over the Grand Tetons in Wyoming.

The truth is, thousands of tiny rocks from the far reaches of space rain down on earth every day. Most burn up upon striking the atmosphere or fall harmlessly into the sea. Grain-size stones can be seen at night as "shooting stars," but some larger ones have landed on cars and houses.

Some scientists who keep track of such celestial events think it's only a matter of time before a "really big" asteroid scores a direct hit. Such a scenario would be catastrophic, especially should ground zero be a heavily populated area.

A blast with the energy yield of the Siberian explosion—estimated to be the equivalent of 30 megatons of TNT—would have wiped out all of New York City and caused widespread destruction in neighboring Connecticut and New Jersey, according to Dr. Kulik.

"If this meteorite had fallen on Central Belgium, there would have been no living creature left in the whole country," he said. "Had it fallen on London, none left alive south of Manchester or east of Bristol."

In 1993, a scientific team from NASA and the University of Wisconsin claimed that a stony asteroid less than 100 feet in diameter caused the Siberian explosion.

"Imagine what would happen if one of these roving monsters decided to drop in during rush hour," one scientist quipped. "It would be like Sodom and Gomorrah. A whole lot of fire and brimstone and nowhere to hide."

Bavaria's "Mad" King

Whenever Ludwig felt particularly melancholy, he'd hop onto a horse and ride out into the woods encircling his fairy-tale castle in Bavaria. Alone in the drifting mists and dark forest, he'd pretend he lived in another world—the mytho-logical world of Tannhauser, Parzival, the Swan Knights and other romantic legends of old.

But Bavaria's tortured young monarch—the moody, wildly eccentric Swan King—was too busy to withdraw permanently into illusion and fantasy. As long as there were more castles to build, more Germanic operas and art projects to underwrite, he had to remain alive and alert, ever tuned to the artistic desires and needs of his talented and temperamental friend, composer Richard Wagner.

Ignoring wars and the palace intrigue raging all around him, King Ludwig dedicated his life and royal treasury to building more castles—Neuschwanstein, Herrenchiemsee and Linderhof, among others. Each of these glittering, dreamlike creations represented a world that for others existed only in history books, mixing the Teutonic, Byzantine, French, Bavarian baroque and Oriental styles of architectures.

Then one day they came for him—commissioners empowered by the Bavarian government—to take away his throne, to put an end to the wild fantasies that had almost bankrupted the realm. That morning, June 12, 1886, they declared the 41-year-old king to be legally insane and sent him away to a lakeside retreat near Munich.

Three days later they found his body floating in the cold waters of Lake Starnburg. The Swan King was dead, along with the psychiatrist who had authorized his removal.

Today, more than a century later, the death of Bavaria's "Mad King" remains one of Germany's greatest unsolved mysteries. Some 5,000 books, plays, films, poems and newspaper and magazine articles have sought to shed light on the deposed monarch's tragic fate.

Was he murdered? Did he kill himself in a fit of rage? Or—as some scholars allege—was the king thrown into the lake by a jilted homosexual lover?

"The truth is, nobody knows for sure," according to Dietrick Schmidt, a lawyer from Fussen, a picturesque village in the Alps nestled in the shadow of Neuschwanstein. "Some old wags like to argue that he never died but was locked up in a dungeon somewhere for safekeeping, or perhaps as punishment—nobody seems to know which."

Most historians insist Ludwig committed suicide, but a growing number of scholars figure he was murdered, a victim of palace intrigue.

"Ludwig's lavish spending habits and bizarre lifestyle made him lots of enemies, both in and out of the government," said German historian Jurgen Braunberg. "There were a number of people who realized he was spending the government into bankruptcy and would have paid good money to take him out."

Part of that resentment stemmed from King Ludwig's insatiable taste for huge, expensive castles such as Neuschwanstein, a soaring, 80-room castle complete with pinnacles, towers and wooden drawbridge. Walt Disney was so taken with the edifice that he used it as the model for the castle of the Magic Kingdom at Disneyland.

King Ludwig was only 18 when he ascended to the Bavarian throne in 1864. A patron of music, he became intimately acquainted with Richard Wagner, the great operatic composer whose creativity and extravagant lifestyle were largely underwritten by the king.

King Ludwig is not known to have had any romantic relationships with women—a fact that gave rise to rumors of homosexuality. Soon after taking the throne, however, he became engaged to his cousin, Sophie, an Austrian princess, but did not go through with the wedding.

As the years passed, King Ludwig withdrew into melancholy solitude, sleeping during the day and spending his nights listening to private recitations of Schiller's poetry or Wagner's titanic operas about Germanic gods and heroes.

He frequently took moonlight rides through the snow-covered forests surrounding his lonely estate in a sleigh decorated with gilded cherubs.

Ludwig's wildly eccentric behavior probably stemmed from an abusive childhood, say some historians. The oldest son of King Maximilian II (1811-1864) of Bavaria and Marie of Prussia (1825-1889), the Crown Prince was raised in a militaristic tradition that ruthlessly suppressed artistic impulses.

To escape the beatings and regimentation, he daydreamed and fantasized about the old Germanic legends. As a young child, he suffered hallucinations and frequently heard imaginary voices as he built castles with toy blocks.

The voices and the fantasies continued as he grew into manhood and ascended to the throne upon his father's death on March 10, 1864. Because of his youth and lack of experience, many Bavarian politicians expected Ludwig to be pliable and easily impressed. Instead, the proud young monarch ruled as he saw fit, neglecting the despised military and pompously issuing bewildering proclamations and orders.

"There was something dark in him," noted Minister of Justice Eduard von Bomhard. "He was mentally gifted in the highest degree, but the contents of his mind were stored in a totally disordered fashion."

Was the king mad? Some say yes, others no—especially his common subjects and modern admirers who continue to honor him each year with festivals and pageants and Oktoberfest— Germany's most popular celebration.

"The king was no madman, only an eccentric living in a world of dreams," said Austria's Empress Elizabeth.

Some speculate that he was murdered because he planned to challenge his removal from power. Others say he committed suicide after killing his alleged lover—the same psychiatrist who had declared him insane.

"The murder and suicide explanation seems the correct one," said historian Ernest Newman. "But it surely proves not the king's madness but his complete sanity. He knew that, for him, life was over," since he had been betrayed, declared mad and imprisoned.

The Money Pit

For more than 200 years, visitors to a small, windswept island off Nova Scotia have searched for a treasure said to be worth millions.

Some say the loot is buried in a water-filled pit dug by the notorious pirate Captain William Kidd. Others suggest it might have belonged to the Vikings or some other group of pre-Columbian explorers—perhaps even Egyptians or survivors from the lost continent of Atlantis.

One theory holds that the fabled treasure was once the property of Spanish conquistadors who had stolen it from the civilizations of Central and South America.

Another suggests that agents working for the king of England buried the fortune then sailed away and forgot about it.

Whatever its origins, the quest to find the lost treasure has cost numerous lives and vast personal fortunes.

The hunt began in 1765 when a 16-year-old boy paddled over from the little Nova Scotian town of Chester to set game traps on uninhabited Oak Island, a small, peanut-shaped isle in Mahone Bay. In a clearing at one end of the island, he found an old ship's tackle block dangling over a curious clay chamber about 12 feet wide.

Undeterred by tales of hauntings and fired by legends of pirate treasure, young Daniel McGinnis recruited two friends—Anthony Vaughn and John Smith—to help him dig up the loot. After months of backbreaking work, all they found was a 13-foot-wide circular shaft dug through flinty clay, with thick oak platforms at 10, 20 and 300 feet.

The dispirited boys soon abandoned their project—but never forgot about the treasure.

In 1804, they told Simeon Lynds, a wealthy Nova Scotia doctor, about their discovery on Oak Island. Dr. Lynds, who was familiar with old legends about buried pirate loot, quickly formed the first treasure company. Within days, teams of workers armed with shovels and pickaxes descended on the island.

The diggers, led by Daniel McGinnis and his two friends, eventually broke through eight oak platforms, three of which were sealed with ship's putty and coconut fiber. Below that, much to Dr. Lynds' dismay, lay 60 feet of water.

Weeks of bailing with buckets and crude pumps failed to lower the level. The next year, Dr. Lynds' crew sank another shaft, close to and parallel with the pit, and at 100 feet they started burrowing toward the "treasure."

They had to scramble for their lives, however, when water suddenly burst into their shaft and filled it to the same level as the water in the pit. The quest left Simeon Lynds practically penniless.

In 1861 a new organization came to the island and began an ambitious bailing project to drain the pit. Steam pumps were used to assist with the work until a boiler burst and scalded one worker to death. Rumors spread quickly that the Money Pit was protected by a long-dead pirate's curse.

Work resumed a decade later, but the treasure remained as elusive as ever. Splinters of wood brought to service by auger bits hinted that loot-filled chests or casks lurked below. Spirits soared when workers hauled up a torn piece of parchment with the letters "v" and "i" on them.

In 1955 a group of wealthy oil-men from Texas began work on the island. They sank several holes into the area and found what they thought was an enormous cavern at 180 feet. Frantic excavation attempts were unsuccessful because the chamber kept flooding—more proof, argued some, that the spirits guarding the island would never allow the treasure to be disturbed.

Ten years later, the Money Pit claimed four more lives, including a famous Canadian stunt driver named Robert Restall. Restall and three co-workers were apparently overcome by gaseous fumes while working in a nearby access pit, fell into the water and drowned.

New hunters came and went, almost on a yearly basis,

sometimes spending huge sums in their quest to conquer the Money Pit. Cranes and bulldozers and other heavy equipment was brought over to expedite the search. In 1965 American geologist Bob Dunfield built a causeway connecting the island to the mainland.

Despite decades of rumor and speculation, the curious Oak Island hole remains as much a mystery today as it did more than two centuries ago when young Daniel McGinnis paddled over to investigate. While some people still believe in the treasure, others suspect it might be a hoax, perpetrated by generations of writers and treasure-hunters trying to raise investment capital.

Rupert Furneaux, author of *The Money Pit Mystery*, has advanced the most plausible theory. Considering the state of the block and rope discovered in 1795, the pit could not have been dug much earlier than 1780, placing the operation in the middle of the Revolutionary War.

In 1778, the British garrison in New York was threatened by Washington's army, and capitulation loomed. The governor held the pay chests of all British forces in America, and it seems likely that, anxious for their safety, he ordered a detachment of Royal Engineers stationed in Halifax, Nova Scotia, to conceal the loot.

Furneaux argues that only a treasure of immense value, such as the pay chests, would call for so complex a hiding place as the Money Pit. And the only group in the area with enough expertise was the British Royal Engineers.

There is no record of the British army losing any great sums of money at the time—a scandal that would have led to the court martial of the general concerned. This may mean that, when the danger was past, the chests were recovered and the Money Pit is, in fact, empty.

Another theory advanced by author William Crooker suggests that British forces under King George III built the Money Pit to dump gold they had captured from Spanish-occupied Havana, Cuba, in the summer of 1762.

Until a thorough geological and archaeological survey is undertaken, it seems certain that the secrets buried within the bloodstained Money Pit on Oak Island's will forever remain a mystery.

Nostradamus

In an age when soothsayers and witches were routinely burned at the stake, it is somewhat amazing that a figure with the reputation of Michel de Nostradame survived to become one of the most famous—and beloved—men in all of Europe.

Part prophet and part witch doctor, the French-born scholar credited with saving thousands of lives during outbreaks of bubonic plague during the 16th century achieved almost saint-like status among the masses and went on to become a close consort to queens and kings throughout Europe.

Some saw his uncanny ability to heal and foretell future events as the work of the devil. Others, however, regarded his strange powers as a special gift and sought to take advantage of it.

Nostradame—or Nostradamus, as he was better known—did not start out on such a favorable footing. Born in St. Remy, France, on Dec.14, 1503, he encountered considerable prejudice early on because of his Jewish ancestry. At Avignon he learned philosophy, classical literature, history, medicine, and grammar. His special interests were herbal and folk medicine and astrology—then generally regarded as a legitimate science.

He also published almanacs, which were popular items in 16th century Europe. Nostradamus's almanacs became best-sellers, filled with the usual predictions about weather and crop conditions, but also containing "secret" prophecies that made them wildly popular throughout France and much of Europe.

When the plague struck France in the early 16th century,

he stopped publishing almanacs and went to work treating patients by administering his special concoction—"Rose Pills," which consisted of ground rose petals, sawdust, iris, cloves, calamus and lignaloes. He refused to "bleed" his patients, the customary treatment for everything from minor colds to the Black Death.

In 1537, plague struck the city of Agen where the famed physician, poet, philosopher and publisher lived with his wife and two children. Although he managed to save hundreds of lives, his own family perished in the epidemic. Devastated, the great healer spent the next six years wandering Europe, questioning his abilities and the meaning of life.

It was during this period of "dark torment" that Nostradamus became aware of another special gift— the power of prophecy. Retreating to his study in the dead of night, he would consult magic mirrors, divining rods, a brass bowl and other "magical instruments" to conjure up visions of future events.

In 1550, he published his first almanac of prophecies. *The "Prophecies,"* written in a curious blend of French, Greek, Latin and Italian, made Nostradamus a household name in Europe. Nearly a thousand prophetic verses were written, each containing four lines, or quatrains. These were arranged in 10 books, called *Centuries.*

The *Centuries* contain prophecies covering nearly the next 2,250 years, until the year 3797.

Nostradamus did not reveal how he arrived at his prophecies. The best guess is that he wrote primarily by inspiration— that is, he wrote down whatever verses came to him while working alone in his study late at night.

Like most prophetic writing, Nostradamus's *Centuries* are couched in obscure, archaic, almost unfathomable riddles, puns, anagrams and epigrams.

His most famous early prophecy, contained in stanza 35 of *Century 1*, apparently concerned King Henry II, though the king's name is never stated.

"The Young lion will overcome the old one
On the field of battle in a single combat;
He will put out his eyes in a cage of gold:
Two fleets one, then to die a cruel death."

On July 1, 559, English King Henry was riding in a tournament against young Gabriel de Lorges, Comte de Montgomery, Captain of the Scottish Guard. The lances of the two riders met and splintered. Montgomery dropped his shaft a second too late and the jagged point pierced the king's gleaming gold visor and entered his left eye, killing him.

Other quatrains predicted the coming of three antichrists. Some scholars have detected references to Napoleon, Hitler and a third "harmful world leader" not yet identified. The verse also has been said to refer to the overthrow of the Shah of Iran and the rise of Saddam Hussein of Iraq.

Some contemporaries saw Nostradamus's prophecies as a curse and burned him in effigy. The Catholic Church also took a dim view of the prophecies—especially when they turned out to be bad—and threatened to burn him.

But one of the prophet's most powerful fans was Queen Catherine de Medici, who not only protected him from enemies but also required regular forecasts of her children's future. Nostradamus was said to have conjured up an angel who showed Catherine a bright and promising future for her children by looking in a mirror.

The prophet fell ill in mid-1556. On July 1, he told friends gathered at his bedside: "You will not find me alive at sunrise."

True to form, he died that night. In his will, Nostradamus expressed the curious wish to be buried standing upright, supposedly so that "boorish" people would not step on his body.

His body was placed within the walls of the Church of the Cordeliers of Salon. The Latin inscription on his tomb reads: "Here rest the bones of the illustrious Michel Nostradamus, alone of all mortals, judged worthy to record with his near divine pen, under the influence of the stars, the future events of the entire world..."

Death of the Wunderkind

He was the *wunderkind* of his age, a brilliant, brooding child genius whose dazzling symphonic and operatic compositions made him an international star long before he was old enough to shave.

Yet when Wolfgang Amadeus Mozart died shortly before Christmas in 1791 at the age of 35, the musical master of the Classical Era—the child prodigy who had composed his first symphony at age 4—was unceremoniously dumped into an unmarked pauper's grave and buried.

For years after his death, rumors swirled through the old capitals of Europe that Mozart had been murdered. Rumors had been fed by the ravings of Antonio Salieri, a mediocre rival who actually claimed to have poisoned the mighty musician himself.

Salieri's claims were generally dismissed as the "wild musing" of a deranged competitor who sought fame by associating his name with the masterful Mozart.

Another theory held that Mozart was assassinated by a conspiracy of Freemasons, even though the young Austrian's own doctors diagnosed the cause of death as a "heated military fever"—quaint 18th century jargon for "beats us."

The truth is, other doctors who examined Mozart's corpse were never quite sure what he died of. Some suspected he had succumbed to tuberculosis, rheumatoid arthritis or streptococcal infection. A common theory today is that he died of uremia following chronic kidney disease.

A more recent suggestion is that the boy wonder probably died of chronic subdural hematoma—a slow leakage of venous blood into the space between the skull and the brain. Miles Drake, a neurologist at Ohio State University who has studied Mozart's skull for clues, theorizes that a crack in the left temple indicates the musician probably fell and hit his head—perhaps while in a drunken stupor.

Mozart drank heavily during the last months of his life, presumably out of frustration at his inability to gain a desirable post and despondent over his poverty.

"In all likelihood, such an injury would have torn veins leading from the surface of the brain, allowing blood to leak into the subdural space, which lies between the dura mater (the brain's protective membrane) and the skull," Dr. Drake said. As the blood accumulated and dried, it would have put increasing pressure on Mozart's left hemisphere. That would have made him subject to the mood swings and depression that characterized the composer's final days.

Dr. Drake said the injury could also have impaired the faculties controlled by the left hemisphere, including his ability to coordinate movements of the right side of his body—and to compose music.

There is no evidence, however, that Mozart's musical abilities were impaired toward the end of his life. On the contrary, it was in 1791 that he wrote one of his greatest operas, *The Magic Flute*. The unfinished work for which he is equally famous, *Requiem*, was actually composed on his deathbed.

Chronic depression, "black thoughts," and headaches figure prominently in Mozart's 1790 letters to Michael Puchberg, a wealthy merchant whom he repeatedly begged for loans. Death was a common theme in his thoughts and letters.

"I thank my God for graciously granting me the opportunity...of learning that death is the key which unlocks the doors to our true happiness," he once wrote. On another occasion, he wrote: "I have formed during the last few years such close relations with this best and truest friend of mankind (death) that his image is not only no longer terrifying to me, but is indeed, very soothing and consoling."

Morbid mutterings like these led some attending physicians to suspect the young musician was suffering from a "deposit on the brain."

"In 18th century neurological terms," said Dr. Drake, "that could have been anything from a brain abscess to a stroke to a brain tumor or a chronic subdural hematoma."

Yet the old rumors that he was murdered would not go away, even though no evidence has been found to support such views. After his death, other myths flourished as well, including gossip about the relationship between his wife, Constanze, and his best friend, Franz Sussmayer. Some musical historians have suggested that Sussmayer, who inherited the task of completing *Requiem* following Mozart's death, might have actually been the real father of Franz Xaver Wolfgang, the son who inherited Mozart's musical inclinations.

One cold November morning Mozart was found slumped unconscious at his desk. He spent the last two weeks of his life in bed, struggling in vain to complete *Requiem*. Shortly past midnight on Dec. 5, 1791, the master of symphonies and author of more than 600 musical masterpieces drew his last breath.

Amid a howling rainstorm, the disease-wracked body of the greatest musician in the history of the world was quietly laid to rest in a common grave because he was unable to afford a proper Christian burial.

Spear of Destiny

Once a week, the huge double doors of Vienna's Hofburg Museum would open and a pale, shabbily dressed young man would step through and head straight for a special exhibit featuring the treasures of the House of Hapsburg.

There, transfixed by the glittering crowns and other jeweled displays behind the glass cases, he would often stand for hours, not moving or speaking until ushered away at closing time.

Of special interest to the young visitor was one particular object, the remains of a spear, dull and black with age.

According to legend, the spear point was none other than the one used by a Roman centurion named Longinus to kill Jesus as he hung on the cross. For his bloody sin, Longinus was cursed to walk the Earth forever—or at least until the time of the Apocalypse.

The year was 1909. The visitor was a struggling young Austrian artist named Adolf Hitler. For the next three decades, until his death in 1945, the fanatical leader of Germany's Third Reich sought to possess the famous spear, not so much for its historical and religious value, but because of its purported mystical properties.

Tradition held that the owner of the Spear of Longinus—also called the Spear of Destiny, the Spear of Hofsburg, the Spear of the Holy Grail and occasionally the Spear of Christ—would possess the power to conquer the world. But the relic also carried a terrible curse—whoever controlled the relic and then lost it, would suffer defeat and death.

Some said Alaric carried the holy lance when he sacked Rome. King Heinrich of Saxony had it in his possession when he defeated the Magyars. Pope John XII is thought to have used it to christen Heinrich's son Otto the Great as Holy Roman Emperor. Otto later used the spear when he defeated the Mongolian Hordes in the Battle of Leck.

Constantine the Great claimed that he was guided by divine providence via the spear in his victory at Milvian Bridge, which established Christianity as the official religion of the Holy Roman Empire. Charlemagne later acquired the spear, then Charles Martel, Frederick Barbarossa and a long list of other great generals, emperors and statesmen who profited politically and militarily.

Some lost the lance and paid the price—Charlemagne died after accidentally dropping it; Barbarossa drowned while crossing a river after letting the lance slip from his hands into the water. Even Napoleon sought the lance, but failed in his attempt to acquire the relic when enemies beat him to it following the battle of Austerlitz.

The spear finally wound up in the possession of the House of the Hapsburgs, and by the early 1900s was part of the collection stored in Hofburg Museum. It was there that Hitler, a young painter living in Vienna, learned about the lance and its mystical reputation.

Dr. Walter Stein, who accompanied Hitler on one visit, said: "When we first stood side by side in front of the Spear of Destiny, it appeared to me that Hitler was in so deep a condition of trance that he was suffering almost complete sense-denudation and a total lack of self-consciousness."

Later, Hitler reportedly said: "I stood there quietly gazing upon it for several minutes, quite oblivious to the scene around me. It seemed to carry some hidden inner meaning which evaded me, a meaning which I felt inwardly I knew, yet could not bring to consciousness. I felt as though I myself had held it before in some earlier century of history. That I myself had once claimed it as my talisman of power and held the destiny of the world in my hands."

Some historians say that Hitler saw the lance as his "mystical connection with generations of conquering Germanic leaders that had come before him."

Soon after rising to power as chancellor of Germany, Hitler moved quickly to annex Austria into his Third Reich. One of his first actions was to claim his "Spear of Destiny" from the Hofburg Museum.

On October 13, 1938, the lance was loaded onto an armored train and sent to Nuremberg, heart of the Nazi movement. There he kept it in a vault at St. Catherine's Church throughout most of the war. To protect it from Allied bombing raids, Hitler had the mystical relic moved to a specially-constructed vault beneath Nuremberg Castle.

Finally, on April 30, 1945, U.S. troops who had fought their way into Nuremberg in the face of fierce resistance entered the vault and came upon the spear. Completely unaware that his treasured artifact had fallen into enemy hands, Hitler committed suicide in his Berlin bunker—just 80 minutes after Lt. Walter William Horn had seized the spear in the name of the United States of America.

Some historians saw Hitler's obsession with the spear as proof that Nazism was more than just a political system aimed at world conquest.

"Nazism," wrote Jean-Michel Angebert, a French historian and author of *The Occult and the Third Reich*, was "only the most recent outcropping of a militant neo-paganism locked in a death struggle with its arch enemy, traditional Christianity, a struggle which will go on to the end of time."

Hitler's own words, uttered in 1944, hinted at the darker side of Nazism: "He who has seen in National Socialism only a political movement has seen nothing."

Today the spear is back in Hofburg Museum, an ancient relic with a notorious past. The shaft is long gone, but the spearhead—held together by gold, silver and bronze thread and containing a nail from the crucifix—remains a favorite attraction, drawing thousands of visitors from around the world each year.

Bizarre Notions

Snowball Earth

Millions of years ago, the Earth was a giant snowball—a barren blob of dirty gray ice and rock floating lifelessly through the primordial void. Then one day the ice began to melt—slowly at first, then faster and faster as temperatures rose and mile-deep glaciers dripped northward.

Then it happened again—another thick blanket of ice moved down from the north, wrapping the frigid planet in a crusty mantle of glaring white ice. As before, the ice finally began to melt, and warmer temperatures returned.

According to scientists, this freeze-thaw process repeated itself many times over the long history of Earth. And while all that was going on, budding young life forms came and went, struggling to survive the dramatic changes taking place on the young planet.

Nobody knows what caused the Earth to freeze, what brought the huge sheets of ice marching down from the harsh northern realms to blanket the globe in a ghastly white pall. Nor does anybody know what caused the glaciers to finally reverse themselves, unleashing the sudden thaw that led to the evolution of complex organisms.

It now seems that the first of these freeze-thaw cycles started about 2.2 billion years ago when gargantuan glacial movements covered the Northern Hemisphere as far south as Panama and Costa Rica. The only forms of life on the planet then—simple, single-celled microbes—probably survived by burrowing underground or under the sea and adapting to chemosynthesis, rather than photosynthesis.

But an even greater catastrophe struck the Earth between 600 and 800 million years ago. This time "monster" sheets of ice reached as far south as the tropics—in essence, covering the entire globe—freezing and suffocating the planet's budding life forms.

Once again, "Snowball Earth" was saved by a dramatic

warming trend. Glaciers melted. Rivers flowed wild. Rising temperatures and the abundance of water led to the rapid development of new species around the planet.

Chemical and isotopic analysis of rocks laid down in parts of Africa shows that the Earth went through at least four deep ice ages, each lasting millions of years. As more ice formed, the colder the Earth got. The dropping temperatures and icy glare reflected the sun's heat back into space, causing the planet to get even colder.

One of the biggest mysteries in science is: What caused each of these ancient ice ages to end? As glaciers grew bigger and thicker, why didn't temperatures continue to fall, transforming the earth into a permanent snowball?

Some scientists theorize that a sudden rise in the amount of carbon dioxide in the atmosphere—perhaps belched up from volcanoes—created a temporary greenhouse effect that led to a rapid rising of temperatures and the bloom of new species. Sea-dwelling snails and worms may have hastened this process along by stirring up carbon-rich sediments in the ocean.

Another theory is that "overturning" ocean currents released large amounts of carbon dioxide trapped on the ocean floor. According to Dr. Alan J. Kaufman, a geophysicist at Harvard University, this process would have warmed the planet significantly.

What would cause the water to "turn over" and liberate carbon dioxide from the depths of the ocean?

"Mid-ocean ridges are continually emitting gas," said Dr. Joseph L. Kirschvink, another Harvard researcher. "At some point the buildup of gases might have become unstable, and like champagne surging from a bottle, this could have created an explosive upsurge of water that would have fractured the ice above and released carbon dioxide into the atmosphere."

This scenario suggests that carbon dioxide spewing into the air trapped heat from the sun and contributed to the planet's steady warming trend.

While this theory remains controversial, most climatologists agree that, one way or another, carbon dioxide probably holds the key to the mystery of ancient glaciations—as well as to the evolution of life itself.

In the words of Harvard University Professor Paul F. Hoffman, "This was the start of the biggest explosion of animal diversity in the history of life."

Cosmic Invaders

About 65 million years ago, a huge extraterrestrial object slammed into the earth, kicking up a global cloud of dust and debris that cloaked the world in darkness and wiped out many life forms, including dinosaurs.

Could it happen again?

Such a doomsday scenario seemed unthinkable—the stuff of science fiction. Now comes alarming new evidence that death-dealing asteroids and killer comets have been frequent visitors to earth—and that a catastrophe similar to the one that annihilated the dinosaurs could happen again.

Scientists who specialize in the study of asteroids say the risk of death from a cosmic strike is greater than being killed in a plane crash.

"The risk is real," admitted David Morrison, a top researcher for the National Aeronautics and Space Administration who recently co-chaired a team of government experts investigating the peril.

A report issued by the team warned that the greatest hazard posed by an asteroid strike "derives from the global veil of dust injected into the stratosphere. An impact would lead to world-wide crop failures and consequent mass mortality, and would threaten the survival of civilization."

For ages, people gazing at the night sky have been fascinated, bewildered and—at times—frightened by sudden streaks of bright light. Comets, fireballs and other cosmic phenomena were usually seen as divine omens or attributed to supernatural forces. Whole civilizations sometimes rose or fell based on their interpretations of celestial fireworks.

But, as Dr. Morrison and other scientists have shown, the reality seems far stranger and more terrifying than ancient stargazers could possibly have imagined.

Using sophisticated land-based sensors and orbiting satellites, researchers have discovered that colossal space rocks streaking through the cosmos bear down on Earth far more frequently than previously thought. Impacts rarely occur because they detonate upon entering the atmosphere.

Should one of these monster intruders get through, however, it could be devastating.

"Such a strike could radically alter life on Earth as we know it," said one astronomer at the Los Alamos National Laboratory in New Mexico.

Until recently, it was believed that rocky objects anywhere from a few feet in diameter to 90 or so feet wide strike seven or eight times a year. New evidence indicates that bombardment occurs more often, perhaps 12 to 15 times annually.

These blasts light the sky with brilliant fireballs but are rarely seen because they often occur over the sea or uninhabited land.

Dr. Douglas O. ReVelle, a meteorologist at Los Alamos, said "At a minimum, these cosmic intruders produce blasts as big as a nuclear warhead of one kiloton, equal to 1,000 tons of high explosive."

In 1908, for example, a speeding object exploded over Siberia with a force of some 20 hydrogen bombs. The resulting shock wave flattened hundreds of square miles of forest and reverberated around the world. A similar impact is thought to have occurred in Arizona about 20,000 years ago.

In the 1980s, a team of astronomers proposed that the planet faces great danger from these giant cosmic intruders. Secret data released by the military after the end of the Cold War seemed to confirm those fears.

In 1993 and 1994, for example, once-secret information showed that Earth had sustained 136 explosions high in the atmosphere from 1975 to 1992, an average of eight a year. The blasts were calculated to have intensities roughly equal to 500 to 15,000 tons of high explosives, or the power of small atomic warheads.

Today, Los Alamos monitors dangerous cosmic activity. Findings reveal that Earth is bombarded, on average, by 10 or 11 objects that are 6 or 7 feet wide and produce explosions equal to 1-kiloton nuclear blasts.

In addition, they report, at least one fairly large extraterrestrial object about 20 feet wide roars into the atmosphere each year, setting off a blast equal to a 15-kiloton explosion.

Such an impact, of course, could have a devastating effect on the Earth. To help guard against such a calamity, the nations of the world are trying to band together in an effort to build a defense system that would include early warning monitors as well as a nuclear shield.

In the early 1990s, disaster was narrowly averted when an asteroid traveling at 46,000 miles per hour and measuring more than half a mile in diameter passed within 500,000 miles of Earth—about twice the distance to the moon.

"On the cosmic scale of things, that was a close call," said Henry Holt, the retired U.S. Geological Survey scientist who detected the asteroid.

Had the asteroid struck, Dr. Holt said it would have been enough to destroy a good-size country.

But had it hit the ocean, "It would have created tidal waves that would have washed over vast areas of coastal regions," explained Bevan French, a scientist in NASA's solar system exploration division. "It would have been a very major catastrophe for which we have had no experience."

Sooner or later, warn astronomers, another major asteroid will collide with the Earth. When that occurs, a cataclysm never before witnessed by humans will occur.

Some fear it could be the end of the world.

The Demon Cloud

Something horrible happened on the morning of Aug. 16, 1984, near Lake Nyos in the African nation of Cameroon. According to witnesses, a "demon cloud" rose from the dark waters and "sucked out the souls" of more than 1,000 villagers on their way to work.

Survivors say it came at dawn and struck without warning.

"There was nowhere for anyone to hide, nowhere for anyone to run," one terrified witness told an American newspaper reporter. The "demon cloud engulfed them all and sucked out their spirits."

Witch doctors believe an ancient spirit came from the lake to punish wrongdoers. They say the spirit appeared as a lethal mist, rising more than 500 feet into the air.

Government officials suspected terrorism was behind the deaths. It was a time of political unrest, and armed bands of guerillas roamed the backcountry creating havoc.

But scientists insist that the spirit was a lethal cloud of carbon dioxide gas belched up from the bottom of the lake.

Dr. David M. Raup, a former professor of paleontology at the University of Chicago, said the carbon dioxide theory offers the only plausible explanation for the catastrophe.

"It's a good thing that someone has brought up this possibility," he told *The New York Times*. "I think we're on the right track."

Periodic eruptions of carbon dioxide gas have been common in the Earth's long geologic past. In fact, say some researchers, the Lake Nyos tragedy is very similar to one that happened some 250 million years ago, when about 90 percent of the planet's animal species were wiped out.

That mass extinction, which came at the end of the Permian period, is thought to have been caused by a tremendous volcanic eruption in Siberia that spewed huge amounts of dust and carbon dioxide into the air. Known as the Siberian

Traps eruption, that event helped reshuffle Earth's genetic deck, making way for the rise of dinosaurs in the subsequent Mesozoic era.

Although carbon dioxide is a normal respiration product of animal metabolism, too much of this compound is dangerous. Dissolved in blood, carbon dioxide forms carbonic acid, which acidifies the blood. Too much causes acidosis, which can kill animals, especially maritime organisms with low metabolic rates.

Few scientists suggest that carbon dioxide released into the air could have reached levels high enough to kill land animals. But air unusually rich in carbon dioxide could produce a heightened greenhouse effect, trapping energy from sunlight and raising global temperatures, which would be dangerous to some animals and destroy habitats needed by others.

Dr. Richard Bambach, a geologist at Virginia Polytechnic Institute and State University in Blacksburg, Va., believes that the Permian mass extinction could have been touched off by the impact of an asteroid such as the one believed to have wiped out the dinosaurs 65 million years ago.

Although the conditions that may have made the Permian seas a killer probably do not exist in modern oceans, certain inland lakes with high levels of carbon dioxide dissolved in deep water pose threats to nearby people and animals.

"It's still a theory, but a very acceptable one at the moment," noted Dr. William C. Evans of the United States Geological Survey.

Chemical surveys at Lake Nyos showed that the content of the water was 96 percent carbon dioxide—an unusual discovery, since decaying organic matter usually causes an equal mixture of carbon dioxide and methane. The study further revealed that the mixture appeared to be volcanic in origin.

The leader of the team of investigators—Haraldur Sigurdsson of the University of Rhode Island—thought he had located the culprit at the bottom of Lake Monoun—a smoldering volcano. In Dr. Sigurdsson's mind, the volcano had perhaps belched a deadly cloud of carbon dioxide that asphyxiated the villagers.

But the results of more tests didn't jibe with his theory. For one thing, there was no detectable sulfur, and the chlorine and fluorine content was low.

"If we'd had a burst of hot volcanic gases," the Icelandic scientist noted, "these should have been high."

Where had the carbon dioxide come from? Sigurdsson reasoned that rather than giving off a sudden, enormous burp, the volcano had been quietly exhaling carbon dioxide into the crater for many years, perhaps centuries.

Because of the increased pressure at that depth, the water can hold much more gas than usual. The bottom layer of the lake had become supersaturated with the deadly mixture.

Sigurdsson suspects that, just before midnight on Aug. 15, an earthquake triggered a landslide that caused Monoun's waters to turn over and allowed the pressurized water to escape.

"The result of the runaway pressure decrease was powerful enough to cause a 15-foot wave," noted Sigurdsson, adding that the possibility of an even larger disaster scuttled an energy project at volcanic Lake Kivu in East Africa in the 1970s.

Today, more than a decade after Monoun exhaled its killer cloud, the people of the region worry if the "demon cloud" will come again. Scientists share their concern.

Some fear that one dark night, when the wind is still and there is a low rumble in the Earth, Cameroon's killer lake may strike again.

The Black Plague

The invisible killer came from the east, riding the night wind aboard creaking old sailing vessels bound for Rome, Marseilles, Lisbon and beyond to the fog-shrouded British Isles. Before it was over, the bodies of some 25 million people—a quarter of Europe's population—lay in the ground.

No other calamity has caused more death and suffering than the Black Plague of the 14th century.

Percentage-wise, the scourge that struck within a four-year period—1347-1351—took more lives than all the world wars combined.

Today it is thought that this devastation was started by bacteria carried by fleas lodged in the hair of a type of far-ranging rat that flourished in central Asia. Victims caught the disease either from the bite of the fleas or from the bodily discharges of infected persons.

To medieval folk, the plague looked like nothing less than God's terrible punishment for humanity's sins.

From Central Asia, the horror traveled to the Crimea with trade caravans, then by ship to Mediterranean coasts, and onward across Europe at a relentless pace. Normal life ceased. Fields were left untilled, cattle turned loose to fend for themselves.

Corpses were soon being buried, one on top of another, in shallow graves, tipped wholesale into pits or consumed by flames.

City life ground to a halt as contagion spread and people fled their homes. Even the air seemed polluted with what a contemporary chronicle described as "an unbearable stench… so fetid as to be overpowering."

The disease had three forms: bubonic, characterized by the swelling of lymph nodes in the armpits, groin and site of the flea bite; pneumonic, infecting the lungs and causing the coughing up of blood; or, most deadly of all, septicemic, in which the bloodstream was rapidly invaded by offending bacteria, making death inevitable within hours.

Bleeding, lancing, laxatives and enemas were common but futile methods of fighting the unknown killer. Various haphazard potions ranging from powdered stag's horn to rare spices and compounds of gold were also prescribed. Aromatic woods were burned to purify the air, the floors were sprinkled with rose water and vinegar—measures that succeeded only in masking the stench of decaying flesh.

As the Black Death continued its sweep across Europe, bizarre religious sects sprang up, including the Brotherhood of Flagellants. A fanatical cult that had originated in Eastern Europe in the 13th century, it soon spread across the continent.

Flagellants believed an angel had brought down a letter from heaven stating that the plague was punishment imposed by God and that He might be brought to relent only by human acts of self-punishment.

The Flagellants would set forth on so-called "pilgrimages," marching in somber lines, two abreast, eyes fixed on the ground. Each carried boards which they used to beat each other mercilessly whenever they encountered onlookers.

The pilgrimages lasted for 33½ days—the number of years in Christ's life—and during those days the flagellants were forbidden to wash or to clean their wounds.

Invisible Killers

For countless eons, they lay hidden in the tropical gloom of the world's rain forests, millions of natural-born killers too small to be seen with the naked eye.

But with the gradual destruction of the ecosystem, many of these ancient predators—highly contagious microscopic organisms with a ravenous taste for blood—have awakened to wreak havoc on humanity.

Tens of thousands of people, mostly from tropical regions in Africa where timber crews, farmers and hunters threaten to destroy the forests, have died from exotic viral infestations since the late 1970s when scientists first became aware of the diseases and started to track their spread.

Death comes swiftly and painfully to those whose bodies

are invaded by the unseen killers. Victims vomit black blood as internal organs "bleed out" and muscle and bone tissue dissolve like jelly. Eyeballs literally pop out. The brain hemorrhages. The heart explodes. The liver turns to pudding. And the intestines fill with blood before the victim lapses mercifully into a coma and dies.

Vampire-like, the hungry agents—officially known as filoviruses—go airborne to seek new hosts, fresh meat. Entire villages have been wiped out in central Africa by a single infestation.

Some authorities say it's only a matter of time before major outbreaks reach the industrialized world. When that happens, millions upon millions of people could die from various viral strains that make AIDS look like the whooping cough.

In recent years, popular books and movies like *The Hot Zone* and *Outbreak* have brought public attention to the reality of emerging viruses and the potential for disastrous epidemics. While these works created some false impressions, the basic message was clear: either the world wakes up to the danger and takes corrective action, or it may be the end of the line for the human race.

Why is all this happening now?

In a sense, say some environmentalists, the Earth is getting even with humans for having disturbed its delicate ecosystem. Centuries of wanton destruction by plows, axes and bulldozers have upset the balance of nature—and now Mother Nature is exacting a terrible revenge.

"The earth is under attack by growing populations of humans," said one microbiologist. "The tropical rain forests are only trying to defend themselves."

Said Richard Preston, author of *The Hot Zone*, a terrifying true book about a near-outbreak in Washington, D.C. in the late 1980s: "Perhaps the biosphere does not like the idea of 5 billion humans...It is beginning to react to the human parasite, the flooding infection of people, the dead spots of concrete all over the planet, the cancerous rot-outs in

Europe, Japan and the United States, thick with replicating primates, the colonies enlarging and spreading and threatening to shock the biosphere with mass extinctions."

Outbreaks of previously unknown viruses—principally Ebola, Marburg and Reston—are increasing rapidly in tropic zones around the world. Scientists gloomily predict that even more deadly viruses will emerge from the rain forests as civilization presses deeper into untrammeled regions.

"I'm sure that we're going to see in the future a lot of new diseases," said Dr. Alain Georges, a virologist. "It's that obvious."

Archaeological evidence shows that the current outbreaks are not the first to wreak havoc in tropical lands. In ages past, as humans cleared brush, plowed fields and pressed deeper into the forests, they stirred up viruses left over from an earlier primeval era. These settlements mysteriously disappeared, along with their populations. One possible reason: repeated epidemics of one or more killer diseases.

The first outbreak of the deadly Ebola virus was not reported until 1977. Although it has spread rapidly—especially in Uganda, Zimbabwe, South Africa, Kenya, Zaire, Sudan, Gabon, Nigeria, Ivory Coast, Liberia, Cameroon and the Central African Republic—the mode of infection remains unknown. Some virologists suspect certain species of monkeys and apes may harbor the virus and pass it along to humans who eat or come in contact with the creatures.

Others theorize that deadly germs are unleashed when saw gangs disrupt the forest floor or bring down the canopies of huge, disease-laden trees where ancient, death-dealing viruses might be nesting.

Emerging killers such as AIDS surfacing from ecologically damaged parts of the Earth appear to be a "natural consequence" of the ruin of the biosphere, Preston pointed out.

"Many of them come from the tattered edges of tropical rain forests, or they come from tropical savannah that is being settled rapidly by people," he speculates. "The tropical rainforests are the deep reservoirs of life on the planet, containing most of the world's plant and animal species."

But, he adds, the rain forests are also the largest reservoirs of viruses, some of them millions of years old, around since the dawn of time. And when viruses come out of the ecosystem, they tend to spread in waves through the human population, "like echoes from the dying biosphere."

In recent years, researchers have discovered dozens of previously unknown viruses, including Lassa, Oropouche, Rocio, Guanarito, Monkeypox, Dengue and Chikungunya. Among newly-found hantaviruses are machupo and Junin.

But a growing number of scientists fear the worst is yet to come—unless we stop trashing the rain forests and learn to better respect the Earth.

Face on Mars

When Professor Tom Van Flandern gazes up into the night sky, he sees the cosmic remains of ancient empires long dead, the dust of civilizations that flowered and died countless eons before humans walked the earth.

According to this Oxford-trained astronomer, the closest visible reminders of vanished celestial kingdoms can be seen on one of Earth's closest neighbors—the planet Mars.

"When we look closely, we can see the ruins of an ancient race of people who flourished millions of years ago," Dr. Van Flandern said.

The evidence, he adds, can be seen in a series of controversial topographical formations on the red planet's surface, first photographed in 1976 by a Viking orbiter. At first glance, many of these formations appear to be artificial; some even resemble ancient Egyptian pyramids.

The most striking formation, however, is located in the Cydonia region and bears an uncanny resemblance to a human face looking outward into space. This so-called "face on mars" has been the subject of intense scrutiny since computer-enhanced images of the photograph were studied by NASA officials in the 1980s.

Some scientists, including Dr. Van Flandern, are convinced that the "face" was built millions of years ago by an extinct race that colonized Mars after their own planet was destroyed in an asteroid collision.

Dr. Van Flandern believes that the main asteroid belt in the solar system is probably the shattered remains of two planets that collided and exploded between 65 million and 250 million years ago. Intelligent life on at least one of those planets evacuated before the collision and launched colonization probes on Mars, Earth and perhaps elsewhere in the solar system.

Alan F. Alford, author of two best-selling books on the subject, *The Phoenix Solution* and *Gods of the New Millennium*, agrees with Dr. Van Flandern.

"The ancient Egyptians and their predecessors had a profound scientific knowledge of the exploded planets, including the causes of these explosions and the subsequent effects on the evolution of life on Earth," Alford writes.

Alford, who lives in England, said NASA has tried to cover up the truth about the "face on Mars" by distorting photos taken by the Mars Global Surveyor spacecraft in April 1999.

"The re-imaging of the so-called 'Face on Mars' by NASA's mars Global Surveyor Spacecraft in April 1998 has done little to dampen the vigorous debate on its possible artificial manufacture by an unknown extraterrestrial race," Alford said.

Officials at NASA insist that the "face" is really nothing more than a natural rock formation—an opinion shared by most astronomers and geologists who have studied the pictures.

"We humans have an infinite ability to see deliberate images where none exist," commented one NASA official.

"Why else do so many people every year see Jesus or the Virgin Mary in tortillas, wall stains or clouds?"

Referring to the new image, chief scientists Arden L. Albee of the California Institute of Technology, was quoted in *The Washington Post* as saying: "Anyone who has flown in an airplane will recognize that this (Face) is natural."

"It's a butte, a mesa, a knob," added Michael Ravine, advanced projects manager at Malin space Science Systems in San Diego, which operated Surveyor's camera. "Nothing jumps out at me and screams, 'This must have been built by the forces of intelligence.'"

Analyst Tom Van Flandern insists that the face is artificial, built millions of years ago by unknown space colonizers from a doomed world.

"The humanoid facial features that first drew attention to this area are confirmed by this new photo despite poor lighting and poor viewing angle," Dr. Van Flandern said. "One feature, the headdress, is so much a symmetrical combination of right-angle linear and rounded features as to suggest artificiality strongly."

After its discovery in 1976, NASA observers quietly filed away pictures of the "Face on Mars," along with hundreds taken on the mission. Two shots from the Viking Orbiter, identified as frames 35A72 and 70A13, show the "face" partly in shadow, which has the effect of strengthening human features.

The "face" is roughly 2,500 meters long (about 1.5 miles), 2,000 meters wide (1.2 miles) and 400 meters at its highest point (about one-fifth of a mile). Several pyramid-like objects purportedly surround the face—objects that some researchers think might constitute a "City Square," complete with four small mounds, a large main pyramid and a fortress just east of the main pyramid.

The exact purpose of the "face" and other suspected artificial monuments on the Martian landscape remains unclear.

"I suspect," said Alford, "that future probes to the red

planet followed up by careful and open-minded study will answer that and countless other questions."

Some die-hard supporters of the "Face on Mars" theory insist it will probably take a manned mission to the red planet before the debate is finally settled.

Ancient Footprints in Stone

Did humans walk the Earth millions of years ago—gigantic beings who might have lived during the time of the dinosaurs?

For years, claims have been made that fossilized human footprints—some of then more than 20 inches long—occur alongside dinosaur tracks in the Paluxy Riverbed near Glen Rose, Texas. The prints, first found in the 1950s by a local rock hound, suggest that a race of human beings more than eight feet tall once lived and interacted with prehistoric beasts as far back as the Cretaceous period.

Such finds conflict sharply with the standard geologic timetable that states humans did not evolve until about 500,000 years ago—more than 65 million years after the dinosaurs became extinct.

Yet, thousands of "giant man tracks" have been found in rocks along riverbeds from Arizona and Texas to Kentucky and Mississippi, leading some experts to theorize that humans interacted regularly with the prehistoric reptiles of old. Over 100 human footprint trails have been studied in the Paluxy River area, while a site in Utah suggests these long-lost ancestors might have actually worn clothes!

Clearly, if these ancient footprints in stone are genuine, then something must be wrong with our fossil records. Otherwise, how is it possible that manlike creatures roamed North America millions of years before the emergence of Australopithecus in Africa and Asia?

While some scientists have dutifully examined the Glen Rose tracks and others, most refuse to consider the possibility that human beings and dinosaurs coexisted.

"Were this momentous statement true, the names of its discoverers would thunder down the corridors of time as individuals who made one of the most outstanding discoveries of the 20th century," says Ernst Mayr of Harvard University.

Finding dinosaur footprints side by side with humans would "counter evidence that humans evolved long after the dinosaurs became extinct and back up the claim that all species, including man, were created at one time," reported a NOVA television special entitled, *God, Darwin and the Dinosaurs*.

On June 1, 1968, William J. Meister, a drafting supervisor and amateur geologist, was searching for trilobite fossils near Antelope Springs in the mountains of Utah when he unearthed an amazing find—a rock containing human footprints along with fossilized trilobites.

Even more amazing was the fact that at least one of the footprints appeared to be wearing a sandal!

The footprint measured just over 10 inches long by 3.5 inches wide at the sole and 3 inches wide at the heel. The heel print was indented in the rock about an eighth of an inch more than the sole. According to one observer, it was clearly the right foot, because the "sandal" was well-worn on the right side of the heel. Several easily visible trilobites were in the footprint.

Since trilobites became extinct many millions of years before the evolution of Homo sapiens, most scientists understandably are reluctant to even consider the authenticity of the Glen Rose, Antelope Springs or any of the other thousands of tracks reportedly found by "con-men" and "pranksters." Most paleontologists who have examined the disputed impressions declare them to be nothing more than partially-registered dinosaur tracks, natural depressions or—

in many instances—outright fakes carved by local residents to sell to tourists.

"None of these claims can be substantiated," argues Glen J. Kuban, president of the Fossil Society of the Cleveland Museum of Natural History.

Kuban agrees that the Antelope Springs specimen does appear to contain several real trilobites, but adds: "The print itself is questionable on several accounts. Upon closer inspection the overall shape is seen to consist of a spall pattern in a concretion-like slab, similar to others in the area. There is no evidence that it was ever part of a striding sequence, nor evidence that it was ever on an exposed bedding plane."

Yet some anthropologists have argued for years that the traditionally accepted time frame for man's existence on Earth is no longer satisfactory. Some creationist-leaning scholars make arguments that various races of humans have appeared on Earth at different times, some of them perhaps millions of years ago.

These fanciful arguments are usually ridiculed by mainstream scientists who generally hold that man originated in Africa at some remote time in the past, then, between 12,000 and 30,000 years ago, began a slow migratory trek that took them first to Asia, then across a now-sunken land bridge into Alaska and the New World.

But that theory has come under fire in recent years. New evidence is emerging to indicate that man might have arrived in the New World much earlier than thought—and that he came by boat, rather than walking from Siberia and down through Canada during the last Ice Age.

One group of scientists even theorized that North America's first inhabitants may have crossed the icy Atlantic Ocean in ages past from Europe's Iberian Peninsula. Belonging to a group known as the Solutreans, these premodern explorers are believed to have originally settled the Eastern seaboard, then gradually spread as far as the American deserts and Canadian tundra, perhaps even into

South America.

Such thinking has led to radical new ideas concerning the age of man in the New World. Jeffrey Goodman, an engineering archaeologist form Tucson, Arizona, now thinks it is possible humans first developed in North America, then migrated westward toward Asia and the Old World.

Dr. Goodman bases his theory on "many individual bits and pieces of information in the archaeological record which, taken together, serve to fingerprint and document specific migrations in reverse."

He added: "Based on the evidence now coming to light, I believe that there was a migration in reverse. Instead of nomadic hunters coming from the Old World to populate the New World, the Paleo-Indians from the new World, the first fully modern men anywhere in the world, traveled to the Old World and woke it from its sound evolutionary sleep."

But even Dr. Goodman and other "America First" theorists are unable to account for the enigmatic presence of human footprints in stone deposits believed to be many millions of years old. These timeless tracks in stone remain one of the greatest mysteries of our time.

In Search of Mammoths

When Thomas Jefferson sent explorers Meriwether Lewis and William Clark on their now famous expedition to the Pacific Northwest in 1804, his instructions included an unusual request—find, study and, if possible, bring back a live mammoth.

Like many leading thinkers of his day, Jefferson believed the lumbering, elephant-like creatures still roamed areas of the world, including the American West. He had seen the remains of some of these shaggy brutes with his own eyes— vast numbers of fossilized bones at Kentucky's Big Bone Lick left behind since the Ice Age—and was determined to find one.

His obsession led to the construction of a museum inside the White House's East Room that he stuffed with tusks and fossilized bones. To complete his collection, he very much wanted Lewis and Clark to bring back a living mammal.

When the 40-man expedition returned in 1806, they brought back many exciting mementos—but no mammoths. Clearly, America's virgin territories sheltered no prehistoric elephants.

Yet we know today that Jefferson's hunch was not so wide of the mark. We know that early Indians hunted and killed mammoths in great numbers. Go back perhaps 15,000 years—the wink of an eye in geological terms—and we find a variety of proto-elephants trumpeting and thundering across the snow-covered tundra and plains of North and South America.

This was the last of the great Pleistocene ice ages, which lasted from about 1.5 million to 10,000 years ago. During that time the world grew very cold. Great sheets of ice, sometimes a thousand feet thick, moved down from the north, gouging out the land. These harsh conditions were ideal for the development of giant mammals like mastodons and shaggy wooly mammoths that foraged the ancient landscape of present-day Idaho.

Early American tribesmen, notably the Clovis people, actually attacked such megafauna with spears, arrows and long knives. Clovis points—sharp, leaf-shaped and fluted arrowheads—have been found in the skeletal remains of American mammoths.

Fortunately for the hunters, their prey were not flesh-eating predators such as tyrannosaurus rex, the fearsome dinosaur that lived millions of years earlier. Like today's elephants, the pro-elephants were peaceable creatures that ate grass, leaves and shrubbery.

Most paleontologists believe elephants evolved about 70 million years ago from a pig-like, swamp-dwelling mammal about two feet high called a Moeritherium. The Moeritheres flourished during the Upper Eocene, when most of the Earth's land surface—according to theory—was connected into one super-continent called Pangaea.

Millions of years after Pangaea broke up and the continents drifted apart, there emerged the famous woolly mammoth, the mastodon and, ultimately, today's Asian elephant and the African elephant. In the minds of many scientists, these giant creatures of the Ice Age might have lived on forever had it not been for the arrival of a deadly predator—man.

From about 20,000 years ago to about 6,000 years ago, almost all of these lordly mammals died out.

Or did they?

Indian legends told of encounters with gigantic "five-legged beasts," which some researchers took to mean elephant-like creatures, perhaps mammoths. The Chitimacha tribe of Louisiana believed that "a long time ago a being with a long nose came out of the ocean and began to kill people. It would root up trees with its nose to get at people who sought refuge in the branches."

A Penobscot myth told of "moving hills without vegetation" that turned out to be, on close inspection, "great animals with long teeth, animals so huge that when they lay down they could not get up." Other Indians related legends about how the great beasts were driven into a distant land by God after the giants had all died off.

Could that distant land be the unexplored wilderness beyond the Appalachian Mountains? That was the thinking of President Jefferson, who in 1803 had acquired 800,000 square miles of trans-Mississippi territory from the French. In such vastness, he reasoned "There is surely space enough for such creatures."

Some scientists think mastodons or mammoths continued to range certain parts of the United States until about 5,000 years ago, when they were probably driven into extinction by Stone Age people.

However, earlier this century, speculation ran high that in some remote corner of the world like Alaska or Siberia, mastodons or mammoths might still be found alive.

In 1918 an elderly Russian hunter told the French Consul in Vladivostok that he tracked down and killed a huge animal with "big white tusks, very curved." The mysterious creature had "dark chest-colored hair, which seemed shorter on the front…"

Could this have been a real mammoth? Perhaps, some scientists acknowledge, pointing to recent discoveries of frozen mammoth cadavers excavated in 30,000-year-old ice crevasses in Siberia. One 40,000-year-old baby mammoth found in eastern Russia in the late 1970s was so well-preserved the body was virtually unaffected by decomposition.

Are there other giant creatures from the Pleistocene hiding somewhere? Early European explorers reported seeing elephant-creatures in North America, but provided no proof. However, it is known that a dwarf branch of mammoths survived on Wrangel Island in the Arctic Sea north of Siberia until just 4,000 years ago—about the same time the pyramids were being raised in Egypt.

Thunder of the Gods

For centuries, people living in the central Montana Rockies have reported hearing strange sounds echoing across the higher elevations. Some say the noise resembles the discharge of cannon. Others liken it to cracking ice.

The Indians called the mysterious noise "thunder of the gods." Whenever the sounds were heard, they said, it meant the gods were angry.

When explorers Meriwether Lewis and William Clark heard about the old stories on their visit to the region in early 1805, they dismissed them as superstitious prattle. Then, in

June 1805, as their expedition pushed deeper into the Rocky Mountains, the famed adventurers began to reconsider.

"We have repeatedly heard a strange noise coming from the mountains," they wrote in their journal. "It is heard at different periods of the day and night, sometimes when the air is perfectly still and without a cloud...It is loud and resembles precisely the sound of a six-pound piece of ordinance."

Two decades earlier, Daniel Jones of the American Academy of Arts and Sciences studied similar occurrences near West-River Mountain in New Hampshire. "Peasants there became obsessed with these oddities," Jones noted, adding that the sounds were similar to inexplicable booming noises heard during Colonial times near what is now Hartford, Conn.—sounds the Indians called Moodus, meaning "strange noises."

Loud, unexplained noises that shatter windows and rattle houses are nothing new in the lore of strange phenomena. Mysterious booming sounds go back thousands of years to the time of Aristotle who wrote of "strange subterranean noises" that frightened citizens, sometimes jolting them out of their beds.

The philosopher guessed that strong winds were responsible, but subsequent theorists have linked these aberrant sounds to everything from collapsing riverbanks, falling meteors, ghosts and cracking ice to earthquakes, falling boulders and parts of the continental shelf falling off.

The fact is, nobody knows for sure what they are—and that's what has a lot of people scared, especially folks living along the North Carolina coast who've been hearing the sounds for years.

"We hear it all the time, a rolling, crashing noise that makes you think every window in the house is going to break," said Fred Schlesinger, a part-time resident of Bald Head Island near Wilmington.

Jim Lanier, director of the North Carolina Aquarium at Fort Fisher, said, "It's pretty dramatic. It sounds exactly like artillery fire, artillery guns, booming way off the coast."

The booms have been heard in almost every country in the world. Known as "fog belches" in Holland, they go by dozens of names elsewhere. The Haitians call them gouffree, the Nova Scotians air quakes or sea farts. In Ontario they are known as Cornwall Thumps, while in Florida they are just "air sounds."

British officials stationed at Barisal in Bangladesh, near the mouth of the Ganges River, knew them as Barisal Guns—the name scientists generally use today when describing the phenomenon.

Since the days of Lewis and Clark, scientists have tried unsuccessfully to solve the riddle of these mysterious "Barisal Guns." The most ambitious attempt was launched in 1978 by the Naval Research Laboratory at the request of the U.S. Congress. Their conclusion: two-thirds of the "events" were caused by supersonic aircraft (even when no aircraft was nearby), while the rest were ascribed to "unknown causes."

Researchers have found that audible booms can be produced by an earthquake's shock wave, which causes the ground to vibrate up and down, sending sound waves into the air just like a loudspeaker. By using a seismometer, microphone and tape recorder during a 1975 California earthquake, David Hill of the U.S. Geological Survey recorded a boom from a shock wave that caused no obvious tremors.

"The sound was a soft rumble, sort of like distant thunder," said Dr. Hill, who thinks that most reported "brontides"—the name used by Italians to describe the phenomenon—have been associated with earthquakes or with distant explosions transmitted by freakish atmospheric conditions.

Thomas Gold, an astrophysicist at Cornell University, agrees that many brontides have been caused by earthquakes, but his calculations show that to produce a very loud boom, an earthquake must be strong enough to be felt.

Therefore, he reasoned, the earthquake theory doesn't account for loud booms unaccompanied by earth tremors. Nor does it account for the many reports that mention booms along with flames.

So Dr. Gold has revived a theory that was used at the turn of the century to explain the "lake guns" heard in upstate New York at Seneca. He suggested that some brontides are caused by high-pressure natural gas that escapes rapidly from the ground and explodes in the air, perhaps sometimes ignited into flames.

Donald Stierman, a geophysicist at the University of California at Riverside who has studied the flow of gas underground, says Dr. Gold's hypothesis has no merit.

"Except in very special circumstances, like geysers or mud volcanoes, gas doesn't escape from the ground quickly enough to produce booming sounds," he said. His guess is that most of the natural booms are caused by earthquakes.

While scientists continue their debate, the Barisal Guns are likely to go right on booming.

Sources and Additional Reading

Adler, Bill, ed., *UFO's*, Dell Publishing, New York, 1967

Andrews, Ted, *Enchantment of the Faerie Realm*, Llewellyn Publications, St. Paul, MN, 1993

Ayer, Brandt, *Treasury of Snake Lore*, Greenberg, New York, 1956

Bach, Marcus, *Strange Sects and Curious Cults*, Dorset Press, New York, 1961

Bach, Richard, William Morrow and Company, NY, 1969

Baker, Alan, *UFO Sightings*, TV Books, New York, 1997

Baring Gould, Sabine, *The Book of Werewolves*, Senate Publications, London, 1995

Barry, J.D., *Ball Lightning and Bead Lightning*, Plenum Press, New York, 1980

Bell, Art, and Steiger, Brad, *The Source: Journey Through the Unexplained*, Paper Chase Press, New Orleans, 1999

Benwell, Gwen, and Waugh, Arthur, *Sea Enchantress*, Citadel Press, New York, 1965

Berlitz, Charles, *The Bermuda Triangle*, DoubleDay & Company, New York, 1974

Bernstein, Morey, *The Search for Bridey Murphy*, Pocket Books, New York, 1978

Bettelheim, Bruno, *The Uses of Enchantment*, Alfred A. Knopf, New York, 1976

Bord, Colin and Janet, *Alien Animals*, Granada Publishing, London, 1980

Bord, Colin and Janet, *The Evidence for Bigfoot and Other Man-Beasts*, Aquarian Press, London, 1984

Bord, Colin and Janet, *Unexplained Mysteries of the 20th Century*, Contemporary Books, Chicago, 1989

Bray, Warwick, Farrington, Ian, and Swanson, Earl, *The New World*, E.P. Dutton and Company, New York, 1975

Brennan, J.H., *Time Travel—a New Perspective*, Llewellyn Publications, St. Paul, MN 1997

Briggs, Katharine, *The Fairies in Tradition and Literature*, Routledge and Kegan Paul, London, 1978

Brookesmith, Peter, *The Power of the Earth*, Orbis Publishing, London, 1984

Burl, Aubrey, *Prehistoric Avebury*, Yale University Press, New Haven, CT, 1979

Bushnell, Geoffrey, *The First Americans*, McGraw-Hill, New York, 1975

Carrington, Richard, *Mermaids and Mastodons*, Rinehart & Company, New York, 1957

Casson, Lionel, Claiborn, Robert, Fagan, Brian and Karp, Walter, *Mysteries of the Past*, American Heritage Publishing Co., New York, 1977

Cavendish, Richard, ed., *Man, Myth and Magic*, Marshall Cavendish Corporation, New York, 1973

Cayce, Edgar, (compiled by B. Ernest Frejer), *The Edgar Cayce Companion*, ARE Press, Virginia Beach, 1995

Ceram, C.W., *Gods, Graves and Scholars*, Harcourt Brace Jovanovich, New York, 1969

Ceram, C.W., *The First American*, Harcourt Brace Jovanovich, New York, 1971

Chaisson, Eric, *Cosmic Dawn: The Origins of Matter and Life*, Atlantic Monthly Press, Boston, 1981

Cherfas, Jeremy, and Gribbin, John, *The Monkey Puzzle*, Pantheon Books, New York, 1982

Clark, Jerome, *Unexplained*, Visible Ink, Detroit, MI, 1999

Cohen, Daniel, *The Encyclopedia of the Strange*, Dodd, Mead & Company, New York, 1985

Costello, Peter, *In Search of Lake Monsters*, Coward, McCann & Geoghegan, New York, 1974

Cotterell, Maurice M., *The Supergods*, HarperCollins, New York, 1998

Cottrell, Leonard, *Lost Worlds*, Dell Publishing, New York, 1962

Daniken, Erich von, *Miracles of the Gods*, Dell Publishing, New York, 1975

Davis, Nigel, *Voyagers to the New World*, William Morrow, New York, 1979

de Camp, L. Sprague, *Lost Continents*, Dover Publications, New York, 1970

Del Ray, Lester, *The Mysterious Earth*, Chilton Company, New York, 1961

Dinsdale, Tim, *Loch Ness Monster*, Routledge and Kegan Paul, London, 1972

Erdoes, Richard, and Ortiz, Alfonso, *American Indian Myths and Legends*, Pantheon Books, New York, 1984

Evans, Christopher, and Wilson, Colin, *The Book of Great Mysteries*, Dorset Press, New York, 1990

Evans-Wentz, W.Y., (ed.), *The Tibetan Book of the Dead*, Oxford University Press, New York, 1957.

Fell, Barry, *America, B.C.*, Demeter press, New York, 1977

Gaddis, Vincent, H., *Mysterious Fires and Lights*, David McKay Company, New York, 1967

Godwin, John, *Unsolved: The World of the Unknown*, Doubleday & Company, Garden City, NY, 1976

Green, John, *On the Track of the Sasquatch*, Cheam Publishing, Aggassiz, B.C., 1968

Grumley, Michael, *There Are Giants in the Earth*, Doubleday & Company, New York, 1974

Guiley, Rosemary Ellen, *The Encyclopedia of Ghosts and Spirits*, Facts on File, New York, 1992

Guirdham, Arthur, *We Are One Another*, Turnstone Press, Willingborough, 1974.

Hancock, Graham, *Footprints of the Gods*, Crown Trade Paperbacks, New York, 1995

Hancock, Graham, *The Sign and the Seal*, Simon & Schuster, New York, 1992

Harrison, Michael, *Fire From Heaven: A Study of Spontaneous Human Combustion*, Pan Books, London, 1976

Hauck, Dennis, *Haunted Places*, Penguin Books, New York, 1996

Herm, Gerhard, *The Celts*, St. Martin's Press, New York, 1975

Heuvelmans, Bernard, *In the Wake of the Serpents*, tr. Garnett, Richard, Hill and Wang, New York, 1968

Heuvelmans, Bernard, *On the Track of Unknown Animals*, Hill & Wang, New York, 1959

Hill, Douglas, and Williams, Pat, *The Supernatural*, Signet Books, New York, 1965

Hoagland, Richard, *The Monuments on Mars*, North Atlantic Books, Berkeley, CA, 1987

Jackson, Donald, *Underground Worlds*, Time-Life Books, Alexandria, VA, 1982

Joseph, Frank, *Synchronicity and You*, Element, Boston, 1999

Jung, Carl, *Dreams*, tr. Hull, R.F.C., Routledge and Kegan Paul, London, 1974

Keel, John A., *The Complete Guide to Mysterious Beings*, Doubleday, New York, 1994

Koestler, Arthur, *Nothing By Chance The Roots of Coincidence*, Random House, New York, 1972

Kubler-Ross, Elizabeth, *On Death and Dying*, Macmillan, New York, 1969

Kusche, Lawrence, *The Bermuda Triangle Mystery-Solved*, Harper & Row, New York, 1975

Leeming, David, *The World of Myth*, Oxford University Press, New York, 1990

Mackal, Roy, *The Monsters of Loch Ness*, MacDonald, London, 1970

Mahan, Joseph, *The Secret: America in World History Before Columbus*, Star Printing, Acworth, GA, 1985

McNally, Raymond T., *In Search of Dracula*, Robson Books, London, 1994

Meurger, Michael, *Lake Monster Traditions*, Fortean Times, London, 1988

Moncrieff, Hope A.R., *A Treasury of Classical Mythology*, Barnes & Noble, New York, 1992

Moody, R.A. Jr., M.D., *Life After Life*, Bantam Books, New York, 1985

Morison, Samuel Eliot, *The European Discovery of America: The Southern Voyages*, Oxford University Press, 1974

Myers, Arthur, *The Ghostly Gazetteer*, Contemporary Books, Chicago, 1990

Napier, John, *Bigfoot, the Yeti and Sasquatch in Myth and Reality*, Jonathan Cape, London, 1973

National Geographic Society, *Vanishing Peoples of the Earth*, Washington, D.C, 1968

Norman, David, *Dinosaur!*, Prentice Hall, New York, 1991

Ouspensky, P.D., *The Strange Life of Ivan Osokin*, Arkana, London, 1992

Pellant, Chris, *Fossils of the World*, Thunder Bay Press, San Diego, CA, 1994

Pinson, Koppels, *Modern Germany*, MacMillan Company, New York, 1966

Platnick, Kenneth, *Great Mysteries of History*, Dorset Press, New York, 1972

Pyle, Robert Michael, *Where Bigfoot Walks: Crossing the Dark Divide*, Mariner Books, Houghton Mifflin Company, New York, 1995

Randles, Jenny, *The Paranormal Source Book*, Piatkus, London, 1996

Readers Digest Association, *Facts & Fallacies: Stories of the Strange and Unusual*, Pleasantville, NY, 1988

Readers Digest Association, *Mysteries of the Ancient Americas: The New World Before Columbus*, Pleasantville, NY, 1986

Readers Digest Association, *Mysteries of the Unexplained*, Pleasantville, NY, 1982

Readers Digest Association, *Quest for the Past*, Pleasantville, NY, 1984

Readers Digest Association, *Strange Stories*, Amazing Facts, Pleasantville, NY, 1977

Readers Digest Association, *The World's Last Mysteries*, Pleasantville, NY, 1978

Reman, Edward, *The Norse Discoveries and Explorations of America*, Dorset Press, New York, 1977

Ribeiro, Darcy, *The Americas and Civilization*, E.P. Dutton, New York, 1972

Roe, Derek, *Prehistory*, University of California Press, Los Angeles, 1970

Sagan, Carl, *Cosmos*, Random House, New York, 1980

Sanderson, Ivan, *Abominable Snowmen*, Chilton Book Company, Radnor, Philadelphia, 1961

Savage, Henry, *The Mysterious Carolina Bays*, North Carolina Press, Chapel Hill, 1982

Science, 153: 1213-20, 9 September 1966

Severin, Tim, *The Brendan Voyage*, McGraw-Hill, New York, 1978

Shuker, Karl P.N., *From Flying Toads to Snakes With Wings*, Llewellyn Publications, St. Paul, MN, 1997

Shuker, Karl, P.N., *The Unexplained: An Illustrated Guide to the World's Natural and Paranormal Mysteries*, Carlton Books Limited, London, 1996

Singh, Joseph, and Zingg, Robert M., *Wolf Children and Feral Man*, Harper and Brothers, New York, 1942

Spaeth, Frank, *Mysteries of the Deep*, Llewellyn Publications, St. Paul, MN, 1998

Speck, Gordon, *Myths and New World Explorations*, Ye Galleon Press, Fairfield, WA, 1979

Spencer, John and Anne, *Alien Contact*, TV Books, New York, 1997

Stevensen, MD, Ian, *Twenty Cases Suggestive of Reincarnation*, American Society for Psychical Research, New York, 1966

Sweeney, James B., *A Pictorial History of Sea Monsters*, Bonanza Books, New York, 1978

Thompson, C.J.S., *The Mystery and Lore of Monsters*, Barnes & Noble, New York, 1994

Thurston, Herbert, *The Physical Phenomena of Mysticism*, Henry Regnery Company, Chicago, 1952

Time-Life Books, *Mystic Places*, Alexandria, VA, 1992

Vaughn, Alan, *Incredible Coincidences*, J.B. Lippincott Company, NY, 1979

Velikovsky, Immanuel, *Earth in Upheaval*, Doubleday & Company, New York, 1955

Velikovsky, Immanuel, *Mankind in Amnesia*, Abacus Books, London, 1982

Vincent, Ken R., *Visions of God*, Larson, New York, 1994

Wambach, Helen, *Life Before Life*, Bantam Books, New York, 1979

Wellhofer, Peter, *The Illustrated Encyclopedia of Prehistoric Flying Reptiles*, Barnes & Noble, New York, 1991

Wheeler, Margaret, *Great Discoveries in Archaeology*, Hart Publishing Company, New York, 1967

Willey, Gordon and Sabloff, Jeremy, *A History of American Archaeology*, W.H. Freeman and Company, San Francisco, 1974

Williams, Stephen, *Fantastic Archaeology: The Wild Side of North American Prehistory*, University of Pennsylvania Press, Philadelphia, 1991

Wilson, Colin and Wilson, Damon, *The Encyclopedia of Unsolved Mysteries*, Zachary Kwintner Books, Ltd., Chatham, Kent, 1987

Wilson, Colin, *Afterlife-An Investigation of the Evidence for Life After Death*, Grafton Books, London, 1985

Wilson, Colin, *The Psychic Detectives*, Pan Books, London, 1984.

Wilson, Colin, *Unsolved Mysteries*, Contemporary Books, Chicago, 1992

Wood, Michael, *In Search of the Dark Ages*, Facts on File, New York, 1987

Index

About the Author

E. RANDALL FLOYD is a nationally syndicated newspaper columnist, motion picture screenwriter and best-selling author of several books including *Deep In The Heart, The Good, The Bad & the Mad, Weird People in American History* and *Great Southern Mysteries*.

A former European correspondent for United Press International, he worked for the *Florida Times-Union* and the *Atlanta Journal-Constitution*. His lectures at Augusta State University helped inspire *100 of the World's Greatest Mysteries*. He lives in Augusta, Georgia, with his wife, Anne, and their son Rand.

Mr. Floyd lectures on a number of topics, ranging from strange and unusual aspects of Civil War history to the paranormal. To contact Mr. Floyd to arrange lectures, guest appearances, autograph signings, or to order books, please call the Augusta office at (phone & fax) **706-738-0354**, or write **Harbor House, 3010 Stratford Drive, Augusta, Georgia 30909.** Or you may e-mail him at **harborbook@aol.com.**

Please allow four weeks for delivery of your order. Mr Floyd would be happy to autograph all ordered books. Please indicate how you would like each book to read.

Other Books by E. Randall Floyd

The Good, The Bad & The Mad	$19.95 Softback	
Deep In The Heart	$24.95 Softback	
Great Southern Mysteries	$8.95 Softback	$16.95 Hardback
More Great Southern Mysteries	$9.95 Softback	$16.95 Hardback
Great American Mysteries	$9.95 Softback	$18.95 Hardback
Ghost Lights and Other Encounters with the Unknown	$9.95 Softback	$18.95 Hardback
America's Great Unsolved Mysteries		$19.95 Hardback

Please add $3.95 shipping and handling for the first book, $2.00 for each book thereafter.
ATTN: COLLEGES, UNIVERSITIES, QUANTITY BUYERS: Discounts on these books are available for bulk purchases. Write or call for information on our discount programs.